WALK WITH MY SHADOW

The Life of an Innu Man

George Gregoire

Canada Council for the Arts / Conseil des Arts du Canada Canadä Newfoundland Labrador

We gratefully acknowledge the financial support of the Canada Council for the Arts,
the Government of Canada through the Canada Book Fund (CBF),
and the Government of Newfoundland and Labrador through the Department of
Tourism, Culture and Recreation for our publishing program.

Cover Design by Todd Manning
Back Cover Photo by Virginia Collins
Front Cover Photo by Camille Fouillard
Layout by Joanne Snook-Hann
Printed on acid-free paper

Published by
CREATIVE PUBLISHERS
an imprint of CREATIVE BOOK PUBLISHING
a Transcontinental Inc. associated company
P.O. Box 8660, Stn. A
St. John's, Newfoundland and Labrador A1B 3T7

Printed in Canada by:
TRANSCONTINENTAL INC.

Library and Archives Canada Cataloguing in Publication

Gregoire, George, 1946-
    Walk with my shadow : the life of an Innu man / George
Gregoire.

ISBN 978-1-77103-000-7

    1. Gregoire, George, 1946-. 2. Inuit--Newfoundland and
Labrador--Labrador--Biography. 3. Labrador (N.L.)--Social
life and customs--20th century. 4. Culture conflict--
Newfoundland and Labrador. I. Title.

E99.E7G749 2012   971.8'20049710092   C2012-905021-0

FSC
www.fsc.org
MIX
Paper from
responsible sources
FSC® C011825

WALK WITH MY SHADOW

The Life of an Innu Man

George Gregoire

St. John's, Newfoundland and Labrador
2012

For Shanut, my children and grandchildren

FOREWORD

GEORGE GREGOIRE approached me in 1995 with a request to help him write a book about his life. We had been friends dating back to 1985 when he invited me to stay with his family – his wife[1], Shanut, seven children, a niece and her baby – in their tent during a traditional Innu gathering in Flowers Bay[2] on the coast of Labrador. In 1992 we had worked together on the People's Inquiry, a Davis Inlet community self-examination after a house fire that killed six children. George served as commissioner during the Inquiry, gathering stories from many adults, elders and children in his community. We were proud of this work, of the book[3] that resulted. We both experienced the power and healing of sharing the story.

George submitted an application for an Explorations grant from the Canada Council for the Arts. We were delighted when he received this grant for new writers. We had no idea that it would take seventeen years to complete his book for publication. The writing and editing of this book has its own story.

For the first few years George periodically sent me handwritten foolscap pages filled with memories from early childhood into adulthood. I typed them up word for word with no edits. I returned the text to him with notes in the margins asking him to elaborate. For example, he wrote about hunting his first caribou. Knowing the importance of this event for an Innu boy, I asked him to flesh out a picture of that day. I wanted all the details. He wrote that he met and married Shanut Pasteen. I wanted to know how he met her, the details of their courtship and I wanted to be there, a guest at their wedding. He sent me wonderful responses to my requests.

George continued to send more pages as the years multiplied. Sometimes he mailed or faxed pages. Occasionally he dropped some off when he came to St. John's. Sometimes I'd collect the latest installment when I was in Davis Inlet. Often the pages came with a box of caribou meat or char, a gift of a Shanut's handiwork: a hat made of caribou hide trimmed with beads and fur, moccasins for my new baby, a beaded

---

[1] Charlotte

[2] Kanishutakashtasht

[3] Fouillard, Camille, ed. *Gathering Voices: Finding Strength to Help Our Children.* Vancouver, Douglas and McIntyre, 1995

hairpiece or necklace. On two occasions George and I spent a week together, reviewing and discussing the manuscript.

From the beginning I struggled with editing decisions. My intention was to meddle with the writing as little as possible. I did not want to simply try to fit George's story within the parameters of conventional literary standards and I wondered to what extent the reader could meet George on his own storytelling terms.

I wondered what George's story would be like in his own language. With years of experience working with the Innu I knew that English and *Innu-aimun* are worlds apart, or more specifically worldviews apart. While I knew George's command of English was strong and that many sought him out as an interpreter, I also knew that *Innu-aimun* words, ideas and concepts often do not exist in English, and vice versa. *Nutshimit*, for example, is a word that translates as *the bush* or *the country*, but it really embodies much more than these two words. It stems from an Innu worldview of a realm and a life alien to my culture. It embodies a notion of home, of comfort and sustenance, which might be the last things non-Innu think of when imagining the Labrador interior. Another word, *utshimau,* is often translated as *leader* or *boss*. Do these English words do justice to the Innu concept: the person who leads the hunt? What are the qualities of an *utshimau* that inspire the trust and confidence for others to follow him? Those qualities strike me as different than those of a boss or leader in mainstream Canadian culture. *Utshimau* pitches up within the Innu word for the provincial department of social services *Mitshim-utshimau* or *Boss of the Food*, or for government *Tshishe-utshimau* or the *Great Boss*. The word *Aueshish-utshimaut*, referring to beings who rule over hunting rites and protocol, is translated by some Innu as Animal Spirits while others refer to them as Animal Masters. There is no exact translation.

Given that George had decided to write and publish in English, I wanted to retain his English voice as much as possible. For a long time I wondered whether to standardize the spelling and grammar. I asked George about his thoughts on voice and grammar. "Just fix it," he told me. I followed his advice. I standardized the grammar, knowing this was the first step to altering his voice, and should he ever do a public reading of his book he would not sound like himself.

George and I discussed whether to insert Innu words into his English text and whether to use people's Innu names and Innu place names. We agreed to insert the occasional Innu word, with an English translation in a footnote. In terms of people's names, most Innu have more than one name: Christian names given to them by missionaries, Innu names (Innu versions of European names or old names passed down through families) and nicknames. George is known among the Innu as Shuash. George and I agreed to use people's Innu names or nicknames with their English name in footnotes. When George thought a person's Innu nickname might sound disrespectful in English he insisted on using only the Christian name. In terms of place names we agreed to use English names in the text, with the Innu name in a footnote the first time it appears in the text. In some instances only the Innu or English place names appear because there is no version in the other language.

The structure of the book also reflects Innu reality. There is a general chronological arch to the narrative, but it also moves back and forth in time and geography – between life in *nutshimit* and in the community, between personal and intimate stories and stories addressing politics that span the province, Canada and even the globe. It is a nomadic structure; George's wandering writing mirrors the traditional Innu way of life. The storyline is circular in the tradition of Innu storytelling rather than linear.

But *Walk With My Shadow* is not a book about linguistic or literary questions. It tells the story of the path traveled by an Innu man through his sixty-five years on the planet. George chronicles his life with an honesty at times stark – the reality both poignant and alarming – within the larger drama of the Labrador Innu as they struggle to find their way through a rapidly changing cultural landscape and the encroachment of Euro-Canadian society during the last century.

George's people, the Innu, inhabit *Nitassinan* – their word for *Our Homeland*, which encompasses a large portion of the Quebec-Labrador peninsula. *Nitassinan* is a vast area of boreal forest, lakes, rivers and barrens. Archaeological evidence indicates the Innu have inhabited *Nitassinan* for thousands of years. Until recently the Innu were known as the Montagnais and Naskapi people. Today they number about 25,000. Most live in eleven Quebec communities. About 2,450 live in two communities in Labrador – 1,600 in Sheshatshiu, where Grand Lake[1] meets Lake Melville[2], and 850 in Natuashish, 300 kilometres to the north

---

[1] Kakatshu-utshishtun
[2] Atatshi-uinipeku

on the coast. The Innu of Natuashish were first settled in Davis Inlet and relocated in 2002.

Before settlement became a way of life during the latter half of the last century, the Labrador Innu lived a nomadic life for most of the year when waterways were frozen and the land covered with snow. George was born into this life, which he describes through the stories of his childhood. Small groups of two or three families would journey to the interior in search of game, walking on snowshoes and pulling their possessions on toboggans. In the summer they traveled by birchbark canoe to various gathering places, including Old Davis Inlet[1], North West River and Sept Iles[2]. Here they traded, arranged marriages and held feasts and other celebrations. They lived off the bounty of the land, hunting small mammals and waterfowl, fishing and gathering berries. At the heart of their culture was the caribou that migrated across *Nitassinan* in the spring and fall. The caribou provided them with food, as well as clothing, shelter and tools. Innu technology was well adapted to their environment. They were experts at making skin clothing, their means of travel — snowshoes, toboggans and canoes – as well as tools, weapons and utensils out of wood, stone and bone. They practised their own medicine. Their diet was very healthy – rich in meats, with few carbohydrates.

The traditional Innu world was filled with spirits related to animals and forces of nature. George writes about some of the spiritual practices that were integrated into everyday activities. Rituals and feasts were held in conjunction with all hunting activities. Shamans communicated with the *Aueshish-utshimaut* or Animal Masters to foretell future hunting, but each hunter could obtain spiritual power through dreams, songs and by performing rituals of respect for all *Aueshish-utshimaut*. Innu spirituality stressed egalitarianism. Humans were seen as equal and integral to nature, as opposed to superior. The hunt was not a conquest. If the hunter showed respect to the *Aueshish-utshimaut*, the animals gave themselves up willingly. After a successful caribou hunt, a *makushan*[3] was held to honour the spirit of the caribou.

George also writes about the fur trade and its impact on the Innu way of life during his lifetime. European trading posts were first set up in

---

[1] Uipat Utshimassit
[2] Uashat
[3] Feast of the Caribou

Labrador during the 1800s, and the Innu were encouraged to trap furs to trade rather than hunt for subsistence. While the Innu became dependent on trading for food and supplies, they also ran into increasing competition with white and settler fur trappers. In the 1930s the collapse of fur prices and a reduction in caribou numbers caused great hardship, even starvation. The Innu were also beset by illness and death from European diseases. They began showing up at trading posts on the coast in a desperate condition, seeking assistance from missionaries and traders who for decades were delegated by the government to distribute food, clothing and social assistance in remote Labrador.

In 1949, three years after George's birth, Newfoundland gave up its status as an independent country to become a province of Canada. Unbeknownst to the Labrador Innu, the terms of this Confederation would have a great impact on them. Unlike their relatives in Quebec, the Labrador Innu were not made Status Indians under the Canadian government's Indian Act. Without this status they were excluded from an expanding range of programs and services provided to Status Indians by the Canadian government. The Labrador Innu had no treaty, no health benefits, no federal money for schools and housing. The decision was to make them "full-fledged" citizens and assimilate them into mainstream Canada. While the Labrador Innu had the right to vote – a right Status Indians in Canada did not receive until the 1960s – they still spent most of their time in *nutshimit*, with little or no knowledge about elections and voting.

In lieu of extending the Indian Act, Ottawa decided in 1954 to provide some funding to the Newfoundland government for medical and other services to the Labrador Innu. This funding fell far short of the level of funding or variety of services the federal government provided to Aboriginal groups elsewhere in Canada. The Newfoundland government decided to use some of these funds to build houses and schools in Sheshatshiu and Davis Inlet in the 1950s and 60s. The province also began to enforce mandatory schooling and threatened to stop welfare and family allowance payments to families whose children did not attend class. Parents were forced to stay close to the village, but living in a settlement meant adults could not make a living hunting and trapping. When the province began to enforce wildlife hunting regulations, the mainstay of the Innu way of life was made illegal.

Settlement coincided with a number of industrial developments on Innu territory, including the mines at Labrador City, Wabush and Schefferville, and the Upper Churchill Falls hydro-electric project which flooded thousands of kilometres of land, including valuable caribou habitat and Innu burial grounds. Forestry projects and road developments resulted in a further incursion into Innu land.

Colonization – the process of subjecting the Innu to foreign institutions such as courts, schools, the church, hospitals and governments, as well as opening their territory to a multitude of developments – stripped them of control over their lives. A once active, proud and independent people became cut off from their culture. George writes candidly about his family's experience of this transition to village life and the subsequent unraveling of his people's social fabric and connectedness. Life in the village turned out to be one of squalor, family breakdown, violence, drunkenness, suicide, accidents, malnutrition and illness.

George's story is also about the resilience of the Innu people and how they never fully surrendered to the process of assimilation. When the government introduced band councils in the two communities in the 1970s, Innu leaders quickly implemented outpost programs to finance the cost of chartering planes to hunting camps in the interior of *Nitassinan* each spring and fall. Whole families embarked on sojourns of up to three months to return to their way of life and ensure that their children would learn Innu practices, skills, language, values and beliefs.

George expounds at length about the band council. From the point of view of both citizen and elected leader he writes about his experience and thoughts about this imposed and foreign structure with its municipal-like mandate. He also discusses the challenges and triumphs of the Naskapi Montagnais Innu Association, which later became the Innu Nation – a regional government established to represent the Labrador Innu in land rights negotiation with the province and Canada. George documents how the Innu capacity to govern within these bodies evolved over the years, at times serving the interests of their communities while other times creating chaos, divisions and dysfunction both within and between the two communities.

George also writes about how the Innu people decided to wrest control of their lives and fight for their rights beyond the realm of band councils and the Innu Nation. In the late 1980s they organized a series of spectacular acts of disobedience – actions that continued into the 1990s and forced the provincial and national governments to pay attention more than once. Through George the reader will gain a first-hand account of a number of these protests. The first one occurred in 1987, when a group of Innu hunters, women, children and elders headed for the Mealy Mountains[1] to shoot caribou where their ancestors had always shot caribou, but where the Newfoundland government insisted hunting was illegal. Women and children sat on the caribou to prevent the wildlife officers from confiscating them as evidence. In court, the Innu had no defense and entered no plea. Instead they read a statement that said, "We believe deeply that this foreign law is not our law, and the right claimed by others to govern us and dispose of our lands and resources is not legitimate." While some of the hunters were jailed, the Innu saw the action as a victory, one that had brought them together and made them stronger and worthy of respect.

The following year, Canada decided to invite its European allies to set up a NATO superbase, to conduct up to 40,000 military test flights and to practice aerial combat and bombings on Innu land. For years the Innu had already borne the brunt of 6,500 low-level test flights at speeds of up to 900 kilometres an hour and as low as 30 metres above the ground. The noise of the killer planes startled hunters, terrified children, frightened the animals. Jet fuel and exhaust polluted the land and waterways. The Innu decided to confront NATO's military might head on. Hundreds camped on the grounds of the air base at Goose Bay. On more than fifteen occasions they marched onto the runways to halt the killer jets before takeoff. Repeatedly, they also invaded the forbidden bombing range near Minipi Lake[2]. Through their actions they attracted worldwide attention. Plans for the NATO base were cancelled and the federal government was forced to put the Innu on the shortlist for land rights negotiations.

These direct actions gave many Innu the courage and the strength to begin to fight their inner demons as well. A healing movement began in the early 1990s and swept through the Labrador Innu communities. Men, women and children – and occasionally all of them together as a family – availed themselves of addictions-treatment services and programs outside the province, in the communities and in *nutshimit*. Dozens of Innu were trained in addictions counseling and began to organize Innu-run healing programs. George shares his own harrowing tale of addiction, as well as

---

[1] Akami-uapishkᵘ

[2] Minai-nipi

some of the challenges and successes of treatment programs and services and his eventual involvement in this healing work.

For the reader who followed the media stories of the land claims negotiations of the Innu with the province and Canada, George shares the backroom and kitchen discussions of the Innu through the whole process. After decades of negotiations the Labrador Innu voted to ratify the 600-page Tshash Petapen or New Dawn Agreement in June, 2011. Although most Innu voted in favour of the agreement, George's account of the negotiating process and the agreement explains why many Innu may still remain unconvinced that a land rights agreement and financial compensation will bring justice or solve their problems.

Walk With My Shadow shows how the Innu continue to live in a constant state of flux and conflict. George writes of his concerns about his children and grandchildren, caught between two worlds, struggling to find a balance between the Innu and Euro-Canadian way of life. People must make difficult choices. The culture of waged work keeps ever-increasing numbers of people tied to the community. More people recognize the need for formal education to succeed in their new reality. Other influences such as the mass media and new technologies also lure them to spend more time in the village. An Innu school board was established in 2008, but much work has yet to be done to transform the school into an institution that promotes Innu culture. The Innu are also working on the devolution of health and social services, and now operate their own medical clinics and social health programs. Many Innu are also involved in a variety of joint venture businesses which, as George writes, have benefited some Innu but also exacerbated divisions and created great discrepancies between the rich and the poor in the two communities.

Fewer Innu now head for *nutshimit* in the spring and fall and for shrinking amounts of time. However, George writes about how efforts to keep the Innu culture alive are evolving.

Over the last few years a number of backwoods snowshoe treks and canoe trips have been organized, involving elders and youth. Reclaiming traditional means of travel and reconnecting with ancestral lands affirm that the Innu culture continues to be passed on from one generation to the next. The Innu are also asserting their culture through the visual arts such as painting, by writing books, creating theatre and dance productions and making films.

Walk With My Shadow is a tough, candid and complicated story written with courage, humour, integrity and no apologies – a book that should help dispel lies, myths and stereotypes too often perpetrated by the media. I invite non-Innu to suspend their worldview and expectations, to make room, to listen and learn from George and his way of telling his story. This story is an important contribution to understanding and rethinking Canada's relationship with First Nations. I hope readers will continue to hear George's voice long after they have closed the book.

Camille Fouillard

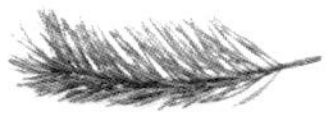

MY NAME IS GEORGE GREGOIRE. My people call me Shuash. I remember as a small boy when we lived in *nutshimit*[1], we didn't ever really run out of food. We ate fish, partridge and other small game. One time when we were camping right close by a lake, my father must have chopped a hole through the ice and left his hooks under water. I didn't know anything about this. My mother asked me if I would fetch some water. I took the bucket and headed to where we hauled the water. I noticed many holes through the ice with hooks in each of them. I pulled on one of them and felt something heavy moving at the end of the line. I knew it was a fish. I was very excited and pulled in the line. As the fish came out through the hole, it wiggled and jumped back into the water. So I filled my bucket with water and ran home, still very excited. What was I going to say when I got there?

"The head of the fish for you came out, but it's gone back in the water," I said to my sister Tshaukuesh[2] as I got inside the tent.

I thought my father and mother would be really proud of me, but my father was very angry.

"You shouldn't have touched that hook," Nutaui[3] shouted at me.

I didn't know I wasn't allowed to touch the hooks, although I guess Nikaui[4] had told me to mind myself and not touch them. I guess I was just too excited. When I felt the fish caught on the hook, I wanted to try and pull it out. Those fish were lake trout and we were somewhere in the Lake Meshikamau area.

Another time Nutaui left and I was told he was gone to Sept Isles[5] in Quebec to get some grub. He was gone a little over one month. While he was away, Nikaui alone had to check the fish net every morning. We ate only fish and partridge while he was away. I didn't find it hard, but my mother must have found it difficult to work alone so hard to keep all of us children alive. We wouldn't have noticed the difference because we were only young.

---

[1] The bush or the country
[2] Elizabeth Penashue
[3] Father
[4] Mother
[5] Uashat

My two sisters Tshestu[1] and Eshkuess[2] were old enough to help Nikaui when Nutaui was away. They were good hunters for partridges and porcupines. They could check my father's traps and it was easy for them to check the fishing net in the winter when it was not cold. But when it was cold, it was very hard on their hands because they couldn't wear mitts to pull the net out. That doesn't mean they were not allowed to wear mitts. They could, but the mitts would be soaking wet in a matter of seconds.

The hardest part of winter fishing was setting the net under the ice. The ice could be as much as four feet thick. I watched my father chop holes in the ice many times with a long pole and ice chisel on one end. It could take him a couple days to make two holes, a week to chop more holes, depending on how long his net was. The first and last hole had to be large enough for the net to pass through. One person could not put a net under the ice by himself. It took two people. After the four holes were made, Nutaui would then cut a long dry pole that could easily be seen underwater. I remember wondering as a small boy how he would get that net under water. He tied a rope at one end of the pole and pushed it underwater directly towards the second hole, where Nikaui would stand. Once the pole touched Nikaui's stick at the second hole, she would call out to my father. He would move to the second hole, and push the pole to the third hole. The two would repeat this until the pole reached the final hole. My father would then pull the pole out, untie the rope, and hand it to Nikaui. He would walk back to the first hole, tie the rope to the net and call Nikaui to pull on it. If the net got tangled up, he would call to her to stop and straighten it out.

This is how the Innu still put the net under the ice during the winter. They have to make sure the net doesn't touch the ice, because if it does it will freeze and stick to the ice. It's hard work but the Innu don't mind. It is one way we support our children. In those days it was the only way.

When my father came back, he chartered an aircraft. The plane couldn't land where we were camping because the ice was too rough. It did finally land on the same lake, but away from our camp. All of us children were very happy.

When I tell this story I can hardly remember because I was so small. In those days, I spent a lot of my time in *nutshimit* with my parents and sisters. These were the good times for us. Now I always wish we could start all over again.

---

[1] Ann Philomena
[2] Mary Martha

2

One time there were many families and elders camped at the end of Grand Lake[1], where we spent a lot of our time when I was a boy. This time there was old Stuinshish[2], Anspuas Andrew, Pien Shak[3], Apenam[4], Pien Selma and Nutaui – elders with sons who were already married.

After freeze-up the men, without their families, went caribou hunting in the Red Wine Mountains[5]. They walked over a hundred miles from the Suzanne River at the head of Grand Lake to the Red Wine Mountains. Each man had to pull his own sled. Some may have had one dog to help pull their load, but there were no dog teams. The dogs were also hunting dogs for porcupines or spruce partridges. I remember Apenam's son Enum was the one who broke the trail. The *utshimau*[6] of this hunt might have been Stuinshish since he was the oldest. They were gone on foot at least twenty days before they got back to our camp. They killed many caribou and the women were very happy to eat deer meat. We were all hungry for it.

Late that spring Apenam, one of the elders, came to visit my father to invite us to join his family. They were going to the Red Wine Mountains in the spring. Nutaui told us about the plan. He would go with Apenam and Enum to North West River to get more grub. They were gone only about a week before they got back to our camp and a few days later we all left together for the Red Wine Mountains. Everyone had his or her own sled, except for us children. We walked, but we were too young to pull a sled. At every new campsite Nutaui and Apenam would go ahead and move our supplies, then the next day we all moved together. So it was like making two trips every time we set up a new camp.

It was hard at times in those days, but we were our own bosses. Apenam was our *utshimau* for this trip. He wasn't chosen to be a leader by my father, but he automatically became the *utshimau* since it was his idea to go to the Red Wine Mountains. He knew where to camp and hunt, and his son Enam was the person who would shoot the game, such as caribou.

---

[1] Kakatshu-utshishtun
[2] Philip Michel Sr.
[3] Peter Jack, Sr.
[4] Old Abraham
[5] Penipuapisk^u
[6] Leader

In the past a hunter who shot an animal would not keep it for himself. The other person with him would get it. If more than two or three persons hunt together, then the oldest one kept the animal. If the same group hunted together for a number of days, others would get their share too if the hunt was successful. If not, only the oldest person would get the kill, whatever animal was hunted: caribou, bear or beaver.

Sometimes the oldest person might have decided to stay behind and only a young hunter would go on the hunt. If he killed one caribou, he would skin the animal and name the person to whom the caribou would be given. Everyone would help carry the meat. When they reached home, each person with meat went directly to the tent of the person who was to receive the caribou. If an elder was with the hunters and one caribou or black bear was killed, the elder would get that animal. The meat would be taken to his tent and he would share the meat with other families. This was the Innu way of life and it still exists today.

We were in the Red Wine Mountains region for a full three months. During that time, I never heard any angry voices, only the sound of the wind, and I remember the feeling of peace all around. I was sad I couldn't go hunting with Nutaui. I was too young to walk the long distances, but I was very happy to be allowed to go with him to haul the caribou back to our camp. I felt very proud to walk behind my father's sleigh. I watched Nutaui tie the caribou onto his sled and start to pull it by himself. He sweated and tired from the heavy load. I felt very sorry for him. I wished I were big enough to help him pull the heavy load. I watched from behind as he hauled the sled over a steep hill and I thought of how much he must love us. He did everything in his power to keep us alive. I was very happy when we arrived back at the camp. Nikaui was really proud of me for having walked that far and I had a very good feeling in my heart.

Sometimes when Nutaui was not around, I played outside. I watched Nikaui carry the heavy wood on her shoulder and I would help her saw it up for the fire. I also felt sorry for her and I wanted to help her out. Inside the tent there was still a lot of work for Nikaui to do, like cooking or tanning and smoking the deerskins. My older sisters also helped.

It was almost summer and our leader Apenam said it was time to move on back to Grand Lake. I was very happy. It was almost a year now since I had last seen Sheshatshiu. We had a very good move on our first day. We hauled a lot of meat. Most of it was dried so it was lighter than raw meat. Every time we moved our camp, we still had to make two trips. At a place called Red

Wine Mountain Lake[1], my father, Apenam and his son did a lot of trapping. They caught a few beavers, minks and otters. We steadily made our way to Grand Lake. Sometimes it was really hard to travel because the snow was very soft and wet. We couldn't move very far in one day. Sometimes we hardly made it past a turn in the winding river.

Once we stopped for tea and I watched my mother coming far behind us. I felt very sorry for her when I thought about the heavy load on her sled. She also had to haul my baby sister Nush[2]. It really makes me sad now when I think about my father and mother, how much they suffered, the heavy work they did in our traveling days.

We reached Grand Lake at the mouth of the Naskapi River[3], which was still full of ice. I thought we were going straight on to Sheshatshiu, but our leader Apenam said we would stay here until after break-up. He told us someone would have to go to North West River to get more grub, so he went with Nutaui and we were left behind.

"What are we going to do here? Why do we have to stop here?" I asked my mother. "Sheshatshiu is not very far away at all."

She must have known that I was anxious to go back to Sheshatshiu, so she explained the situation.

"Apenam is our *utshimau*[4] on this trip," Nikaui said to me. "We are staying here because the migratory birds will soon arrive. Your father and Apenam will hunt the ducks and after the ice breaks up we will move on to Sheshatshiu."

I wondered why they wanted to kill ducks and geese since we had plenty of dried and powdered meat. But I understood what my mother was saying. Besides, I didn't mind anymore because I wanted to see what duck hunting was like.

About a week later the men returned with flour, lard, tea, tobacco and lots of gun shells. As they approached the camp from a distance we noticed there was one more person besides the three of them. We didn't know who that person might be. It was Kanatuakueshiss[5], Apenam's grandson. He is now my brother-in-law, married to my sister Tshaukuesh[6]. We used to play together,

---

[1] Penipuapishku-nipi
[2] Rose
[3] Meshikamau-shipu
[4] Leader
[5] Francis Penashue
[6] Elizabeth

Kanatuakueshiss, Tshaukuesh and me. My sister must never have thought about marriage to him in those days. I don't know how old we were then. I was probably about ten years old and the two of them were a bit older.

By the middle of April it was so good to hear the songs of the geese and ducks as they arrived from the south. Then I really understood why we had stayed. Sometimes I would go with Nutaui and Nikaui. We paddled a canoe and it was easy to kill ducks and geese. We laid a white piece of board in the front of our white canoe. We were well camouflaged. Amidst the ice floes in the open waters of spring, the birds could not tell the difference between the white canoe and an ice floe. Once the ice and snow were gone, people used boughs and green paint as camouflage in the same way.

I learned a lot that spring. I never thought about going back to Sheshatshiu anymore. We had a new friend with us and duck hunting was a good experience for a boy my age. I thought we could only dry caribou meat, but I learned that any wild meat could be dried, including duck. The only difference was that there were no bones in dried caribou meat. Nikaui would leave the bones in the duck's meat when she was drying it. She would first loosen the joints of the bird like the wishbone, legs and wings, and then open them wide. She dried the meat inside the tent, but it could also be dried outside in the sun. When it rained she would bring the meat inside. It seemed easy for her, but I don't know how easy it would be for me. It might take only a couple of days to dry the meat.

Near the end of June, we ran out of flour, tea and tobacco again. My father and Apenam wanted to smoke real bad. Our *utshimau*[1] said it was time to move on to Sheshatshiu, but the ice was not broken up and was starting to float back and forth. As we made our way, sometimes we had to spend a few nights at one camp because we were icebound. Other times we had to walk around along the shore. My father and Enum carried the canoes. This was the most difficult time during our whole stay of one year in *nutshimit*. Once we reached a place called Ashkashkuaikan-shipiss[2], we were free of ice and we could paddle all the way to Sheshatshiu.

We landed on the beach in Sheshashui at the R.C.[3] Mission building. Many people came to greet my father. I was kind of shy so I was happy when Nutaui and Nikaui had finished setting up the tent. Later that evening many elders

---

[1] Leader
[2] A place halfway up Grand Lake on the north side; translates as Log Cache Box Brook
[3] Roman Catholic

came to see my father to hear the stories about our trip in *nutshimit*. My mother shared dried meat and ducks with them. While we were in *nutshimit* my father had prepared a small *makushan*[1] with the caribou bones for me. Now he asked me to give it to Shuashim Ashini[2]. I took that little bit of *makushan* or *pimin*[3] to Shuashim. He was very happy and really appreciated the gift.

A priest also came to visit my father. He said to my mother that we should go to school, so the next day we went. I didn't feel like going, but I had no choice because the priest ordered it. The elders respected the priest and everything he said had to be done.

The only teacher in the school was Father Pierson. It wasn't much of a school at first. We learned mostly about religion. I was kind of scared of so many things about the Catholic religion. I felt I was bad person. I thought if I didn't do what the priest said, I would die and go straight to hell. All those things really affected my life, not in a good way but in a very painful way. I thought people who were not Catholics were bad people. Now I can never forgive myself for having been disrespectful to those people.

In those days we never stayed very long in the community before we headed back to *nutshimit*. This time we went to Amitshuatan, a portage of the Naskapi River. It was late fall and we went with the families of Matshiu[4], Shimun[5], Tanien[6] and Mishen[7]. We all walked up to the higher ground, to a place called Kauauiekamast[8] where we spent our time until after freeze-up. That's where my father got very sick.

Shushep[9] made a *matutishanitshuap*[10] for him. I was only young and I had no idea what it was. The elders decided when a sick person needed a *matutishanitshuap* and someone to blow hot steam into their wound. After the sweat my father must have caught a cold and his illness got worse, so Matshiu and Mishen took the long walk to North West River to get help. Two or three days later a chopper arrived at our camp to pick up my father and

---

[1] Feast of the Caribou
[2] Old Shuashem Ashini
[3] Bone marrow, which rises to the surface of the pot when boiling the crushed bones of the caribou
[4] Mathew Ben Andrew
[5] Simon Pone
[6] Daniel Pone
[7] Michel Jack
[8] Translates as Round Lake
[9] Old Joseph Ashini
[10] Sweat lodge

take him to the North West River Hospital to see Dr. Tony Paddon. I was really worried about what would happen to us.

Dr. Paddon was well-known to most Innu and no one was concerned about his medicine. We were all very happy that my father was alive and well. The *matutishanitshuap* would have worked too if my father hadn't caught a chill right after the sweat. He should have stayed inside for three or four days after the sweat, but my father was a hunter and trapper and he couldn't wait that long. He had to go check his traps and that's why he got sick again.

Dr. Paddon's kind of medicine has been around since I can remember, but the Innu didn't use it much back then. Innu medicines were better than *Akaneshau*[1] medicines. During our stay in *nutshimit* that full year, others fell sick. They used Innu medicines that worked for them, because they followed certain rules. The problem with my father was that he didn't follow the rules.

One day after my father was taken to the North West River Hospital, our *utshimau* Joseph Ashini said we all had to move to another place. I had no idea if my mother was asked about this move, but she told us we would go too. We only made it halfway the first day, but by the end of the second day we had reached Utshashku-nipi[2]. We stayed there until late January.

One day I was inside the tent with my mother when we heard someone call out in a loud voice, "Someone is coming." My mother stood up to look outside. Every one of us in the camp came out to see someone heading towards our camp pulling his sled.

"That must be your father," Nikaui said and I knew immediately she was right.

"Can I go meet him?" I asked. She gave me my mitts, coat and cap. He was still about a half mile away. As I walked slowly but directly towards him, I kept thinking, "Is that my father or is there someone else headed this way?" Finally I recognized him. I was so happy to see him alive. He hugged and kissed me and asked me to sit on his sled. He looked so healthy. My mother must also have been very happy to see him.

We stayed a long time at Utshashku-nipi. From there we must have gone to the Naskapi River and later to Mulligan[3], where my brother Makiss[4] was born near Jim Baikie's house with the help of Jim's wife who was a midwife.

---

[1] White
[2] Translates as Muskrat Lake
[3] Maunakan
[4] Max

After the birth we went to a place called Minapakun-utshu[1] where Nutaui did some trapping. He'd collected just a few furs when my brother Shimuniss[2] got very sick. We moved back to Mulligan and from there Nutaui had to haul my brother all the way to North West River. We went with them. The day we arrived my father's sled broke. This was an omen. Nutaui knew something bad would happen when his sled collapsed.

Shimuniss was admitted to hospital and that summer he died of tuberculosis. There was no cure for TB. When I saw the priest coming to see my parents, I knew there was a problem. Nutaui and Nikaui went to the hospital across the river by canoe. I didn't stick around and went out playing with other kids. Just before I reached our tent that evening, I heard Nutaui, Nikaui and my sisters crying inside the tent. I knew right away that my brother had died. I didn't go inside the tent. I was afraid to face my mother and father. I don't know why. I had never seen an adult person crying in my life. I thought adult people didn't cry.

Later that summer Nikaui told us how she felt about my brother's death. She said the day she kissed my brother with tears in her eyes, his body was still warm and she believed he went straight to heaven to be with God. My father also told us that he knew my brother would die. He talked about the trip from Mulligan to North West River and how the ice was very rough when he hauled our sick brother on his sled. He had no problems with the sled until we came to land at the point of North West River, when one of the runners on his sled broke.

"That sled was mean to me," Nutaui told us. "That was the end of your brother's trip. It was sad, but I didn't want to tell you. I knew when the sled broke, this meant your brother would die sooner or later."

This is what my father told us. That's all I can remember about when I was very young.

---

[1] Translates as Old Man's Beard Mountain and is found north of Mulligan
[2] Simon

ONE SUMMER THE R.C. MISSION built a one-room schoolhouse. All the children were in the same class with only one teacher. That's where my school days really started. I was about ten years old and our teacher's name was Mr. Nash. He was very friendly and we often went fishing or berry-picking together. Sometimes Father Pierson would take his turn to teach us religion. At first I really enjoyed school, but after awhile I got tired of it.

Fortunately every year my family still spent time in *nutshimit* with other people from Sheshatshiu. Nutaui was a very good friend of a Settler from North West River, Cyril Michelin, who would take us in his big motorboat to the head of Grand Lake[1] where Nutaui did some trapping west of the Suzanne River[2]. In March we headed back to Sheshatshiu. We children would go to school, but my father was always on the move. He hunted a lot, especially in the Mealy Mountains[3] where there were a lot of caribou before the government imposed a hunting season and closed it. I was still too young then to go with my father.

I can remember very well when Nutaui got work at the old I.G.A.[4] Hospital in North West River. The hospital used to burn wood and my father was hired to supply the wood. It was a seasonal job and in the spring my father would go up Grand Lake to cut wood. He didn't make much money, only sixty dollars for one thousand logs. We children were young, but we were able to help Nutaui and Nikaui cut wood. It didn't take us that long to cut one thousand logs, maybe only one week.

I never heard my father use the word "lazy" and we could never use it to describe him either. When he wanted to do something, he'd just go ahead and do it! He helped many Settlers in his life. He also cut wood for them, although he didn't make that much money. He seemed to love this work.

"Last night I dreamt I ate all kinds of trees," I heard Nutaui tell Nikaui one time.

---

[1] Kakatshu-utshishtun, translates as Raven's Nest
[2] Pekissiu-shipiss
[3] Akami-uapishkᵘ
[4] International Grenfell Association

"In your life you cut many thousands of trees," she said. "Maybe that's why you dream that kind of dream."

In the summer the Innu would move their tents closer to the beach in Sheshatshiu. They'd set their nets to fish just off from where the old band council building now stands and all the way past the bridge. The nets were no more than thirty feet apart yet people would catch many salmon and trout. Every morning I would watch the elders check their nets. Sometimes, as many as five elders would be out at the same time in separate canoes.

The Innu were free to hunt anywhere in the Sheshatshiu area in those days because there were no game wardens or federal Fisheries Officers. We could hunt and fish anywhere without any worries about foreign laws. We were happy because outsiders never bothered us. Even the Settlers from across the river were friends with the Innu.

There were not many Innu people employed back then. A few teenagers, including me, worked when the Hudson's Bay and Grenfell boats arrived each spring and fall. The Hudson's Bay boat was the Pierre Radisson and I think the Grenfell boat was called the Lady Grenfell. We were hired for only two or three days. The Hudson's Bay boat brought stuff like flour, tea, sugar, lard, clothing, some fresh food and junk food. Because the ship anchored outside North West River, a motorboat had to bring all the stuff from the barge to shore.

The children went to school in the summer and quit in the fall to go to *nutshimit*. In August my father would get three months' relief from the welfare worker. If we couldn't get everything we needed, Nutaui would get credit from the Hudson's Bay Company. He'd pay back this loan if he got any furs. I was always anxious to go back to *nutshimit* because by then I was allowed to use a gun. We'd come back to Sheshatshiu after Christmas, but we never stayed long before we headed back to *nutshimit*.

A few years later a bigger school with two classrooms and a teachers' residence was built. Many Innu stopped going to *nutshimit* because their children had to go to school. But the new school didn't stop my parents. They still went to *nutshimit*, but now we didn't travel that far. My father was still doing well with his trapping back then.

We spent some winters at Grand Lake Rapids[1] where my father's main occupation was still to cut wood for the Grenfell Hospital or for Sid Blake and his son Edward. I didn't mind staying away from the community to help my

---

[1] Akutueshtinu, outlet of Grand Lake

11

father cut wood. My sister Tshaukuesh and I would also set snares for rabbits and sometimes we went trout fishing.

In the summer most people would settle in Sheshatshiu with their tents. I hated staying there because every morning I had to go to church. My mother would wake me up before 6:30. The church bell rang at 7:00 and my mother wanted me there as an altar boy. Sometimes I was very angry when she woke me up, but I didn't say anything because I was afraid of her. All Innu children were afraid of their parents. Children used to respect their parents.

My mother never drank alcohol until my sister got married. I don't even remember when my father started drinking. He may have been drinking all his life. I was really afraid of them when they were drunk, but they used to drink for only one day and they would stop the next day.

The priest was like a police officer back then. Father Pierson would go wherever anyone was drinking. Some people were afraid of him. Children were really afraid of him. Why were people and children so afraid of the priest? Maybe it was because we were afraid of God. I was afraid because I didn't want him to hit me in school while other children watched. If we didn't show up for Sunday Mass or for school on Monday, the priest would be really angry with us. He'd also remind us about our parents when they were drunk. We were ashamed when he said this to us with lots of other kids around.

One time Father Pierson scolded a young boy about my age who spent time at Kenamu River[1] with his grandparents in the summer. One day that boy came to school.

"Did you see God at Kenamu River?" Father Pierson asked the boy.

"Yes," the boy said. He looked so scared.

"That was not God you saw. That must have been a caribou," Father Pierson shouted at the boy. Then the priest laughed and we were all laughing too. I wonder how that boy felt? He must have felt shame. This is how the priest used to control the Innu in Sheshatshiu.

In those days the American military had a base at North West Point, about three miles from Sheshatshiu. The military men who were Catholic used to come to Sheshatshiu to attend Sunday Mass. In the afternoon they'd come back to show movies in the old schoolhouse. Every Sunday afternoon children anxiously waited for the military jeep to arrive. Once we saw the jeep, we knew there'd be a movie. They showed mostly Western or Bible movies. That was the first time I saw a real movie. I thought the things we saw in the movies

---

[1] Tshenuamiu-shipu

were really happening in other countries. In the cowboy and Indian movies I thought Indians were bad people, but I never thought about myself. I was always hoping the cowboys would win the war. I should never have thought that.

Father Pierson didn't mind seeing the military men come to Sheshatshiu. Maybe it was because he collected a lot of money from them, especially on Sundays. Even in the winter the military people used to come from Goose Bay[1] to attend Sunday Mass. There was no road, but there was a winter trail for snowmobiles – the kind only the military had that could take about ten passengers.

On Christmas Day every child would receive a Christmas gift from the Mission. I have no idea where all those toys came from, but maybe it was from the military men too. Father Pierson also received food and used clothing from them for the Innu. I remember some Innu used to dress in military clothes. They'd pull off the stripes and badges from the clothing. I'm sure they didn't like to wear these clothes, but they didn't have any choice. People didn't have the kind of money needed to buy expensive clothes from the Hudson's Bay store. Some adults used to dress in homemade coats and pants made by women. These clothes were not like the ones sold in the store. The women used buttons instead of zippers on the front of the shirts or coats. Some people wore Mountie pants and boots. The Mission gave away some of this old clothing. I don't know if people had to buy it. Maybe they paid a very cheap price to the Mission.

When someone got married in those days, they'd have a good time. They drank only homebrew. The priest would allow the Innu to have a *teueikan*[2] dance, but he'd decide on the time when they should stop. He used to own an Innu *teueikan*. Someone from Sheshatshiu must have given it to him. He'd rent out his *teueikan* for an Innu dance. Many elders also owned a *teueikan* for their own use when they were in *nutshimit*, but the priest didn't like elders to sing with the *teueikan*. Although he didn't have any proof, he thought drumming was the devil's work. He was only guessing. Once I saw the priest disrupt the *teueikan* dance. "Your time's up, time to quit," the priest said to the elders. I wasn't inside the tent so I don't know if he took the *teueikan*, but I saw he had it when he headed back to his place. The priest must have hurt the elders real bad when he took their *teueikan*.

---

[1] Kuspe
[2] Innu drum

The priest did many things to extinguish different parts of the Innu traditions and culture. In those days there was no band council. When the priest appointed the first Chief, there were no councilors or funding. A house was built for the Chief, but where did the money come from for that? The first Chief was Shushep Ashini[1]. I remember before he was appointed, he went to Ottawa to meet Queen Elizabeth. Who paid for that trip? Maybe he was invited by the Queen. Maybe that's how he became Chief. He was a very religious person and helped the priest out a lot. Every morning he'd start the fire in the large wood stove down in the basement of the church. He was also a well-respected person in Sheshatshiu.

---

[1] Old Joseph Ashini

I N MY TEEN YEARS I learned how to hunt and trap on my own. One time we set up camp halfway up Grand Lake at a place named Ashkashkuaikan-shipiss[1]. Before freeze-up we moved to higher ground to a place called Big Lake[2] where we had our main camp.

When the Innu went out to *nutshimit* in groups, they usually chose an area where they'd spend three to four months. They'd set up their main camp, but then go off hunting somewhere else, not just for one day but for as long as two or three weeks. The women stayed at the main camp. Without any difficulty we'd spend at least a week away. We brought an extra tent and stove for hunting and trapping away from the main camp.

This one time at Big Lake, Nutaui and two brothers-in-law headed further north to trap beavers, otters, minks and martens to sell the furs to the Hudson's Bay Company. A marten would fetch only about $15 to $20, mink $20 to $30, otter $30 to $40, lynx $60 to $70. Nutaui would receive no more than $1 for a muskrat fur and $30 to $45 for beaver, so in my trapping days I never made that much money. Whatever I got, I gave to Nutaui anyway. He told me that in the 1930s a silver fox fur sold for $1000 in Quebec. That was a long time ago.

The one thing I really liked to do in *nutshimit* was to hunt beavers. Sometimes we'd find a beaver lodge in a small pond. It could take us only one day to kill all the beavers, not an easy feat for one day's work but one we did many times. The beaver lodge is not the only place where beavers live in the winter. When the beaver builds his lodge he also builds dens that serve as emergency shelters in different places around the pond. Those dens are built underwater and lead to dry ground. The lodges can easily be seen, but it's very hard to notice the dens. The only way to find them is by feeling around with a stick. Usually the ice is thin near the den so we have to make sure the ice is strong enough to walk on for our own safety. Usually in the fall during the first few days of freeze-up, it's not safe. We have to use a stick about six feet long to test the ice. If we can't break the ice with the stick, it's safe to walk but we

---

[1] Translates as Log Cache Box River
[2] Mishta-mishkumi, translates as Big Winter Lake

have to test it every few feet. Once we've found all the dens there's no other place for the beavers to hide. Then we can kill all the beavers in one day, although we aren't always so lucky. There are times when we find it difficult even in a small pond. In the old days when we couldn't get all the beavers, my father wouldn't let us break the beaver lodge.

"If you break the lodge, the beavers will freeze," Nutaui told us once. "They need a warm place to stay for the winter just like we do. And maybe the Missinaku[1] doesn't want us to kill its beavers." It sounded like he was talking about a human being.

One time when we were supposed to check our trap line, Nutaui asked me if I could cut down a small tree. I didn't know why he needed a stick but I took an axe, headed out and chopped down the tree. When I tried to split it I accidentally cut my foot. I was really afraid, although I didn't feel the pain. I tried to run as fast as I could with my snowshoes. When I got to the camp my brother-in-law Penute Ashini took off my moccasin and looked at the wound.

"Why did you have to cut your foot when we need to leave tomorrow?" Nutaui asked me. He must have been really frustrated because now I wouldn't be able to go trapping.

Nikaui treated my wound. She cut a small juniper tree and sawed it into short pieces that she then boiled in water. She carefully peeled off the bark. I didn't know what she was doing. She brought a log that was already peeled inside and another smaller one about two feet long and two inches in diameter. She rolled the bark into a ball and pounded it with the stick. I was wondering why she wasn't using an axe or a rock. She said it was better to use this stick to pound the sticky bark because the bark belonged to the stick and that way it would help to heal the wound faster. After the bark was pounded, it looked and felt like gum. She put this gum on my wound. She changed the poultice every day and in no more than one week my foot was healed.

The next day after I hurt myself Nutaui and two brothers-in-law left to check their beaver and mink traps. During those days I went with Nikaui instead to check her traps. She got two minks and my sister got one too. The second time we went out to a lake called Kainipassuakamat[2] where we saw a fox. I was hanging on to my dog with a rope tied around its neck. When the dog saw the fox she pulled so hard I let go of her and off she went to chase the fox. When we reached the end of the lake we saw fresh caribou tracks.

---

[1] Beaver Master
[2] A lake with many small islands north of Big Lake

16

We advised Nutaui about the tracks and he told us to move our camp. My brother-in-law headed out with his gun to track the caribou. He didn't bother to help set up the tent. About an hour later we began to anxiously listen for a shot but it never came. I was very disappointed. If I hadn't let that dog run free I knew my brother-in-law would've killed that caribou.

After we'd checked all our traps my brother-in-law Matshiu[1] left to go to Grand Lake. He told us he would not stop at our main camp but go directly to the place where he'd left some stuff. On his way he killed three caribou. He also found our dog that had been missing for three days. He headed back to the main camp and he was already there when we returned. The next day Nikaui asked me and my two sisters if we could go down to Grand Lake to pick up some bags of flour. We headed out to pick up not only the flour but other supplies as well.

Stuinshiss[2] was camped at Grand Lake along with his son[3] and Enum Abraham, but all the men from that camp were gone trapping for a few days. Our aunt, old Mani Nush[4] ,was very happy to see us. She told us her granddaughter, Mani Anish[5] , had been badly hurt when a tree fell on her chest. The next morning a military chopper flew over our camp. We didn't see it coming. Old Mani Nush shouted at us to wave them down, but it was too late. The chopper had already passed our camp and it didn't circle around. Who would have been the spokesperson if the chopper had landed? None of us could speak English.

Later that day we headed back to our main camp. It took us a whole day but I didn't mind walking that far. In those days I never thought about traveling with machines such as skidoos or outboard motorboats.

I heard Nutaui talk many times about going back to Sept Isles in those days, but he'd always say he couldn't leave Sheshatshiu because of my late brother. He'd talk about the different traveling routes to Sept Isles. He named all the

---

[1] Matshiu Ben Andrew
[2] Old Philip Michel
[3] Philip Junior
[4] Mary Rose
[5] Mary Agnes

rivers and lakes along these routes and he described the way if we decided to move back. He was getting old but he still knew how to get there very well. The problem was that Sheshatshiu was the place where he wanted to die because of my brother. He must have loved him very much. My brother's Christian name was Simon, the same as my father. We called my brother Shimuniss which means Little Simon.

During those years, we always went back to Sheshatshiu in late January. Many times I didn't feel like going because I didn't have anything to do there. I could only go to school and church. Besides that I didn't like to see Nutaui and Nikaui getting drunk. When springtime rolled around, at least there were many Innu who hunted ducks and geese and there was a little bit of wild meat available.

One September, Cyril Michelin took us from Sheshatshiu to Happy Valley[1] in his motorboat. We then traveled with an elder Settler as far as Muskrat Falls Hill[2]. We portaged around the falls. Tsheniu Shimiu[3] and his son Sepastien were with us. We paddled all the way from Muskrat Falls Hill to Gull Island[4]. The only portage from Happy Valley to Gull Island is called Gull Lake[5]. It was always a very good place for trapping, hunting and fishing.

It took us two weeks to get to Gull Island. We had to take some of our gear ahead of us. Nutaui happened to have two canoes on this trip, and my mother and I used one. We sometimes spent two or three days in one place because my father was hunting a lot of porcupine and partridge. The porcupines were everywhere.

We had to pass three rough rapids to reach Gull Island. I watched Nutaui use a long pole while he stood up in his canoe. With every push the canoe moved smoothly through the rapids. It looked so easy for him but I never learned how to pole my way through rapids with a heavy load in the canoe. I should have but I guess Nutaui never let me try. After he passed the rapids he came back for us and guided the other canoe. I marveled at the skill he had to pole himself through those rough rapids.

Tsheniu Shimiu's son Sepastien was about the same age as me. We stayed around Gull Island until after Christmas. Sepastien and I had a good time

---

[1] Apipani
[2] Manitu-utshu, translates as Evil Creature Mountain
[3] Old Simeo Pastitshi
[4] Tshiashkunish
[5] Tshiashku-nipi

18

hunting porcupine and spruce partridge together with a dog. In the summer it was very difficult to find any porcupine without a dog. It was much easier in the winter because we couldn't miss any kind of animal tracks in the snow.

One time on my own I found porcupine tracks leading into a cave. I tried to crawl inside and when I was about halfway in, I realized the den was not very big. I tried to move backwards but my heavy coat got stuck on each side of the cave. It took a long time before I could take off my coat and free myself. "Never again in my life will I ever try to get inside a porcupine's cave," I thought after I'd freed myself.

Another time I went hunting with Nutaui before freeze-up and we found a beaver lodge in a small pond. He told me that in the evening before dark the beavers would come out and we should wait for them in a spot close to their dam. We sat very quietly and Nutaui spoke in a whisper. Just before the sun went down we saw one beaver swim across the pond. It turned and swam toward the dam. Then we saw a second one swimming towards the end of the pond. The one near the dam was close enough to shoot. I didn't know why Nutaui wasn't shooting it. The beaver dove again and came out a few seconds later. This time it was so close but still Nutaui wouldn't shoot. It was only when the beaver turned toward the other end that my father took a shot. Then I knew why he didn't shoot earlier. He was waiting for the beaver to turn around so he could shoot at the back of the beaver's head.

"Sit still. The other one will come this way to find out about the shot," Nutaui whispered. He was right. We saw the other beaver swimming towards us. She dove and came out closer yet, dove again and a few seconds later lifted her head and sniffed the air before diving again. She did that a couple more times and finally swam towards the dam. As she turned to swim across the pond my father shot her. We retrieved one of the beavers but the other sank. Nutaui said it would surface by morning so we had to stay the night.

"How are we going to spend the night without a tent and stove?" I thought. "How will we get any sleep on such a long fall night?" I wondered but I didn't say anything. That was my first experience of sleeping outside without any shelter. Later that night Nutaui made a small fire to boil the kettle. After we had something to eat he cut more logs, both green and dry ones about eight feet long. We didn't have a watch so we didn't know the time. The night was clear and I lay down beside the fire looking at the stars and the moon. I didn't feel sleepy but I must have dozed off. When I awoke Nutaui wasn't around. Where was he gone? The next thing I knew I could hear him cutting wood nearby. I stood up and ran to help him carry the wood back. Even though it was my first time I really loved sleeping under the stars.

"In years to come if you are alone outside or in the tent, don't be afraid even if you see or hear someone," Nutaui explained to me later. "It can happen many times to anyone. People can see someone who looks like a human being, but it's a Spirit who looks after us." I accepted and respected what he said.

The next morning after breakfast we went back to the pond where Nutaui had shot the beaver. We approached the beaver dam and found the beaver that had sank the day before. It was still early when we left for home and I carried one of the beavers on my back. We checked a few traps on the way. We found a lynx caught in one of the traps and it was still alive. Nutaui told me to shoot it in the head. He said if I tried to hit it with a stick, it might come loose from the trap.

Late that fall before freeze-up we moved our camp to the other side of Gull Island where Nutaui set his traps again. By this time he always invited me to join him. One time the two of us set out with very little gear, only a tent, a stove and a little bit of grub. We didn't just travel steady. We found two or three beaver lodges in different places along the way and stopped for a few days to set our beaver traps. While we traveled Nutaui also picked out the best place for me to set my mink trap. Although I didn't do very well that year I did help my father catch the animals. The price of furs wasn't that good but whatever we got helped us buy grub for the family. We camped three times before we reached our destination.

"We are going back tomorrow but not the same way we came," Nutaui told me about a week later.

"But that was a good trail we came on," I said.

"We'll see if we can find more beavers on the way back," was all Nutaui said.

The next morning I watched him pack our gear onto his sleigh. I didn't have a sled. All I carried were a few steel traps and my gun. Nutaui hauled everything on his sled. We were just about ready to go when he told me that this time I would break trail. I was surprised. Why did he want me to break trail? Maybe it was part of my training. I took the lead and it wasn't as easy as

I thought. I got lost so often. I tried to be very careful about where I was heading but I often went in the wrong direction. I'd stop and not know where to go. Nutaui would catch up and point out the hills and valleys to me, indicating the way I should go. Again I'd take off in the lead but the same thing happened over and over again.

"Don't pick the open areas that make it easy for you to walk," Nutaui said to me this time. "That's why you get lost. You only pick the best spots to walk." He finally took the lead and I pulled his sled. Luckily his load wasn't that heavy. I watched my father break trail. He never picked the open areas but ploughed straight through heavily wooded places. He never bothered to go around those hard places. It didn't take us long before we came across our main trail. We reached the last pond before Gull Island and I knew we'd reach home in a couple of hours. However, my father said we'd spend the night. That was okay with me and after we set up our tent I was able to cut enough wood for the night.

Before I went to sleep, Nutaui told me a story about a *kakushapatak*[1] called Uashaunu. Nutaui said the old man used to perform a lot of miracles. He talked about how Uashaunu sometimes ran out of tobacco and his *Mishtapeu*[2] would bring him some.

"I saw this with my own eyes and he shared that tobacco with me," Nutaui said. "But the tobacco tasted different."

Uashaunu told Nutaui that a *Mishtapeu* moves like a flash of light and that maybe the tobacco blew away out of his hand. My father also told me that during a shaking tent ceremony a *kakushapatak* would invite all kinds of *Aueshish-utshimaut*[3] to come inside the tent. Any person could talk to any of these spirits with the help of an interpreter. The person had to be outside the shaking tent but would hear the *Aueshish-utshimaut* inside. My father might have gone on with his story but I guess I fell asleep.

The next morning we headed down to Gull Island and it was still early when we reached our main camp. Nikaui must have made homebrew while we were gone because after lunch Nutaui started to drink. They were both drinking. My brother-in-law Penute[4] and my sister had their own tent, so Nutaui asked me to take a large mug of homebrew to Penute. Penute had his own

---

[1] Shaman
[2] Spirit Master
[3] Animal Spirits or Animal Masters
[4] Daniel Ashini's father

homebrew and he sent me back with a dipper of his for Nutaui. I made many trips back and forth.

I really wanted to taste the homebrew. Every time I took a mug to Nutaui or to Penute I drank a little. Finally I could feel it in my head. I was very excited about how it made me feel like an adult person. I felt proud, like a show-off. I just can't really describe how I felt this first time I drank. If we'd been in the community I don't know what would have happened. Maybe people would've made fun of me for drinking at my age. Eventually my father caught on that I was drinking. He wasn't angry with me. Instead he offered me some of his brew. I must have been drunk. I didn't remember anything when I woke up later that day. I had a very bad headache and a hangover.

"Never again will I taste any alcohol in my life," I thought to myself.

That evening me and my sister Tshaukuesh went to check my mother's rabbit snares. I was very sick but I went anyway. As we walked through the woods she reminded me of what had happened that morning. She told me the things I said when I was drunk. I was really ashamed and I wished she'd stop talking about it. When we got home she again reminded me and I thought I'd never drink again.

At the end of that year at Gull Island we all went back to Lake Melville[1] after Christmas. We traveled as far as Happy Valley and Nutaui decided to stay put. I have no idea why but I think the reason might have been to visit with old Tshetshepateu[2]. The only Innu who was a permanent resident in the Happy Valley area, Tshetshepateu was originally from Davis Inlet[3] and worked at the American base for many years. Nutaui had met him in Old Davis Inlet[4] in the 1930s, so I guess they were always friends. The two were about the same age. Tshetshepateu would often invite Nutaui to his house for a drink.

About a month later a priest from Sheshatshiu Father Pierson came to visit us. It wasn't just a friendly visit. He told my parents that we should move back to Sheshatshiu so the children could go to school. He even arranged

---

[1] Atatshi-uinipeku, translates as Cut Off Sea
[2] Nickname for old Edward Rich, which translates as *He walks early in the morning*
[3] Utshimassit, translates as Place of the Boss
[4] Kauishatukuants

transportation for us and the next day a big truck arrived at our camp. All of us, including other families at the site, moved to Sheshatshiu where I didn't do anything. I just went to school.

I remember later that spring three couples arrived from Davis Inlet. They'd walked and canoed all the way to Sheshatshiu. They arrived by canoe after break-up. It amazed me how they had come all the way overland from Old Davis Inlet to Sheshatshiu. They stayed two or three years in Sheshatshiu before they headed back.

IN THE SUMMER the Innu and Settlers from North West River used to play soccer games just outside the Mission building. These were not rough games, only for fun. I used to play with other boys my age. This was the only recreational game Innu children played in those days. Father Pierson also played soccer with us. The games took place after mass on Sundays or in the evenings on weekdays. There were also canoe races and ball games but these were adult games.

Girls and boys weren't allowed to stay out late into the night. Many evenings Father Pierson would patrol the community with his flashlight. When we saw someone with a flashlight, we knew it was the priest. We'd run through the woods in all different directions so that the priest couldn't catch us. There were times when he'd be really nice to us and there were other times when he'd be really angry with us.

In the afternoon Father Pierson would take his turn to teach us in school. We had to be in the classroom before he arrived. Every one of us would wait patiently. Usually he held a flat stick in his hand and if he walked into the classroom with a smile on his face we were all happy. If he came in with his face all red we knew he was angry. Without saying a word he'd make the sign of the cross and we'd all stand to pray.

Before the bridge was built between Sheshatshiu and North West River many white Settlers used to leave their trucks on our side of the river. Some Settlers built their own garages. Sometimes the kids would break in or steal something from the garages. Once the Settlers found out they'd report it to Father Pierson, who would then come to school and ask us who stole that thing or who broke into that garage. He had good reason to be angry with us then.

Father Pierson didn't like it when the Innu drank. I saw the priest come many times to see people who were on the booze. Some Innu would go see the priest when they were drunk. They'd argue and say things they wouldn't dare say when they were sober. They must've been very frustrated about the way the priest was trying to control the whole community. They said all the things that they didn't like about what the priest was doing.

Innu people drank alcohol back then but not that often. Innu weren't allowed to buy yeast at the Hudson's Bay store because they used it to make homebrew. The priest must've talked to the store manager and told him not to sell any yeast to the Innu but that didn't stop the Innu. Many were friends with Settlers from across the river and so they didn't have any problem getting yeast. Once in a while I'd drink in those days when I was still in school. My two sisters Nush and Tshauskuesh also went to school. By this time I'd learned everything about hunting and trapping.

Sometimes the priest would be gone for one to three months and a priest from Davis Inlet would replace him. When a new priest came, many Innu would go to confession. Why was this? In those days I didn't know whether or not the church was doing a good job with the Innu. The thing I didn't like was when the priest forced us children to go to church every Sunday and to be home before ten o'clock every evening. I felt the church was mistreating us. Everyone should have the right to make his or her own decisions about these things.

When the Innu were not drinking I never saw them sing with the *teueikan*[1] but when they drank they'd sing traditional songs to the beat of the *teueikan*. Why wouldn't they sing when they were sober? They were probably afraid of the priest. The Innu weren't born to be Catholic. They were forced into being baptized in the name of Jesus. According to our elders we used to have our own spirituality. One time I heard an elder, Shuashem[2] Nui, say that the priest thought it was evil to perform the shaking tent but Shuashem believed the ceremony was a gift from the Creator.

My parents had good reasons to keep taking me to *nutshimit* with them. If I'd stayed behind and gone to school all the time I would've learned only things that don't belong to my culture. I'd probably have a good formal education, but I'd be a useless person in our culture.

It was 1965 and the next fall we headed for Gull Lake again for the last time. We went with my brother-in-law Matshiu and the late Shenum[3]. After the

---

[1] Innu drum
[2] Joachim Nui
[3] Jerome Pokue

hydro dams were built on the Churchill River[1] in 1967, the Innu stopped going to Gull Island although it had always been a very good place to trap, hunt or fish.

We left a bit late that day and it was getting cold when we reached Porcupine Rapids[2]. We happened to stop for tea at a place called Sand Bank Beach[3] on the Churchill River, where we saw some geese a distance away. Shenum took his shotgun and told us to wait for him. He headed through the woods and was gone about an hour when we finally heard a shot.

"We must go now. He'll probably wait for us to come there," Nutaui said. Although it was very cold we were still using canoes. When we arrived we were really surprised. How had Shenum killed seven geese all by himself with one gun? I'd never seen anyone kill seven geese all by himself!

Shenum's father was supposed to come with us to *nutshimit* but he was too old and stayed in Mud Lake. He was the last *kakushapatak*[4] in Sheshatshiu. In the 1960s he performed a shaking tent for the last time at Kenamu River just across the bay from Sheshashiu. I never saw a shaking tent myself but I've heard a lot of information about it. I visited this *kakushapatak* a lot and one time I asked his wife if she had the powers.

"Your grandfather is getting old so I have more power than him," I was surprised to hear her say. I said "grandfather" but that doesn't mean he was my real grandfather. In our culture we call any elder Mushum[5] or Nukum[6].

Back then I thought the shaking tent was an evil thing because Nikaui would say that. I guess she was brainwashed by the church. I should've listened to Nutaui who talked about how the shaking tent was not evil and helped many Innu to survive in *nutshimit*. I was confused and caught in the middle between the two cultures.

Three days later we made it to Gull Island. Our first day of hunting was very successful. Matshiu and Shenum killed eleven caribou. The next morning most of us at the camp went to pick up the meat. It was so peaceful to have lunch outside with fresh caribou meat.

Nutaui didn't do much trapping that year. He killed a few beavers, minks and a couple lynxes. We all went to Happy Valley before Christmas and spent

---

[1] Mishte-shipu
[2] Kaku-paushtikuʷ
[3] Kaishpanekaut
[4] Shaman
[5] Grandfather
[6] Grandmother

a few weeks in the area before moving on to Sheshatshiu. Later that spring we went caribou hunting in the Mealy Mountains with my father and brother-in-law. We went by dog team and made it all the way in one day. The day we left was cold and windy. We weren't facing the wind but we weren't dressed that warmly. There was no such thing as skidoo pants or skidoo boots in those days. After we passed Kenimich River we traveled to a marsh area called Mishta-massek[1] where we met Kamikuakueuiet[2] and his three dogs. He'd tied the dogs' noses together. I don't know why. Maybe he didn't want them to bark. He might've thought they were making too much noise. He must've had a good reason. The dogs were tired and a lot of hot steam was blowing out of their mouths.

That evening Matshiu and I made a big fire outside to cook a meal for our dogs. I was kind of lonely because we were still close to Sheshatshiu and I must've been thinking about my girlfriend. There was no one to talk to about her, only Nutaui and Matshiu.

There weren't many signs of caribou in the area because they were being hunted year round. Too many hunters must've driven most of the herd further inland. I set out to hunt with Matshiu, and Nutaui stayed behind to look after the dogs. We couldn't go to the top of the mountains because of the bad weather and it was hard to see where we were going.

A couple of days later the weather cleared up. This was our last try to find any caribou. We hadn't walked far when we came across fresh caribou tracks. Matshiu could tell the track was only a few hours old. We continued to follow the trail but after a couple of hours we still could find no sign of the caribou. We continued on their tail. Finally we saw one young caribou. Both of us had 30-30 Winchester rifles and we shot many times but we didn't hit the target. That lone caribou leaped straight up the hill. We followed it to the top where we found the rest of the herd. We had them cornered. The only way out to get down the hill was for them to pass by where we stood. We killed eight caribou and only two escaped.

I was fifteen years old this first time I killed a caribou. I thought I'd better not show how I felt because I was with Matshiu and I knew he'd killed many caribou in his life. But inside my heart I treasured the feeling. If I'd been alone I would've been very proud and showing off. We headed back to the camp, a very long walk, and we only made it back late that night. The next morning

---

[1] Translates as Big Marsh
[2] Old Simon Pasteen

we moved our camp closer to the kill because we had to haul all the caribou to the camp. We left three caribou behind on the first haul. Two of them were for us and the other was for Matshiu. A week later the two of us went back to get the rest of the caribou. When I got back to the community I was so excited to tell my mother and friends about how I shot the caribou. Some of them were very interested to hear my story.

That fall I also shot and killed a beaver for the first time. We were again at Porcupine Rapids[1], near Gull Island. I'd killed a beaver with a steel trap but not with a gun. I was hunting with Nutaui all the time and that morning we left early, just the two of us. We passed many ponds but found no sign of beavers. We shot only one porcupine and a few spruce partridges.

In the late afternoon we decided to turn back. On the way home we came across a very large pond – maybe one mile long and one-quarter mile wide. We saw about six beavers on the other side and Nutaui said we should wait for them at the mouth of the pond. After about an hour none of them had swum our way. Nutaui directed me to walk toward a point halfway around the pond and wait for them there. I was very happy to be on my own. I had my 22 rifle and walked right over to the point and waited. After a long time I saw two beavers swimming away from their lodge. One of them was swimming straight across towards me. The other one swam along the shore towards the mouth of the pond.

I was ready to shoot the one swimming my way, but something reminded me that I had to wait until it turned and headed towards the other end. I was also nervous because I wondered what Nutaui would say if I missed it? As the beaver turned I aimed and shot. Bull's eye! I hit the target. My first beaver with a gun. Later I heard another shot. When I met up with Nutaui and told him I'd killed a beaver I found out he'd killed one too. It was almost dark so Nutaui said that we should spend the night at that spot. That was my second time sleeping outdoors overnight and once again I enjoyed it.

---

[1] Kaku-paushtiku

I'll never forget what I learned from Nutaui. My father taught me how to take care of myself alone in the bush. I learned to know the land well. For example, if I was hunting alone I had to make sure I didn't get lost. When I returned in the night I had to know how many small streams I'd crossed before I reached my camp. I had to know the hills and ponds I'd passed over earlier. Even if I didn't come back the same way I'd notice these hills and ponds. He also taught me to make sure I didn't get lost walking at night. It's not easy, especially if you don't know your way. You have to make sure you know where you're heading. Innu have to be able to return home safely. This is the most important thing to know for any hunter or trapper.

I also learned how to set up a tent just by watching others do it. It's a little bit harder in the winter than in the summer. In deep snow a tent can be set up anywhere in a wooded area. I know how to erect a tent to last a week or longer. First I mark out the spot with my feet and then level off the surface with snowshoes. I cut small trees for tent poles and use the branches as insulation along the sides to help the tent stay warm. I also pack snow along the sides as insulation to help keep the drafts out and the tent warm. If the tent is twelve feet by twelve feet, I need about thirty or more sticks, including poles for all along the inside walls of the tent as well as poles for the outside. Poles are also needed as legs to hold up the sheet metal stove. The poles are stuck deep into the snow below the inside tent floor and hold the stove about one foot above the ground. Long sticks are needed for these stove legs, partly for safety and also to make sure the stove does not move when something heavy is placed on it, like a pot of crushed bones in water to boil for *Makushan*[1]. Once the tent is set up, the women place spruce boughs on the floor for more insulation. We don't need to keep the fire going all night, but if someone is cold in the middle of the night they get up and make a fire and the tent heats up in a matter of minutes. A small tent needs a small stove while a larger tent needs a bigger stove.

It's a little bit easier to set up the tent in the summer but we still need the same number of sticks and boughs for the floor. I feel very comfortable sleeping

---

[1] Feast of the Caribou

in the tent either in winter or summer because of the fresh air I breathe. The smell of the boughs and wood smoke brings back a lot of memories of the old days.

I learned other survival skills such as how to stay outdoors during the night, in case of an emergency in the community, if I got lost or for any other reason. I learned many things from my father, and my sisters learned other things from my mother.

As I got older my father started to go to *nutshimit* by himself sometimes for two or three months, all alone. I was at school but I was really proud that I'd learned everything about life in *nutshimit*. I didn't do anything in Sheshatshiu other than just go to school and drink. I got tired of school so I quit. All the time I was very anxious to get back to *nutshimit*.

ONE FALL WE CHARTERED a plane and I went back in *nutshimit* with Nutaui and my brother-in-law Tuminik[1]. Chartered planes weren't that expensive in those days. Before we left we cut a lot of wood for my mother to make sure she had enough fuel while we were gone. We landed in a place called Kauipushkakamat[2]. Other people were already there including my other brother-in-law Penute along with his brother-in-law Ponus Nuke, so we couldn't trap. We had to move farther away to Mitshishu-utshishtun[3].

One morning I got up and dressed. I put on my snowshoes and headed out into a beautiful dry day. I crossed the lake and I could see the sparkling snow all around as I watched each step I took with my snowshoes. I was walking on unpolluted land. I reached the other side of the lake and continued straight into the woods until I came across another lake. I set my first trap and kept going to the end of the lake where I set my second trap. I then decided to go through the woods just to see if there were any signs of martens.

I hadn't walked far when I came across a porcupine track. I followed it and soon caught up with the porcupine climbing a tree. That's when I made my first mistake. I knew female porcupines were fat about this time of year. I figured the only way to find out if it was female was to cut down the tree and have a closer look. I discovered it was male because male porcupines are skinny right after they mate in the fall so I let it go. I didn't bother to kill it. I kept going to set my third trap, this time for marten. I then walked back to the lake to follow the brook. It was fall and the day was very short. I decided to boil up water for tea, and after I finished my lunch it was time to head back. I took a shortcut and as soon as I reached the lake where we were camping I decided to set a fox trap. It was my first time. I'd never seen my father set a fox trap but he'd explained it to me so I followed his instructions. I made it home just before dark and told my story about what I did with the porcupine.

"If you don't respect the animals you're going to find it hard to find them again," Nutaui said. That was the first time he told me about respect for the

---

[1] Dominic Pokue
[2] Translates as Burnt Area Lake
[3] Translates as Eagle's Nest Lake

porcupine. I wondered why he'd never mentioned it before. He had told me to respect all animals but he never explained that I should not check to see if a porcupine is male or female. According to Innu beliefs I should've just killed that porcupine and taken it home. I should've known better. Maybe I'd been too young for my father to teach me this but what he said that day is exactly what happened. For the next three years I never saw even a sign of a porcupine. Uhuapeu[1] gave me a three-year penalty. I felt sorry that I didn't know that female porcupines had shorter tails than males. I could easily have recognized the length of the tail. I'd made a mistake that I would never repeat in my life.

The next day I set out with Nutaui to check his traps. It was snowing but we didn't mind. We found only two minks so Nutaui told me he'd set more traps. I headed further downriver and came across two fresh sets of otter tracks. I followed them and suddenly they turned sharply to the right into the open water. The otters must've heard my father setting traps. I walked back to tell him about the otters. It was late afternoon and he said that maybe they'd come out of the water later. We moved closer to the open water and waited for them. Finally one came out but she was too far away to shoot. She didn't want to come out on our side of the pond. Nutaui told me to walk across the pond and wait for her. I didn't have to wait long before she came out again. She was very close and I shot her.

Nutaui said that if we spent the night the other one might come out early in the morning. I told him I couldn't spend the night and I was going home. I didn't want to. The nights were too long in the fall. I didn't think it was worth spending the night there just to wait for one otter. We were only about three or four hours' walk from our tent. Finally I convinced him to head back to camp.

I was breaking trail. I didn't mind because I didn't want to spend the night outdoors in this weather. Nutaui followed behind. Every once in a while I had to wait for him to catch up. As I reached the long narrow lake where we were camping I decided to stop again and wait for him. Night had fallen. The sky was clear and a full moon shone across the lake. I looked westward over the

---

[1] Porcupine Master

lake and saw someone coming toward me. I knew there was no one else in the area besides us and it clearly was not an animal. I thought it must be my brother-in-law Tuminik. The silhouette walked with snowshoes and carried a gun on his shoulder. I looked back to see if my father was coming. Seconds later I turned my head but the person had disappeared. An Akaneshau[1] would have said it was only my imagination. My father came out from the woods a moment later. I started to walk again. The person I saw never showed up at our camp. I wasn't scared and I didn't care. Whoever he was, I'd never know.

We reached our camp late in the night. I made a fire and chopped some wood. We didn't have a bucksaw so I had to use an axe. My brother-in-law arrived that night. I told him about the person I had seen but he said it couldn't have been him.

There are many burial grounds in *nutshimit* but not around where we were. Someone must've died in that area but a very long time ago, beyond anyone's memory. Many times I've heard Innu speak of how they saw a person in many different places in *nutshimit* – places where Innu had died long ago. I thought it could be a dead person's Spirit that I'd seen. Or I might've seen an outside Spirit – one who keeps an eye on Innu people, according to what the elders say.

The next day we moved to a nearby pond where Tuminik had spotted a beaver en route to our camp. Nutaui and Tuminik set their traps at the entrance of the beaver lodge and I set other ones in places where beavers usually hide. The pond was small so I thought it would only take a few hours to kill all the beavers. After three days we still had not caught one single beaver. On the last day a beaver suddenly appeared out of the water in the middle of nowhere. For three days we continued to study the pond but again no sign of the beavers. We knew they were in the pond but where? Even my father's hunting dog had proven useless. Suddenly on the fourth day the beaver's head surfaced about thirty feet away from us. Tuminik shot it. That afternoon I headed to the big lake nearby with only a 410 shotgun. As I reached the mouth of the lake I looked over to the open water at the other end. A large beaver came out of the water. I could only see its nose. I shot it with my 410 shot gun but I wasn't sure if I'd killed it.

That night back at our tent just as we were about to go to sleep we heard the dog bark. At first we didn't pay much attention because she often barked

---

[1] White person, or White English-speaking person

but later my father said we should check to see if she was okay. Tuminik and I went out and found her with a beaver by the tail. She'd probably stopped barking when she grabbed the beaver and then dropped it just long enough to bark again. It must've been the beaver I'd shot earlier. A wounded beaver cannot stay underwater. It has to be on dry land. The following morning we moved back to our first camp. We'd only hunted down two beavers although we knew there were more from the size of the lodge. I went to check my traps and found a mink, a marten and a fox. It didn't seem like much but it was better than nothing. That fall I was still giving my father whatever I found in my traps.

On the 18th of December, Tuminik left early for his camp where a plane was meant to land that day. He arrived just in time to ask the pilot to return for all of us on December 21st. On the 20th we moved all our gear to his camp. Only four days before Christmas and we wanted to be home for the celebrations. We couldn't go anywhere and just waited anxiously to hear the sound of the plane's motor. It was about noon when my father said that if the plane didn't show up soon we'd be late for Christmas. We decided to pack our gear and head out by foot. Tuminik said he'd wait a couple more hours and if the plane didn't come he'd catch up to us. I felt bad. I thought we should wait for the plane rather than walk another 100 miles to Happy Valley. When we stopped for tea and Tuminik caught up with us I was happy. I didn't have to think about Tuminik landing in Sheshatshiu that same day while we slowly made our way through the deep snow.

We didn't travel far that first day because we'd left in the afternoon. We made it as far as Gull Island on the second day. On the 23rd of December we passed Porcupine Rapids[1] near Muskrat Falls Hill. We decided to stay in Bill Michelin's tilt. We thought it was actually Christmas Eve so my father cooked beaver meat for our midnight dinner. He took out his rosary and we all prayed. We ate our supper and went to bed. Early next morning we hit the road again. I thought for sure we'd make it to Happy Valley that day. I was very happy when we passed a pump house that evening. I knew that we'd soon reach Tshetshepateu's house about a mile ahead. Tshetshepateu was very happy to see my father. He invited us into his house and his wife cooked up some food for us. Tshetshepateu told us it was only Christmas Eve. Nutaui told him we'd already celebrated Christmas Eve. Tshetshepateu gave Nutaui and Tuminik a drink of homebrew.

---

[1] Kaku-paushtik^u

Homebrew is made by mixing lukewarm water with brown sugar or molasses and yeast and then letting it brew overnight and one day. If you want it to brew three or four days, you add more sugar and a little molasses. If the water is too hot you cook the yeast and it won't brew. A good homebrew is much stronger than beer or wine. Tshetshepateu was from Davis Inlet where people made spruce beer by boiling spruce boughs with prunes and water.

I was drinking too that day but not very much. By midnight, Tshetshepateu, his wife, Nutaui and Tuminik were drunk. I wasn't drunk, only feeling all right. My brother-in-law wanted to head out for Sheshatshiu. He said he'd pay the taxi fare. Where would he get the cash? We didn't have any money. Tshetshepateu didn't have a telephone but there was another building close by with a phone. Tshetshepateu sent his daughter to call a taxi. In those days a taxi was not that expensive, only twelve dollars from Happy Valley to North West River.

We left our dog at Tshetshepateu's place. She must've gone back to our camp in *nutshimit*. That spring Pien Shushep[1] and Pien Shak[2] went to *nutshimit* on foot with their sons. Sometime in April they found our dog. Imagine how that dog survived for over three months. My father was so happy to have his dog back.

It took us only an hour to get to Sheshatshiu by taxi. Tuminik fell asleep in the back seat and it took me a long time to wake him up when we finally arrived. As soon as he woke up he went straight to Father Pierson's house to try and borrow money from him. Father Pierson must've given him some and Tuminik paid the taxi driver with cash.

It was Christmas Day in Sheshatshiu. I had nothing to do except go to church. In the afternoon all the schoolchildren were invited to the old school hall to receive Christmas gifts – mostly Christmas stockings filled with candies, apples and oranges. Some boys and girls got clothing, like pants and gloves. Parents were also invited and some elders got a small gift from the priest.

I don't know how Father Pierson got all those gifts and donations from the military people in Goose Bay. He must've been well known in Goose Bay. He must've had respect for the children and elders or he wouldn't have gone looking for these donations from Goose Bay. But at the same time he wanted the children and all Innu to follow him to his church. That was his mistake. People should've been able to make their own choices about whether or not

---

[1] Pien Selma
[2] Peter Jack Sr.

35

they wanted to be Catholics or whether they wanted to continue their own ways with their own religion. I just watched as the priest handed out the gifts and hoped I'd also receive one. I waited for nothing. I didn't get anything because I hadn't gone to school that fall. I didn't really care anyway.

"What I'm learning from my father about our own traditional way of life is far more important than White man's education," I thought to myself. "Once I complete my own Innu education I'll use it in a very good way for many years to come."

BY THIS TIME I WAS already drinking heavily but I wasn't really sick. I didn't know anything about alcohol and how it affected my body. In the fall we again chartered a plane into *nutshimit* from a company called Wheeler Northern Airways. This time my whole family came, along with the families of my two brothers-in-law. The pilot was Pat Mornie and the aircraft was a Norseman, which was bigger than a Beaver plane and wider and higher on the inside. On floats it could carry less than when it was rigged with skis in the winter. Although it was shorter than a single Otter aircraft, it could carry heavier loads. With a full load the plane would sink halfway into the water but airborne it could still fly with the help of the wind. Nowadays bush pilots don't carry that kind of load anymore, I guess because of government regulations.

When we went into *nutshimit* we needed to bring a couple tents, a stove, flour, tea, tobacco, candles, sugar, guns, enough ammunition, three or four axes and a canoe – all for one family. If we were travelling by plane we'd take only one canoe, even if there was more than one family.

That fall my brother-in-law Tuminik, his family, my sister Nush and I went on the first plane. We set up our tent and Tuminik and I went hunting. He headed west and I went east. I hadn't walked far when I spotted three otters in a small pond. I only had a 22 rifle. I shot several times but only killed one. There was no way I could get that otter because it was in the middle of the pond so I continued to walk further east. I knew the otter would eventually blow to shore and I figured I'd pick it up on my way back home.

That day I didn't score any other animals. Early next morning my sister Tshestu[1] asked Nush[2] to fetch some water. She grabbed the bucket and was only gone a few minutes when she came back. She said she'd seen some spruce partridge on the beach. Tshestu told her it must be whisky-jacks. I took my gun and went to see for myself. Sure enough, there were spruce partridges, in fact, many of them. I must've killed over thirty of them.

Around ten o'clock that evening a second plane arrived carrying my other brother-in-law Penute and his family. We helped them quickly set up their tent.

---

[1] Ann Philomena
[2] Rose

Penute also had a canoe and once he'd cut enough wood for the night he told us we should do a little bit of canoeing, like we'd just go a short distance. We'd paddled about halfway across the lake when we saw something floating and moving across the water. We stopped to have a good look. It was a caribou crossing the lake. We knew we'd never catch up to it. Tuminik hit the side of the canoe with his paddle. He said if it was a bull caribou and he heard us, he'd wait once he reached the shore. The last we saw of him, he was swimming around the point. As we slowly passed the point we spotted a big bull standing on the beach. Tuminik was ready and he just shot it.

A bull caribou is not very good to eat during the mating season because he eats the moss on which female caribou have urinated. The taste of the meat is very strong. Some people like it but most young people don't. Even the bone marrow has a very strong taste, although I like it very much. Some elders will dry the meat and then the taste is not strong. However, the skin of a bull caribou at this time of the year is perfect for moccasins.

Together we skinned the caribou and cut the meat into small pieces. We continued our journey to the end of the lake and killed three more caribou before we headed back to camp. It was already dark when we reached the camp. We were surprised to find Nutaui and Nikaui there because we hadn't heard the plane land. My mother was very happy when she saw the meat. She was sorry we hadn't returned earlier so she could have sent deer meat back by plane to my other sister Maniaten[1] in Sheshatshiu.

My parents were drinking and they shared their homebrew with us but we didn't get drunk. The next day we went to haul the meat back to our camp. We also killed three otters and many spruce partridges.

Another day we went to Penute's old campsite, a lonely looking place at Kauipuskakamat[2]. We killed four beaver and one caribou. We would've killed more caribou but it was still too warm to keep meat for very long outside. After freeze-up we headed back to our camp and the caribou moved north. We should've killed the caribou while we had a chance. We thought they would be around all fall but we never saw any more signs of them. We only ate porcupine, along with the odd beaver and spruce partridge.

One day my mother and father left for a couple days to hunt beavers. By this time we were really short of flour. We used two different kinds of flour – a very white one and the other a brownish colour. At that time Tshestu's twins,

---

[1] Mary Adele
[2] Translates as Burning Lake Area

Shimun and Tshani[1], were still babies and bottle-feeding. A couple of days after my parents had gone, Tshestu asked me if I would take a bag of brown flour to my mother to exchange for white flour. The twins had run out of milk and she didn't want to feed them brown flour mixed with water. She thought they'd get sick if she fed them brown flour.

I left early the next morning on this mission. I followed my parents' trail and as I approached their camp I heard a shot nearby. I continued on my way. When I reached the camp I could see my father was working on something. I approached and saw a dead otter lying in the snow. Nutaui said he hadn't seen the otters coming and only had time to shoot one. Another escaped but he knew it would be somewhere in the brook so he was setting a trap. He caught that otter before he even finished setting the trap. I headed for the tent but Nikaui was not there. I could see her over on the other side of the cove. When she returned to the tent I told her I wanted to exchange some flour with her. It was still daylight when I got back to our main camp later that afternoon.

While we were in *nutshimit* there was no such thing as relaxing. We'd always find something to do every day. Days flew by fast until December rolled around and we started to haul up our traps and pack our gear. We'd booked a plane to pick us up on the 15th of December to bring us back to Sheshatshiu. We cut a few small trees to mark the spot where the plane was to land. We waited around the camp expecting to hear the sound of the plane. It never came. The next day I went to haul wood and when I was about halfway across the lake I heard the plane. I ran back to our tent. My father, my mother and some of the kids went out on the first trip. The rest of us followed on the second plane.

I was bored back in Sheshatshiu with nothing to do. I drank and when I wasn't drinking, I'd sometimes cut and haul wood. My sister Tshaukuesh[2] got married that summer to her old friend Kanatuakueshiss[3], whom she'd known ever since she was a young girl. Another couple, Sepastian Pastitshi and Mani Katnin Nuna[4], also married that day. The wedding was beautiful. I never

---

[1] Simon and Charlie
[2] Elizabeth
[3] Francis Penashue
[4] Kathleen Nuna, and Kathleen Pastitshi after she married

thought my sister Tshaukuesh would suffer so much in the years that followed her wedding day.

The problem was alcohol. The first few years after Kanatuakueshiss married my sister everything went pretty well. Their first child Peter was born and they must have loved him very much. Kanatuakueshiss was also a great hunter and trapper. But a few years later the marriage wasn't looking so good. At first my sister didn't drink but Kanatuakueshiss did, although only once in awhile. But the year the government opened the beer store in Goose Bay alcohol really hit the community of Sheshatshiu. Peter was about five years old when his father really started to drink more often. Kanatuakueshiss and I were great drinking buddies. We were both really useless in our drinking days. I wasn't a very good person when I was drunk. Many times I got into fights and I still hate to think about those fights today.

I remember Tshaukuesh telling me a story about Peter when he was just a small boy. He told my sister he was going to be an airplane bush pilot, that when she'd be in *nutshimit* and saw a plane fly over her tent it would be him behind the controls flying the plane. He probably never thought as a boy that one day he'd become the leader of all the Innu in Labrador, and later be elected and become a cabinet minister for the government of Canada.

The year my sister got married, I kind of missed her. My mother must have felt the same way too. I never asked Tshaukuesh how she felt after she got married. I thought she was very happy and maybe she was. The priest told us that an unmarried person who died would not go to heaven. I guess the church had brainwashed our parents.

The summer when my sister was married there were three French girls from Montreal who came to Sheshatshiu. They were Jose Mailhot, Andrée Michaud and Madeleine – I don't remember her last name. They were student anthropologists. They were doing a study of the Innu in Sheshatshiu and I volunteered to help them out. This was the first time I'd seen White people come to research an Innu community on how we had lived in the past. People in Sheshatshiu liked the girls and they were very friendly. They liked the Innu right back.

At that time I was drinking homebrew every day. Later that summer after our friends left, I had a seizure. That was the first real sign of my alcohol problem. I went to see Dr. Paddon at the North West River hospital. He sent me to St. John's for further examination. I was admitted into the St. John's General Hospital and examined by a middle-aged doctor. A couple of days later that same doctor came to tell me there was nothing wrong with me.

"You have two choices," the doctor said. "Stop drinking now or you'll suffer for the rest of your life." That was all he said. I left for Goose Bay the next day and went on to Sheshatshiu. The doctor's warning made no difference to me. I continued to drink heavily every day. I wasn't worried. I could stop anytime I wanted.

I was still very interested in *nutshimit*. That fall my brother-in-law Kanatuakueshiss, his father Kantuakuet[1], his uncle Pien[2] and I flew by plane to Mishtashini[3], south of the Mealy Mountains. That was my first time south of those mountains and Pien explained all the names of the lakes and brooks to me. Shenum[4], his two sons and the late Mashkap[5] were also at the camp.

Two days earlier I'd packed all my gear: my gun, some grub, snowshoes and clothing. I wanted to make sure I didn't forget anything. During these days I really wanted to be with my girlfriend. I knew I was going to miss her but *nutshimit* and following my way of life were more important to me. I had to go. I told her I'd be back in three months. I asked her if she could wait that long and she said she would. I was only about 18 and she was probably 16. I kept thinking about her that whole last night. As the sun came up the next morning I was already up and feeling very excited. Our charter arrived in Sheshatshiu about ten in the morning. I felt very happy as we loaded the plane but as we took off I felt a deep hurt about leaving my girlfriend behind. I'd be lonely and homesick and not just for my girlfriend. This was my first time in *nutshimit* without my family. Still I figured I was better off enjoying life in *nutshimit* rather than staying home to be sick.

Our first morning in *nutshimit,* Kanatuakueshiss, his cousin Antuan[6] and I took off for Kamishikamat[7] by canoe. I was in the rear steering. We paddled down to a narrow brook where we ran into a fallen tree almost blocking the

[1] Mathew Penashue
[2] Pien Penashue
[3] Translates as Big Rock
[4] Jerome Pokue
[5] Joseph Rich
[6] Tony Penashue
[7] Translates as Big Lake

brook. As we got closer the current kept getting stronger. We tried to pass around the tree but the canoe hit it sideways and tipped over. Kanatuakueshiss and I jumped into the water. Fortunately it wasn't too deep. Antuan managed to grab and hang on to the fallen tree. He couldn't touch bottom. We were all laughing. I finally grabbed Antuan and pulled him to shore. He wasn't that old at the time. We lost three guns. With a long stick we managed to retrieve two of them. My 22 rifle was still underwater but the water was too deep to reach it. The canoe wasn't damaged so we headed back to camp. Kanatuakueshiss's father asked us why we were back so soon. We told him the story and he laughed too.

For all of October and November I only had a 30-30 Winchester rifle with me. This was a problem. One time I went hunting to a place called Uapinatsheu-nipi. I couldn't walk in the middle of the lake because the ice was not thick enough so I walked along the shore. I ran into three otters. My first shot with the rifle was good but the skin on the otter was badly damaged because of the high-powered gun. I tried to shoot the other two otters but missed. I also found a dead caribou that day. I could only see its head under the ice and thought it was a bull caribou. I had no idea what might have caused his death. Later I took a shortcut through the woods back to our camp. It was already dark and the night sky was clear. No matter which direction I walked I could see my own shadow reflected from the full moon. I was headed west and the moon came up from the east. One minute my shadow would be in front of me when I walked in one direction and then it would move to my left or my right. I soon began to feel like someone was walking beside me. I felt like I was walking with my shadow.

Back at our camp I told Pien about the dead caribou. He said that during breeding season caribou sometimes kill each other. He reminded me about the gun I'd lost. He figured the water had probably gone down since then and I'd be able to retrieve the gun. The next day I went with Kanatuakueshiss to the spot where I'd lost my gun. Pien was right. The water was running very low and I was able to easily recoup my gun.

During those two months I watched Pien and Kantuakuet closely when they killed beavers to see if their methods were different but they used the same ways of my father. I realized that Innu people in this area hunted the same way as other Innu from other territories. I knew then that the culture is very much the same for all the Innu throughout Nitassinan[1], in both Labrador and Quebec.

---

[1] Innu Homeland

Near the end of that season Pien suggested we move our camp to Unikush Lake[1] where Shenum and his two sons had already gone. It wasn't far and we arrived early in the afternoon about two days later. We stayed about a week and then took up all our traps. Pien suggested that we go to Sheshatshiu and send a plane back to pick up the elders and all the gear. We didn't know the way so Pien drew a map for us outlining an old trail. The next day Kanatuakueshiss, Antuan, Maskap and I headed for Sheshatshiu with only a small tent and a stove.

On our first day of travel we almost reached the Kenamu River. We hadn't taken any food so we ate a bit of spruce partridge and beaver meat we hunted along the way. On the third day we ate porcupine for breakfast and supper. We didn't bother to set up a tent that afternoon. We just made a fire and took turns keeping the fire going all night. Early the next morning we reached Mud Lake, thanks to the trail that Pien had so clearly mapped out for us. I wondered how he could remember all the ponds and small brooks along the way. He'd not missed a single one. When had he last traveled that route? He must've had a good memory to be able to indicate so clearly each feature along this old Innu trail. We went to visit an old Settler in Mud Lake. His name was Shipiss, or "Little Brook" in English. We asked him for bread and he gave us a loaf. Later that afternoon we were in Happy Valley and we caught a taxi to Sheshatshiu. I was really tired but so happy to be home.

The following spring we went, this time by dog sled, to the same place we'd been in the fall. My father and I had four dogs. Kanatuakueshiss and his father Kantuakuet also had four dogs. We didn't have skidoos back then. I couldn't imagine traveling any other way than by foot or dog team. We might've reached our destination more quickly if we'd had a skidoo but a skidoo might've broken down. We couldn't pull the heavy komatik that a skidoo was able to cart but it would be loaded down with more gear than we needed. We'd have to pay for and carry gas, lube and spare parts for the machine. A skidoo made a lot of noise and scared the animals away. We'd have traveled by night, bent on getting to where we wanted, and worn ourselves out. A dog team may

---

[1] A lake along the Mistashini river south of the Mealy Mountains.

have been slower but we could still get to our destination. We had to carry dog food, which we cooked and fed to the dogs every evening. It was a lot of work but it was better than travel by skidoo. Dogs could even be rigged up to carry stuff on their backs. They could really help carry meat. They could even swim with loads on their backs.

Travel by foot would've been even better because we wouldn't have had to carry anything but our basic gear. Dogs made a lot of noise in the morning and during feeding. When they weren't tied down they chased animals away. If we had traveled by foot with a sled we would have had no worries because we'd have been on our own. We could have hunted as we traveled and camped wherever we wanted. We would've seen more of the land and we might have discovered a new travel route. If I could go back to my old ways I'd take my family out in *nutshimit* and teach my children how to travel by foot. They would find it hard but at least they'd know how the Innu felt when they traveled by foot.

Anyway we left Sheshatshiu that day with our dogs and headed across the bay to Kenamu River. From the mouth of the river we traveled another day following another river that ran southeast. As we reached higher ground we headed south again. This route led us to Mishtashini Lake where Kantuakuet picked up his canoe from last season to bring back to Sheshatshiu. It took us four days and it was a very special trip. One morning Kantuakuet and I were in the tent when we spotted an otter outside nearby.

"How would you like to have an otter for yourself?" I asked Kantuakuet.

"I'd like that," he said. So I took the shotgun and walked slowly to the edge of the lake. Each time the otter dove in the water I'd run. When it came out I'd stop and walk very slowly. The otter was no more than thirty feet from me when I shot but I missed! I tried a second time. Missed again. I felt pretty sure I'd be able to kill that otter, but my guess was that I couldn't because of my promise to Kantuakuet. I was too sure I'd be able to kill the otter. I should have known better. Maybe *Missinak*[u1], the *Aueshish-utshimau*[2] of the otter, heard me make that promise and decided he wouldn't let me kill the otter. It was strange.

Kanatuakueshiss and Kantuakuet led on this trip, and Nutaui and I followed behind.

"Let's stop here for tea," Kantuakuet said to Nutaui one beautiful April spring day. Kanatuakueshiss and I started to cut dry sticks to make a fire. We

[1] Master of the Water Dwellers
[2] Animal Master

could see both north and south a long way across the lake. I had my transistor radio with me and the NHL[1] playoffs were on. Two nights earlier we'd listened to a play-by-play of Chicago against Montreal. They were tied now at three games each. This was the seventh and tie-breaking game, and CBC was broadcasting live at three o'clock.

"Let's listen to the radio and check out the score," I said to Kanatuakueshiss. The game was almost over and the score was 4 – 0 for Montreal.

"My team is Montreal," my father joked to Kantuakuet. He was cooking spruce partridge while Kanatuakueshiss and I listened to the game. I was cheering for the Chicago Black Hawks. About three minutes before the end of the game Bobby Hull scored for Chicago. That made it 4   1 for Montreal but it was too late. Montreal had won the Stanley Cup.

After we drank our tea we continued on our journey. I was kind of sad my team had lost the game but it was a beautiful afternoon. No matter which way I looked I could see beautiful hills dressed in full forests. Further away the hills seemed blue. I wanted to be up in those hills but we were traveling to Mistassini Lake. We only spent two weeks in *nutshimit* before we headed back to Sheshatshiu. It took only three days to get home.

Back in Sheshatshiu I spent a lot of my time hunting with my friend Sepastien[2]. One summer day we paddled by canoe up Grand Lake as far as the Red Wine River[3]. We got a few porcupines, a couple of beavers and one black bear. We didn't stay too long because we didn't want the meat to spoil. On our way back to Sheshatshiu the wind started to pick up just as we reached Cape Caribou[4]. Sepastian suggested the wind might help us travel faster. We stopped for tea while Sebastian cut a couple of sticks. He tied them near the front of the canoe and we covered them with canvas to rig a sail. The canoe was only about 16 feet long. We were just having fun. We weren't scared because we figured we were good swimmers. As we tried to pass Cape Caribou

---

[1] National Hockey League
[2] Sebastien Pastitshi
[3] Kamikuakamiu-shipu
[4] Kaneshekat translates as Protruding Rock Mountain

the wind blew rough and we almost capsized. We were very lucky. The wind calmed down and we were able to paddle again to make it home that evening.

Another time we went to Hamilton River, which is now Churchill River. We call it the Mishta-shipu. We paddled our canoe as far as Edward's Brook[1]. We had to portage around Muskrat Falls Hill. I didn't know who would carry the canoe. I'd never carried the canoe on a portage. As we landed on shore, Sepastian said he would carry the canoe first and then we'd come back for the rest of our stuff. He was older and he must have learned from his father how to carry a canoe. It looked so easy to me but I knew the canoe was heavy for one person to carry.

We didn't know there were other people on the Churchill River. We met Misheiss[2] with his family and son-in-law Katshistushis[3]. They'd killed a caribou and offered us a good meal. We ended up staying in *nutshimit* for a month, just the two of us. We didn't stay with Misheiss and his family very long. We moved further west along the Churchill River. On our way back, Misheiss and family decided to head back with us.

We went as far as Mud Lake with them and spent the night. The following day we made it back to Sheshatshiu. My father and mother were really worried about us. Nutaui had gone to visit his old friend, Sepastian's father Mishte-Shimiu, to ask him how we were doing in *nutshimit*. The next day Mishte-Shimiu came to tell my father that we were okay. He knew by using his spiritual powers. My friend's father must have come in spirit to see how we were doing.

Even after Sepastian got married we still hunted together.

The next spring my father, my friend Etien[4], my brother-in-law Tuminik and I headed by dog sled for the Big Lake area, north of Grand Lake. We'd been there many times before. By the third day we'd passed Big Lake and walked as far as Kaushe-Tauakamat[5]. We travelled all the way to a lake called Kainipassuakamat[6] where we camped for the night.

---

[1] Etuat-shipiss
[2] Michel Pasteen
[3] Simeo Rich
[4] Etienne Andrew
[5] A lake north of Grand Lake
[6] A lake with many islands found north of Big Lake

Early the next morning as we continued on our journey we spotted two otters at the end of the lake. We discussed among ourselves the best way to kill them. Should we shoot them or hit them with a stick? Tuminik, Etien and I thought we should chase them and try to kill them with sticks. Nutaui disagreed and told us to let the dogs loose to chase after them. Once the dogs had them we could hit them with sticks. As we continued to argue about their execution the otters started to run towards us. We thought we'd catch them easily but just before they reached us my brother-in-law whistled at them. Once they heard us, the otters ran straight into the woods. We started to chase them but they were faster than we thought. I took a shot before one otter could escape. I must've hit it as it turned and ran toward the open water. Nutaui was keeping an eye on the dog that caught the otter before it could reach the water. The other otter escaped. If we'd listened to my father we would've killed them both.

On this beautiful day we continued on our way to the end of the lake where we saw fresh caribou tracks no more than an hour old. Etien and I took our 22 rifles. I also had a 30-30 Winchester. We hadn't walked far before we saw a small herd of about thirty caribou. I started shooting first. Etien took a shot too but we only killed one caribou. My father didn't complain because he knew we were still learning. My brother-in-law was surprised to see only one caribou after he'd heard so many shots.

My father suggested we set up camp in that area. After the tent was up he skinned the caribou. I watched him and wondered how many times he'd done that in his life. We stayed about a week and we left for home on another beautiful day. The snow was hard and we didn't need to use our snowshoes until late in the afternoon. It was still early when we reached Kaushe-Taukakamat and heard some geese. We thought the geese might have landed in the open water near the mouth of the lake but we couldn't see them. These were the first geese of spring. Tuminik had a 12-gauge shotgun and I had my 30-30 Winchester. We crawled along the ground until we got close enough to shoot them. We killed two.

The next day we walked halfway around the lake and stopped for tea. While my father boiled the kettle, Etien and I went for a short walk to the top of the hill. I didn't take my gun with me but my friend had his 22 rifle. We didn't expect to see anything but just as we were on our descent we spotted a small herd of caribou. Since I didn't have a gun I hoped my father and Tuminik would be waiting on the other side of the lake. It was quite a narrow lake so we could see them from where we were but we couldn't call out to them because the caribou would hear us. The only way to contact them was to whistle. As Tuminik turned to look our way we waved at him. He must have known why we were waving because he brought me my gun. We killed four caribou that day.

By this time we already had a heavy load on our komatik. Nutaui suggested that we just take the main bones in case we couldn't make it back later to pick up the rest of the meat. The ice on Grand Lake was getting bad. The next day we were back in Sheshatshiu and three days later the three brothers Etuet, Shinipest and Etien[1] left to pick up the meat we'd left behind. Nutaui and I left in the evening and caught up with the others at Ashkashkuaikan-shipiss. I didn't know my father had brought along some homebrew. That evening he and Shinipest got drunk. I didn't know how strong this homebrew was. I did not enjoy drinking outside the community.

The next day we made it to the spot where we'd left the meat and the following day we headed back home in the rain. We set up camp about halfway to Grand Lake. That evening Shinipest used wet snow to carve a goose. He said that if he carved this goose the weather might turn cold and the rain might turn to snow because he was born in the summer. It didn't work. He might've been playing a joke on his brother Etien. But it's true that some people who were born in summer can do such things. They can carve a rabbit or goose with snow but it can only work in the springtime. This time it only rained harder. No one complained. We just laughed. Two days later we arrived back in Sheshatshiu.

---

[1] Edward, Sylvester and Etienne

WALK WITH MY SHADOW

I N 1966 THE GOVERNMENT built houses in Sheshatshiu. The contractor, Benson Builders, brought in some of its own men but many Innu were also employed. I was working too and my job was to survey. I made $1.50 an hour and that was a lot of money. I was drinking heavily and each morning I drank before setting off for work. The work didn't last long. As soon as the surveying was finished I was out of a job.

No one really knew where the money was coming from to build these new houses. We didn't understand what it would mean to move from tents to wooden houses in a permanent community. The store manager was in charge of the housing. My father was on the list for a new house and just before Christmas we moved into our new residence. It didn't take us long to find out it was better to live in a tent than a cold and empty house. It had not been built properly. The houses looked good from the outside but the walls weren't well insulated. There were no storm windows and on the floor there was only plywood and a thin covering. The kind of wood stoves installed could never heat the whole house. Every morning we had to close the bedroom door to keep the heat in the kitchen area.

That same year a big hydro development was started at Churchill Falls[1]. No government people ever came to sit down with the Innu to talk about such a development. They never explained to us how much of our land would be flooded. Some Innu worked on that development in different areas: Flour Lake[2], Overflow Lake[3], Sandgirt Lake[4], Lobstick Lake, Sail Lake and Windbound Lake[5]. All those lakes became joined together into Lake Meshikamau, one big lake now almost the size of Lake Melville. We heard the government people say many times that they were trying to protect the animals and waterfowl. In fact they were the ones who killed the animals when they flooded the Meshikamau area.

---

[1] Mishta-paushtiku is the Innu name for the original majestic falls that existed before the hydro development
[2] Nushkuau-shakaikan
[3] Piashtipeu
[4] Kanekuanikau
[5] Menutinau-nipi

In the 1960s I paddled in that area from the overflow Piashtipeu to Lobstick, Sandgirt Lake, Flour Lake and Churchill Falls. We portaged from Flour Lake to many different ponds and the last one where we camped is where the dykes are built near Churchill Falls. Now the area is totally unrecognizable.

While the Lower Churchill hydro-electric project was being built, a new school was built in Sheshatshiu. Both the federal and provincial governments were scheming and making plans. They must've thought that if they kept the Innu in a community, it would be easier for them to start all kinds of developments on our lands. Maybe they thought a new school and some houses would keep the Innu quiet and that's exactly what happened. Innu people found out about the hydro project but they didn't say anything. They never complained. They began to settle down in Sheshatshiu. Some people were happy about the school and others weren't.

Anspuas Andrew was one of the people not happy. One day he came to visit my father and they talked about the school. I didn't pay much attention to them but I did overhear a few comments.

"The school is so big," Anspuas said to my father. "Our grandchildren will never be able to learn our way of life. Our culture will be replaced by the White culture."

"I never went to school my whole life," my father said. "I've trapped and hunted, travelled to many different places. That was my education." My father and Anspuas were still talking when I left. I should have stayed behind and listened to them.

If the Innu had known the kind of games the government were playing with them they never would have taken the houses and accepted the school. I don't think the government ever did any studies about the effects of damming the Upper Churchill River. When I first heard the dam was being built for hydro-power, I wondered what kind of machine they'd use to build a dam at these great falls. I'd seen their work camps but not the dams. A few years later when I crossed the bridge at Churchill Falls I noticed the river had gone dry. I didn't ask anyone why the river was gone. I didn't want to ask because I wouldn't have believed what anyone might have explained to me. The road construction from Churchill Falls to Goose Bay was already underway. Most men working on this road were heavy-equipment operators, while a few women worked in the main office. Why were so many roads were being built? I'd heard about hydro-power but an Innu person like me could never imagine that our land could be lost forever. Many of us thought the hydro project was not a big issue because we weren't consulted anyway.

I often heard people describe their visit to the underground site of this hydro dam. One time when I travelled with my mother to Esker to catch the train from Churchill Falls to Esker, she told me about the area before it was destroyed for Innu people.

"This is where people used to stop for tea," she told me, as she pointed across the lake.

"Was it in the winter or summer?" I asked.

"In the summer," she said. "We suffered a lot in those days but the land and the animals took care of us and we survived. Now we suffer more because all we can do is watch helplessly as our land is destroyed, polluted, flooded."

She told me how the once beautiful and mighty falls *Mishta-Paushtik*[u1] were now almost dried up. The cold steam that would rise up in the winter was no longer visible. No more rainbows could be seen crossing the falls. The Innu could no longer use the land in the flooded area. Many thousands of trees drowned and how many animals were also drowned that we'd never know about? With all the trees underwater we could no longer safely travel by boat. Fish weren't safe to eat anymore because of the methylmercury. Small animals that eat fish also couldn't be eaten because of the methylmercury. My mother said the best place for caribou in the old days had been in the Sandgirt Lake and Meshikamau areas, and now the best feeding grounds for the caribou were all flooded. Many Innu gravesites were flooded, and Innu lost steel traps and canoes too.

Before the construction of this hydro project the Innu used all this land that was now flooded. Some Innu continued to use the land near Churchill Falls and east of the Meshikamau area as well as inland from the Naskapi River but the flooded area was a dead lake to them. Now that it was too late we understood that our land had been damaged. In the meantime, Hydro- Québec was selling millions of dollars of electricity to Americans – electricity generated from Churchill Falls, really from Innu land. The Innu got nothing for that power.

---

[1] Churchill Falls, an older Innu name is Patshishetshuanau

I didn't ask my mother any other questions. I knew how she felt when she thought back to her younger days when people traveled by canoe or by foot. That day she rode in the truck and it took only eight hours to drive from Sheshatshiu to Esker.

That year of 1967, Premier Joey Smallwood came to the new town of Churchill Falls. A White friend told me what Joey said during this visit. "This is our river, this is our lake, and these are our forests," Smallwood claimed. The Innu were not awake at that time. Joey could say whatever he wanted. But had Joey Smallwood been there a few decades later and tried to say the same thing, I'm sure he would've heard Innu voices and seen many Innu protesters.

Twenty-five more houses were built during the summer of 1967. I was now working with Brinco. One day my boss Old John Michelin and I were flown from North West River to Lobstick Lake. He was looking for silver, which he'd found forty-two years earlier. For almost two weeks we canoed many different places in the Lobstick Area prospecting around Overflow Lake, the place where he'd first discovered silver. We flew overhead. John was having difficulty reading the map but I didn't want to tell him what to do. He was my boss. I didn't know why he was looking for that silver now. He must've heard that the whole area had been flooded.

There were a lot of caribou, beaver, black bear and fish in the area but we only hunted once because Old John was afraid of the game warden. I wasn't afraid of anybody. One day he put out his net for about a half hour and caught many lake trout. As we canoed and portaged our way to Churchill Falls we passed many old Innu campsites. Sometimes we found old steel traps hanging on trees. Some had fallen to the ground. I couldn't take them because I was working. It made me wonder about the thousands of other things belonging to the Innu that were now all underwater.

As we reached Flour Lake we stopped for the night. After supper I went for a walk. I came to a spot where a lot of trees had been chopped down but I didn't see any around. I thought they must have been burnt. What was this clear-cutting all about? Perhaps it might be for a road or an airstrip but it didn't really look like that. I knew about the hydro dam but it was over 50 miles away. I returned to the camp and figured I would never know why so many trees had been clearcut. I never thought that the floodwaters would reach so far across so much land.

In a couple more days we were about five miles out of Churchill Falls, the town, where we decided to set up camp. We hitchhiked into town and got picked up by a truck driver. You couldn't really call Churchill Falls a town. It was more like a camp. I went back to our camp that night because I didn't feel like spending the night in a trailer with strangers from Quebec and Newfoundland. Our tent was on the other side of the pond so I had to cross by canoe. I slept in late the next morning and woke up to someone calling my name. I looked outside and saw John and two other guys looking for me on the other side of the pond. I crossed the lake to pick them up. The truck was waiting for us on the road. I didn't bother to have breakfast. I just packed the tent and all the gear into the canoe. The truck took our canoe and gear to Mount Hyde Lake where we camped the next four days.

John made a few phone calls to North West River. I guess he was told to keep looking so we chartered an aircraft and made two more trips to Lobstick Lake. We canoed to the west end of the lake but found nothing. Finally John had to give up. We headed for Flour Lake where we got a free ride to Churchill Falls.

I was finished with Brinco, but was soon hired by the provincial Forestry Department. I worked with them for a couple of months before I quit. The forest rangers were like game wardens, so I couldn't work with them. I didn't want to hurt my own people. Besides that I'd promised a French girl I'd be in Sept Isles in September. Instead I ended up in Montreal.

I'd met this girl in Sheshatshiu the previous summer. I went to Montreal to visit her for a couple of weeks during the fall of 1967. I was very anxious to see her. Maybe that was part of the reason why I quit my job as a forest ranger. During these two weeks in Montreal I didn't do very much. I just drank every day. A can of beer was only 25 cents in any store that sold food. Only once did my friend and I go see Expo' 67. We also went to her father's summer house outside of Montreal. At the end of two weeks my friend must have been getting worried about my drinking. She paid my way back to Goose Bay. She escorted me to the airport and that was our final farewell.

By this time I was drinking a lot but I wasn't worried. I thought I could stop whenever I wanted. I was 21 years old and still healthy. The alcohol wasn't making me sick yet. When the liquor store opened in Happy Valley it sold beer first and liquor later on. At first the Innu weren't allowed to buy liquor or beer. Maybe the priest had ordered this prohibition. We had no idea why the Innu couldn't buy alcohol from this store but it never stopped us. We'd just give our money to the taxi drivers and they'd buy us the booze.

One day I decided I'd stop drinking for a while and try to get a job. I got one at a nearby sawmill owned by the provincial government. During the winter we piled up the logs and in the summer we sawed them. I worked there the whole summer. Although I didn't make much money I enjoyed the work. I found it hard to quit drinking for more than two weeks. I'd drink in the mornings but still I never missed work.

By the end of that summer most Innu had their own houses. I was very interested in working because everyone in the community had a job. Everyone was making about $1.10 an hour. It wasn't much but it was better than welfare. By the end of the summer the people who didn't drink had saved enough money to charter an aircraft to *nutshimit*. I'd managed to not spend all my money on beer. Some of it went to my mother.

When I went into *nutshimit* that fall with my father and my two brothers-in-law I didn't think this would be my last time. Nutaui was still strong and prepared to go anytime he wanted. At 21, I was still very interested in hunting and trapping. It was the middle of October and I went on the first plane with one brother-in-law. We were meant to land the plane at Kauipuskakamat. I sat up front with the pilot, Hector Baikie, a former trapper from North West River. As we were flying over many frozen lakes and ponds he told me we might not be able to land because most lakes were frozen. I didn't say anything. I was just hoping we'd be able to find a lake with open water. I could see a long distance ahead and I could tell the lake where we were meant to land was already frozen. The plane circled around looking for open water but we couldn't find any. We headed north, then traveled east. Finally we spotted a lake that was still open in the middle although the edges were frozen. We landed and the pilot managed to break the thin ice right to shore.

It was getting late as we set up our tent. The autumn daylight was short. We went off in different directions to hunt. We each got a porcupine and a few spruce partridges. We hoped the lake would remain open until the next day when my father was meant to land with my other brother-in-law. We wanted to send the porcupine home on the plane. I wrote my mother's name on a small piece of paper which I tied to the porcupine's head. My brother-in-law did the same thing. We left the two porcupines in an open space where they could easily be seen when my father arrived so that we wouldn't have to wait for the plane. We went off looking for small game and I was only a few miles away when I heard the plane land.

When I got home that evening I could smell porcupine meat cooking before I got inside the tent. I thought my brother-in-law Penote[1] must have killed another porcupine but then I learned that the pilot had seen the unfrozen portion of the beach and had landed there. They had missed the porcupines we'd left behind. There was nothing more to do except eat them.

My father had brought homebrew with him. After supper we started drinking but I didn't get drunk. We made more homebrew and in the morning my father was still drunk and we couldn't move to the place where the plane had been supposed to land. That was our last day of drinking. In a couple of days we were able to reach our destination and begin our trapping season.

We spent over three months in *nutshimit*. We hadn't asked the pilot to pick us up again so we walked back to Sheshatshiu. That was the last time we went to *nutshimit* by plane at our own expense. But my hunting days weren't over. I'd still hunt for small game like ducks, porcupine, beaver or partridge in the Lake Melville and Grand Lake area. I'd sometimes travel inland a bit by foot. I was happy to use the ways my father had taught me.

---

[1] Penote Ashini

THE FIRST TIME I MET SHANUT[1] I'd been admitted to the hospital in North West River because I had a seizure from drinking too much alcohol. She'd come from Davis Inlet that same week. She was also in the hospital but it couldn't have been because of alcohol. She never touched any alcohol before she married me. The year was 1969.

I didn't feel much like talking to Shanut on that first day. I was still too sick. The next day when I was feeling a little better I went to see her. She was sitting in the television room. I already knew her name because my sister Nush[2] had told me about her. The two were friends.

"Are you Shanut?" were the first words I said to her.

"Yes, that's me."

"Would you like to walk downstairs and go outside for a few minutes?"

"I might not be allowed to go out."

So we stayed inside and I loaned her my watch, which she returned the next day. She told me she'd heard about my drinking problems but she didn't seem to care. She must've heard this from Nush. I was discharged from the hospital but I kept going back to see Shanut over the next few days. We began to know each other well. I'd never thought I would marry someone from Davis Inlet but things happen unexpectedly.

A week later Shanut went home to Davis Inlet. I kind of missed her but I thought, "Who cares?" to myself. I just kept on drinking. I'd make homebrew and whenever I had money I'd buy beer. The education I'd learned from my father seemed lost in those days. I was a heavy drinker but this did not mean that I forgot what he'd taught me about life in *nutshimit*. The things he'd taught me were stronger than alcohol. My thoughts were always the same. I wanted to be back in *nutshimit* with my family. I always wanted to do everything to make them happy. It was my turn to pay them back for their teachings. I found it hardest when fall rolled around during those drinking days because it was the season I loved most in *nutshimit*. Every time I saw geese overhead flying south it would bring back a lot of memories about my hunting days.

---

[1] Charlotte Pasteen
[2] Rose Gregoire

A couple of months later Shanut came back to Sheshatshiu to work at the hospital. I was happy to hear about her return. When I was sober I wouldn't feel much like seeing her. I was kind of shy when I was sober that first month but we got along well anyway. Then we began getting into trouble. Even before I married her we were always fighting and arguing. I don't remember how I asked her to marry me. I must have popped the question when I was drunk and the next day she reminded me about it. I couldn't reverse my decision then. In our culture it's easy to say to a woman that you want to marry her. After a couple of months we decided we should get married. We thought that maybe after we were married things might change between us. I told my parents. They also thought my drinking habits might go away if I got married. We went to see the priest and told him the news. He was also happy to hear the word "married." He didn't like to see unmarried couples hanging around together.

We were married in October. I didn't have any money at that time because I wasn't working. I didn't even have anything to wear, so I borrowed a suit from a former teacher. Shanut also borrowed a wedding gown and we even borrowed the wedding rings. On our wedding day my friend and I headed for Goose Bay to pick up some booze. Drinking was part of my plans for the celebration although it wasn't in Shanut's plan. I would've married her just the same without the alcohol but I was so dependent on it. I had to have a drink every few hours. When the church bell rang I was still at my friend's home all dressed up and drinking. I wasn't shy by the time I got to the church. The next day we returned the things we'd borrowed.

I was very nervous that day I got married. I can't say I was excited. I was sick and I was drunk. I wasn't in a hurry to get married. I guess I didn't want my girlfriend to be taken away by someone else. She must have felt the same way too. Shinipest and Manimei[1] Rich were also married that day. The church was full. Sam Nui was my best man and there was a *teueikan*[2] dance that evening. After the church ceremony, Father Pierson had his camera ready. He took a picture of Shinipest and his wife Manimei but he never took a picture of us. He didn't like anyone who drank alcohol so I never even got a picture of myself on my wedding day. It didn't really bother me. I figured a picture was just a piece of plastic and paper, just the image of the people.

---

[1] Sylvester and Mary May Rich
[2] Innu drum

"A picture won't bring us any happiness," I thought to myself. "I'm Innu and proud to be Innu. When I'm gone, I'll be gone for good. No picture of me will bring me back to life." Shanut reminded me many years later how we went straight home after the wedding. She said she hadn't even known that the wedding cake was also for us.

During those early days of our marriage my wife wasn't drinking but I used to drink every day. I ended up in the hospital many times. I hate to talk about what I was like when I first got married. Our marriage was miserable. I beat my wife many times even though I'd be very sorry about it the next day. Our main problems were that we didn't trust each other and I was so dependent on alcohol.

Shanut says I was always trying to control her. She says she was a battered woman but she didn't know any different. She'd seen her father and mother fighting all the time. She thought it was just part of the Innu culture. I beat her before we were even married. She remembers crying out in pain, scared of what I'd do next. One time she ended up in hospital with a black eye. She says it wasn't really my fault. She'd had a problem with her eyes for as long as she could remember. Every two years they'd change the prescription of her glasses. But maybe she was trying to protect me and the black eye I gave her was really part of the reason she ended up in hospital.

Shanut thought I beat her because she didn't know how to help me during those first few months after we were married. She didn't know how to do the cooking and washing. She says she thought I was always angry with her because she didn't know how to show respect for her husband. One time she boiled a whole dozen eggs in a very small pot. I didn't want to eat her cooking but by and by she learned how to cook.

For a long time Shanut didn't seem to care how I treated her but eventually she learned that to abuse a woman is criminal.

The fall we were married my wife and I went camping on the Goose River[1] for a couple of weeks with my father. In Sheshatshiu I drank every day and found it very difficult to live without alcohol. My father-in-law, Tshenish Pasteen[2] in Davis Inlet, must've heard about our marriage problems so he

---

[1] Uashikanashteu-shipu
[2] James Pasteen

invited us to move there. We didn't have any money to travel so we asked the priest to arrange for transportation through the hospital plane. He must have talked to Dr. Paddon and a week later he came over to say there was room for us on the hospital plane. The next day we left for Davis Inlet.

I brought some yeast with me so I could make some homebrew when I got there. We landed and many people had come out to meet the plane. Some people were playing jokes on me. They teased me, saying things and laughing. I didn't care. We just went straight to my wife's father's house. Many people came to visit. People invited me over for drinks, especially those I'd met in Sheshatshiu.

The day I arrived in Davis Inlet I was very excited to see the barren mountains. I thought to myself, "No wonder people here call themselves the *Mushuau Innu*[1]." I did love the community very much and people were very nice to me. It was a beautiful place to live in the summer. At first the *Mushuau Innu* dialect was hard for me to understand but after awhile I got used to it. My wife would tell me the names of some of the places in the area. The community was on an island and surrounded by water but back then it was a good place to hunt and fish for those who were interested.

There were a few ten- or twelve-horsepower skidoos in Davis Inlet but the majority of people were still using dog teams to travel out to *nutshimit* or to haul wood. Few families could afford to buy skidoos although they cost less than a thousand dollars. Dogs were more important and people were really proud of their dogs. Some families had five or six dogs, which they treated very well. They would cook for them and feed them every day.

A few months after we were married, my father-in-law invited us to go to Sango Bay[2]. He wanted us to bring his niece Shanin[3] along because her father was already camped in Sango Bay. As we reached a landing about a quarter of the way to Sango, Shanut and I stopped to argue. We didn't even see our dogs take off with the komatik and Shanin inside. I also had a bucket of homebrew on the komatik. Shanut didn't care about the homebrew but she was worried about her niece. Fortunately Shanin fell off the komatik before the dogs had gone too far. I went after them but I would never have caught up with them if they hadn't stopped on their own.

---

[1] People of the Barrens
[2] Shankut
[3] Jeanine Pasteen

We were headed to a place called Kamatshiteuiashkuiat[1] where Shanut's brother had his camp. Our first stop was Ustinitshu, about halfway to Sango. The place is named after a *kakushapatak*[2] called Ustinitshu. The late Shushepiss[3] told me he'd buried Ustinitshu in the winter. They couldn't bury him underground so they'd built him a log casket and laid him on the cliff. Now when you go to this place the logs are all rotten but the bones are still there. This was before the missionaries had come up the Labrador Coast.

On this day, Napess Toma[4] and Matshitu-napeu[5] were camping at Ustinitshu. We had something to eat with them and left again. It was late in the evening when we arrived at the camp. We'd been so angry with each other that it had taken us the whole day to travel to Sango. We'd wasted too much time arguing.

During that fall I'd often hear this one person's name, Napeu[6], who was out in *nutshimit*. Just before Christmas I heard he was back in the community and he and his wife came over to my father-in-law's house. I began to know him well and we became fast friends.

Napeu was the last person to travel from Davis Inlet to Mistastin Lake[7] by dog team. After that, people would still go to *nutshimit* but never that far away. As for me I wasn't able to hunt anymore. I loved to hunt but I was always too drunk. Shanut said that after three months in Davis Inlet it was the same as before we were married. Our problems had found their way back to us. Nothing had changed.

Later that spring, Shanut and I went back to Sheshatshiu. I tried to stop drinking but a couple of days later I had a seizure. This happened many times. Sometimes I'd end up in the hospital for a few days. Shanut was expecting a baby sometime in July. I was worried about what was going to happen to our baby. Would we be able to take care of him? I thought we might

---

[1] Translates as Wooded Point
[2] Shaman
[3] Late Old Joseph Rich
[4] Joseph Toma
[5] Raphael Rich
[6] Sam Napeu
[7] Kameshtashtan translates as Where it is All Blown Away

be okay because Shanut wasn't drinking but I went right on drinking, just trying to drown all my worries. The doctors kept warning me about what would happen if I didn't stop drinking. One priest also came to speak to me but my answer was always the same.

"I don't care what happens to me. It's my life!" I'd tell them. "Even if I stop drinking today I'll die just the same." I repeated this many times to anyone who'd ask me to stop drinking.

There were times when I was really sick. I'd be short of breath and I'd find it very hard to swallow when I tried to eat. Two or three times a night I'd get up to have a drink and then try to get back to sleep again. When there was no alcohol nearby I'd get very nervous wondering what would happen to me next.

To become an alcoholic is the worst thing that could ever happen to anyone. Alcohol is like a deadly weapon, like someone pointing a gun at your head and telling you that if you don't drink you'll die. That was what I was feeling. If I didn't take a drink I'd die. Alcohol was like a medicine to me. I thought it could help me solve my problems and heal my sickness. I didn't realize that my drinking just kept piling on the problems.

On July 25, 1970, our first child Gerry was born in Sheshatshiu. After the birth we moved back to Davis Inlet to stay for good. I was a proud father and hoped I'd stop drinking but that didn't happen. I worked as a labourer that summer.

One day the priest, Frank Peters, helped me find a job at the store. Frank Peters was also working for the International Grenfell Association at the time. He was the doctor as well as a priest. I'd sometimes wonder whether, as a priest, he should be allowed to see a woman's body when she was sick.

In those days the only people who had year-round, full-time jobs were Shuashem Nui, Tshenu[1], Antuan Tshakapesh, Etuet Piwas[2] and me at the store. Shuashem and Tshenu were both working at the power plant and Antuan was working at the school. Some people were fishing for a living. Other available jobs were mostly labour and part-time work but any job was better than welfare. Some people managed to work enough weeks in the summer to claim U.I. (unemployment insurance) in the fall. Those of us who were drinkers would get up early, have a drink and go to work at 8:00. During our coffee break we'd drink and also again at lunchtime.

---

[1] Joachim
[2] Edward Piwas

I worked as a store clerk for almost three years. Even though I drank every day, I was still able to support my family and I never really missed work. One day I had a seizure at work. Afterwards I didn't remember a thing. I totally blacked out and the next thing I knew I was in the clinic. But I was still able to work the next day.

Another time I went to work feeling very sleepy. The store manager was in his office. I was behind the counter. Since we didn't have any customers I moved away from the counter and sat on top of a pile of rope. The store sold all kinds of hardware stuff. I must've fallen asleep until my first customer arrived.

"Get up! You're supposed to serve us, not sleep while you're at work," this customer said as he woke me up. The manager threatened me with a layoff slip. I didn't mind because I was drinking too much.

After freeze-up in the fall many of my drinking buddies went out hunting. They often invited me but I always found an excuse not to go. It wasn't that I didn't like hunting. I wanted One winter's day, as I stood behind the counter waiting for customers, I looked through the window and saw Pukue[1] walking toward the store. He was my first customer of the day. He walked in and I went over to serve him. "I want to buy snowshoe frames," the old man requested.

"What will you need them for?" I asked him.

"I'm going to set up camp about a mile south of here," he said. "I'll need snowshoes out there. But today I'm going out to the hospital. I'm just on my way to pack up my tent and clothes and then I'll wait for the mission plane."

The plane arrived within an hour. My co-worker looked out and saw a big crowd surrounding the plane. I told him to go and check out what was happening. A few minutes later he came back to tell me the sad news. Pukue, who'd just been in the store no more than an hour ago, had been killed by the plane. He must've walked straight into the turning props and got hit in the head. I wondered why the pilot had started up the plane before his passenger was inside. I thought of what the old man had just said to me about the place he'd go where he'd need snowshoes. It seemed like he'd known he'd die that day. At first I thought he was only joking about the snowshoes. I thought he'd just need them to move around his tent. He was too old to be able to hunt. Once in a while I'd visited him at his tent. He was the kind a person who liked

---

[1] Old Charles Pokue

people my age. This was one of those times when an Innu elder had spoken in parables and no young person could understand what he meant.

When I worked at the store, people would come to sell the furs they'd trapped. In exchange they'd get credit for food. One winter we were told the government store would no longer take any furs and people would no longer get any credit. They'd have to pay cash for any food. The store was only open from Monday to Friday and closed all weekend. This made it very hard for the people to buy food, especially for people who didn't have any money on Friday. Some people who were on U.I. or employed were lucky enough to get their cheques on time. Those who didn't have any income or who didn't get their social assistance on time had no choice but to accept this new policy. The children would expect their parents to buy food for the weekend, but if there was no money there was nothing to be had. It's safe to say the children were the ones who suffered the most.

Years later a much bigger store was built but it had the same amount of stuff. It didn't supply any more food than before. The coolers were the only new thing but there were times when the coolers were empty. We were told the store didn't make any profit, that every year it lost money. The store never had all the things that people needed. It was no wonder it lost money. Some of the canned or packaged foods often had expired dates but they still sold them for the same price. Some business from St. John's must've been dumping its old stock on us. The old store also sold guns but now anyone who wanted a gun had to order it from outside.

One morning I went to see the store manager. As usual I'd been drinking. I asked him if I could buy some food on credit but he refused. I grabbed him and tried to choke him. He must've called the police. When they arrived to see me, I didn't even try to defend myself. I told them straight out what happened. When the court came to Davis Inlet I pled guilty and got six months in jail. I felt very ashamed and I really missed my wife during my time at Her Majesty's Penitentiary in St. John's. After four months I got my parole just in time for the last boat run from Goose Bay to Davis Inlet. As soon as I got back to Davis Inlet I started on the bottle again.

That fall we traveled to *nutshimit* by boat with my father-in-law Tshenish, my brother-in-law Shan Shushep[1] and his wife Shunin[2], and the families of Miste-Etuet[3] and Napess[4]. We went to an island called Kutshinapess in Okpatik Bay. We got a few seals and spruce partridges but no other animals because we were on an island.

One day Miste-Etuet and I moved our gear to a spot where we'd spend the rest of the fall. The next day everyone moved together. The ice was very salty, which made it hard to travel with a komatik rigged with steel shoes. Eventually we made it and as I was looking for a long pole to set up our tent I saw signs of a porcupine. I followed them and killed it. When I got back to the camp I walked right by the first woman I saw – Upuameukush[5]. I didn't even stop. I just went right by her and gave the porcupine to my mother-in-law Meneshkuesh[6]. I later found out that I should have given that porcupine to the first person who saw me return with it. That was my mistake. I didn't know that the culture of the *Mushuau Innu* was a little different than in Sheshatshiu. I was supposed to give the porcupine to the man's wife, who would decide who should get the porcupine. If it had been a fur animal, the man would've made the decision.

I learned that although the Quebec Innu and Labrador Innu have the same culture, there were certain things they did differently in the way they treated the animals. Another thing I had to learn about the ways of the *Mushuau Innu* was that if a person caught a lake trout it had to be eaten in the one tent after it was cooked. You could not send it to your neighbour's tent. You had to invite others to your tent to share the trout. The otter also had to be eaten in one tent. In Sheshatshiu you could send the meat out to different tents.

During our stay in Obtik Bay we drank in the morning and in the evening. I was able to hunt for a whole day without alcohol. Every one of us was drinking except my wife and my sister-in-law Shunin. One day I went out hunting

---

[1] Charles Joseph
[2] Julianna
[3] Edward Mistenapeo
[4] Joseph Toma
[5] Mary Toma
[6] Theresa Pasteen

without a drink. I knew I'd be sick but I didn't really care. I left anyway. I killed one porcupine, which gave me the strength to walk another mile. This was not a spiritual strength. It could happen to anyone. I had a different feeling after I killed that porcupine. I was more motivated to walk a little further to hunt some more. I killed a few spruce partridges and decided to turn back when it was almost dark. As I walked through the night, alcohol was the only thing on my mind. I was tired, sweating and short of breath. As soon as I stepped inside our tent I asked for a cup of homebrew. After downing a couple cups I was okay and able to eat.

I was always worried about what might happen to me if we ran out of homebrew but I was still able to do a lot of hunting. I hadn't forgotten the lessons from my father. Many times I'd think I should stop drinking so I could stop worrying about everything. My father-in-law was also a heavy drinker at that time but he didn't get sick when he couldn't have a drink.

The second week of December, Shan Shushep, Miste-Etuet and I took our families back to Davis Inlet. I was happy to see all my drinking buddies. After New Year's, Shan Shusep and Miste-Etuet headed back into *nutshimit* but my wife and I stayed in the community.

The next summer I got up early one very beautiful morning. The sun was just coming up over the high mountains and the water was calm as far as I could see. Smoke swirled from chimneys. I was headed to see my friend Mishen[1] who lived in the last house at the end of the community. I decided to walk on the beach. I passed many freighter canoes and komatiks along the beach. Mishen was usually up early in this kind of weather. I thought he might have gone for a walk to the graveyard where he often went in the morning.

I was about halfway across the community when I saw Tuamas[2] shove his canoe into the water. He told me he was going to check his net. I continued on to my friend's house. By the time I reached his house he'd already left to visit friends. I walked back along the beach and saw Tuamas again just back from checking his net. I waited to see if he'd caught any char. As he beached his canoe, I moved closer for a better look. I'd never seen so many char and their size was amazing, some as big as salmon.

"Help yourself," Tuamas said to me. "Pick any fish you want." I took one large char and before I walked away he pointed to just across the cove.

---

[1] Gilbert Rich
[2] Old Thomas Noah

"That's where your father used to put his net," he said to me. "This whole place is called Shimun Kapishtauat or The Spot Where Simon Cast His Net."

"Thanks for the fish," I said as I left. Shimun was my father's name. I looked over at the cove and wondered at how my father had traveled by foot all the way to Old Davis Inlet from Sept Isles.

A S THE YEARS WENT BY, my drinking problems only got worse. It was hopeless. I'd never stop drinking. I was very much interested in going hunting with other people but I was ashamed of my drinking problem. I was afraid of what my friends would think if I took homebrew with me on hunting trips. Hunting was always on my mind but I just couldn't go. I was so dependent on alcohol. I'd go as far as Flowers Bay[1] and Sango Bay for partridge hunting but I'd always bring along a little bit of homebrew in a bottle. I could only hunt if I could also temporarily drown my worries.

In 1972 our second child Shakanin[2] was born. This was the first time I really tried to stop drinking. I was sober almost five months. I was able to hunt with other people and most days I would take any available job in the community. During this time I began to know Kaniuekutat[3] before he ever became Chief. He was about fifty years old but he was always very healthy. He spent a lot of time out in *nutshimit*. He was the nephew of my father-in-law and he would often call me his brother-in-law. Sometimes he'd just call me his friend. I never had my own house during the 1970s and we lived with my father-in-law. Kaniuekutat would visit his uncle everyday. I was always interested in hearing his stories although I never talked to him much myself.

One time I traveled to Old Davis Inlet, then to Jack's Brook[4] and all the way to Katshistaputshikuanut[5]. That evening I left my skidoo by the lake and walked over to the next pond. I came across the fresh tracks of two otters. I waited a few minutes for them to come out but there was no sign of them. I headed home before dark. Kaniuekutat was at our house when I got back and I thought I'd tell him about the otters. That was the first time I really talked to him. He said he'd get up early the next morning to find those otters. We both knew that otters were always on the move early in the morning. He came back to visit the next morning around 10:00 with a story about how he'd killed the

---

[1] Kanishutakashtasht
[2] Jaqueline
[3] John Poker
[4] Tassiputakan-shipiss
[5] Translates as the place to wash your face

two otters. When I'd told him there were two otters in that pond, in our culture it was like I was giving him the authority to go look for them. I'd have gone to get them myself but I figured Kaniuekutat was older and more experienced. He was a great hunter and he'd know how long to wait before the otters came out of the pond.

One time we all went to Nutakuan River[1] all the way to Mistastin Lake. I was very surprised to see how well Kaniuekutat remembered the trail. We were in Mistastin Lake for a couple of days but there was no sign of caribou. Kaniuekutat was the *utshimau* and he suggested we leave the following day. It was snowing and blowing the next morning. He didn't seem to mind so we just packed our gear and left. He broke trail with his small skidoo. Even in this bad weather he could easily find a place called Kanakashkuaikanisht[2]. There was still no sign of caribou so we continued on our journey until we'd reached Kauauatshikamat[3] where we set up camp. We didn't have much wild food, only a couple of partridges.

The next morning we continued on our way and ran into some two-day-old caribou tracks around noon. Kaniuekutat suggested we camp at Barren Lake[4]. As we were setting up the tent, Kaniuekutat took off with his skidoo. When he returned he told us he'd spotted more white partridges. He handed me his gun and told me to bring back some of those partridge for supper. I was kind of nervous that I wouldn't be able to kill any. I started up my skidoo and headed out. Minutes later I ran into six partridges and managed to kill five. Later that afternoon Kaniuekutat suggested we head back to track the caribou before dark. We didn't get far because it was too windy and snowing. We saw fresh tracks but we didn't bother to look any further.

The next day the weather was okay although still windy. An elder Maskutiskam[5] was with us but he didn't come along. Kaniuekutat told me later that Maskutiskam would've been the next *kakushapatak*[6] if he hadn't died. Five of us set out that morning: Kaniuekutat and grandson Prote, Phil Jeddore, Kaniuekutat and me. Phil was a Mi'kmaq from Conne River and a good friend of Kaniuekutat. I still didn't know Kaniuekutat that well. As we crossed the lake where we'd seen the fresh tracks we could no longer see any sign of the

---

[1] Nutakuanan-shipu
[2] Translates as Long Stick Used to Cache Dried Meat
[3] Translates as Small Winding Lake
[4] Kamushuauakamat, translates as Barren Area Lake
[5] David Rich
[6] Shaman

caribou. We continued across the lake and headed into the barren hills. Suddenly I saw a caribou appear out of nowhere in the valley. Prote started shooting and I grabbed my gun and jumped off my skidoo. My gun jammed after the first shot. The empty cartridge got stuck in the barrel. I asked Phil for his knife and managed to free the cartridge.

We killed fifteen caribou that day. Kaniuekutat was very happy. He said if we'd not taken this route we'd never have found these caribou. We had our komatiks with us so each of us had to haul one caribou. I was planning to give mine to Maskutiskam. When we arrived back at camp Kaniuekutat gave his caribou to Maskutiskam. I also gave him mine. I was surprised to see Kaniuekutat show this respect for Maskutiskam because he was older than his friend. Kaniuekutat must have known what kind of person Maskutiskam was. In the afternoon we returned to the site of our kill to haul the remaining animals back. We left very early the next morning for Davis Inlet. We'd been very lucky to get so many caribou after we'd lost all sign of them.

That was the first time I ever went hunting with Kaniuekutat. He must have kept a close eye on me to check out my hunting skills. After this hunt he'd often come to visit and tell me stories about his past. I'd also tell him about my life in *nutshimit*. We continued to hunt and fish together in both the summer and winter. I learned many things from him.

One day Kaniuekutat told me a story about the time around 1946 when the Newfoundland Rangers were trying to capture Tuamas Noah[1]. They never succeeded. Tuamas was like a fugitive and he managed to hide away. Kaniuekutat never told me why the police wanted to arrest Tuamas. Kaniuekutat said one time he and his brother-in-law Metshitunapeu[2] were setting a net near Old Davis Inlet by a camp on the Hudson's Bay store side of the island. They were just about ready to canoe back across the Bay when they heard someone call their names. Kaniuekutat said he was kind of scared but then he remembered Tuamas. He turned around and sure enough it was Tuamas. His clothes were all torn up and he looked very weak. Kaniuekutat said he was surprised that Tuamas had managed to survive. What did he eat?

---

[1] Thomas Noah
[2] Raphael Rich

He thought Tuamas must have eaten wild berries or maybe his wife brought him food during the night.

I was very interested to learn more information about this story. I'd often remind Kaniuekutat about it but he wouldn't tell me more until years later. He told me how an elder and his two sons had tried to help the police capture Tuamas. Another elder was also in on this plan and a Ranger called Cyril Goodyear. It didn't work because other Innu heard about the police's plan. The news spread to other families and to the late Meshkea[1] who was a *kakushapatak*[2]. When he heard the news he went directly to see one of the elders helping the Ranger and told him to stop. Meshkea didn't want to see Tuamas betrayed by his own people, so the elder and his sons decided to pull their help after that.

My good friend Mishen was the son of the late Shushepiss[3] but he wasn't one of the sons who wanted to help the Rangers capture Tuamus. Mishen told me the story was true but I never asked him about his father helping the Rangers. Mishen told me another part of the tale.

"You must have heard about the move to Nutak," he said to me.

"Yes, I heard about it."

"Well, people say the government moved the Innu from Old Davis Inlet to Nutak just to capture Tuamus. They thought this relocation would be the only way they would be able to arrest the guy. They figured he'd be on the boat moving people up to Nutak. And that was exactly what happened."

When the boat was transporting the people, Tuamus was on board hiding inside the hold where they kept the firewood. Most Innu were on board although some were still in *nutshimit*. The boat anchored outside of Nain and the Rangers came over in a small boat to search the boat. They found Tuamus hiding inside the deck and arrested him. Mishen also talked about how the Innu had been told they'd be trained as fishermen once they moved to Nutak. I wondered if his father had got all this information about the move to Nutak because he was helping the police.

The Innu were only in Nutak for about a year and a half before they made their way back to Old Davis Inlet. I never heard the elders talk about being trained to become fishermen. Did the government supply boats and motors for the Innu to fish in those rough waters around Nutak? I later read documents

---

[1] Old Sam Rich
[2] Shaman
[3] Joe Rich

about how people were moved there because the store in Old Davis Inlet was going to close down.

My five months of sobriety ended abruptly when I slipped off the wagon and started drinking again. My oldest child Gerry was a little over two years old. My wife didn't seem to mind my drinking. Maybe she was afraid of me. I certainly was not the only one with drinking problems in Davis Inlet.

Almost every couple had a record player in those days. Every morning as I stepped outside after a few drinks I could hear country music somewhere in the distance. People would open their windows in the summer and point a loudspeaker playing country music outside. I liked to listen to country music when I was drinking. Most of the time I'd play Charley Pride or Conway Twitty. I'd sometimes get up as early as one o'clock in the morning. After a few drinks I'd visit my friends. I knew they'd also be up early. I'd often wake up my wife before I left and ask her to cook up something for when I got back. I'd come home again after daylight. I'd try to eat but I couldn't. The only thing I could manage to get down was something soft, like soup. When I tried to eat meat it would almost choke me. Many times I thought to myself that this would probably be the day I was going to die, but if I kept on drinking I'd live. Every time I'd see someone sleeping I'd wish I could sleep that good. I suffered so many ways because of alcohol. There's no one word to describe this in *Innu-aimun*.

During the seventies we'd buy hard liquor from the CN ferries. Sometimes we'd have to pay the bootleggers as much as a hundred dollars for a twenty-six-ouncer. Things got even worse when a Hopedale businessman started to sell beer in his store. One time we returned from Hopedale with forty-five dozen beer in our komatik. We had many visitors that night. I took off to Sango Bay the next morning with a couple dozen beers on my skidoo. I kept stopping to drink a bottle of beer and when I'd reached my buddy's camp I shared what I had left with him. When we finished the beer I went back for more.

I never thought to save any money for my two children. I knew my kids needed me more than I needed alcohol but I just didn't care. My little boy was growing up fast. Many times when I'd go out to Goose Bay I'd promise Gerry that I'd buy him something to bring back but as soon as I got there I forgot about my promise. All I could think about was drinking. I'd return to Davis Inlet with nothing to show my little boy. I'd only bring back yeast and hard liquor. I'd tell Gerry that the next time I went out I'd buy him something. There was always a next time but it never came. When my children had grown up, I did something to them that is very shameful to think about today.

Early one morning when our children were still in bed, Shanut and I left to go look for a drink. It was about 8:30 when we got back to our house. Gerry, who was about five years old, was trying to start a fire in our woodstove. I guess he was trying to please us and he was probably afraid of us. There were times when we hardly had enough wood to heat the house and I'd tell my children not to burn all the wood while we were gone. I wanted to save the wood for myself. I didn't really care if my children were cold or not. All I cared about was myself.

My enemy was alcohol. I did love my children very much but why didn't I care about them during those drinking days? I can never forgive myself for what I did to my children. I know they have forgiven me and now respect me as a father, but I also know they were the ones who suffered the most. For a long time, whenever I'd think about what I did to my children I'd hug one of my boys and in my mind I'd tell him I was sorry. I never said the words out loud, just in my thoughts.

Now I hope and wish none of my children suffer the way I did with alcohol. When I see couples drinking and their children don't seem to mind, it reminds me of Shanut and me. The children might look happy but I know they are deeply hurt inside their hearts as my children were. Now when I stop drinking I feel like a whole person again but I can never forget my drinking days. It still really hurts to think about those times in my life.

For years I tried many times to offer my wife a drink but she wouldn't take it. In the seventies, about eighty percent of the adults in Davis Inlet were drinking, both men and women. It was rare to see young people under eighteen drinking but most adults and elders did. When there was fighting in the community the priest would often call the police. News of this would spread around the community real fast and people would hide their homebrew. The RCMP would search all the houses and if they found any homebrew they'd throw out the bucket.

The RCMP were also like wildlife officers. People were afraid to hunt while the RCMP were in the community but the priest, Frank Peters, would encourage us to hunt.

"You have nothing to be afraid of," the priest would say. "This is your way of life." He was really standing up for the Innu but he was also trying to control the whole community.

When we were sober we felt like a bunch of useless people but after a few drinks we'd be out visiting again. We might talk about what we should do together the next day, about whether to go hunting but that day would never come. It was just as well. Hunting and drinking together is not like hunting at all – just a good time in a bad way.

One summer I was working in the fish plant in Davis Inlet. It wasn't much of a fish plant, only a building with natural ice and a scale to weigh the fish. I really liked the job although it was hard work. Most people who bought fish at the plant were Innu. Some Innu fishermen – like Shuashem Nui, my father-in-law Tshenish, Kaniuekutat[1] and Miste-Etuet – did really good fishing that summer. Of course the White people made good money fishing with their bigger and faster boats.

One time my father-in-law was asked to take thirty drums of gas in his motorboat to a fish camp at Hunt River[2]. My wife and I and other couples were invited along. On our way back we stopped on one of the islands to pick wild eggs. I hadn't taken any homebrew and I was very nervous. I had a 12-gauge shot gun. There were many ducks around and we killed quite a few. On my last shot everything went black. I had a seizure and the next thing I knew I was on the boat with my wife. I was perfectly okay after that and nothing happened.

That evening one of the couples who'd been on the excursion with us came to see me. The man asked me if I'd ever used a shotgun before. He seemed to think I didn't know how. "Yes, I've used a shotgun before." That's all I said. I let him think I was no hunter at all. He didn't know I probably would've been a better hunter than him if it hadn't been for the alcohol. He must've thought all hunters his age were skilled hunters. I didn't want to hurt his feelings and I respected what he thought. Maybe he thought he was a great hunter and he should teach me how to use a gun. He hurt me a lot when he said those things but I just didn't want to say anything.

I can hardly remember those years in the seventies. I don't know what year it was that my wife and I separated for a while. It was not because we didn't love each other. I guess I was just drinking too much. She looked after

---

[1] John Poker
[2] Kapapisht-shipu

our children and I went to Sheshatshiu, where I could always be close to the beer store in Goose Bay. I cheated on my wife and she must've done the same thing to me. I went with single girls even though I didn't like what I'd done when I was sober. My wife and I were not bad people. We didn't trust each other, which was why I cheated on her. I heard she was also drinking and had cheated on me too. I didn't complain because I'd done the same. I saw with my own eyes many husbands and wives always cheating on each other. I figured it happened in all Innu, Inuit and White communities.

One day when I was in Sheshatshiu I got a call from Davis Inlet to tell me my wife's brother had passed away. I headed back for the funeral and my wife and I got back together again even though we'd both heard the stories of what we'd been up to during our separation.

In those days my elder friend Mishen spent a lot of his time in Flowers Bay with his wife and grandson. I'd often visit them and although Mishen was a drinker I was always interested in hearing his stories. He'd talk about the old ways and how he wished we could live as our fathers had – in peace – without having to worry about our children. He talked about his travels through *nutshimit* and I could almost picture in my mind the times his father had with mine in the bush. His grandson hunted partridges although he was young. I saw that Mishen must be teaching him many things about hunting and the Innu way of life. It made me think that one day I should stop drinking and become a hunter again.

I did stop again for a few months in 1974. When I stayed sober no one could force me to drink. Some people say other people force them to drink. No one ever did this to me. I couldn't blame anyone for my drinking problems because it is me who took the drink. When someone would ask me why I had started to drink again I'd have all kinds of excuses but I couldn't blame anyone else.

One time when I was still drinking I took my family to Sango Lake[1]. Napeu[2] and his wife accompanied us and we traveled in a small boat with a four-horsepower motor. We reached some rapids along the Sango River[3] and

---

[1] Mishta-natuashu
[2] Sam Napeu
[3] Sango-shipu

I wondered how to get through them. Sam had crossed those rapids many times in his life although it must not have been with an outboard motor. He said he knew where the water was deep and he should handle the motor. We were both drinking. We were just above the rapid when we hit a rock but luckily we didn't damage the boat. We didn't care. We were just laughing. We tried again but this time we towed the boat with a rope.

It took us two days to get to the end of the lake, where a number of people had already set up camp. The next day the men went caribou hunting. Sam and I took along some bottles of homebrew. At the end of the day we headed back to camp empty-handed. How could we find any animals? We were just walking with our heads down and alcohol on our minds. It wasn't worth even trying to hunt. We needed to be sober to respect everything on earth, even every step we took. The next day we returned to Davis Inlet, not from what you could call a hunting trip. It had just been a gathering for drinking.

Another time, Kaniuekutat[1], Miste-Etuet and I went caribou hunting in Fraser Canyon[2], north of Nain. Each of us had our own Elan skidoos, not big machines but good for pulling loads. We met many hunters on the way. White hunters passed us with their faster machines. This time I wasn't drinking. I was one hundred percent healthy with nothing to worry about and very happy to be with these two elders. We had a hard time finding a place to camp along the high cliffs on either side of the Fraser Canyon. The next morning we drove our skidoos without our komatiks because we had to climb a very steep hill. We reached the top of the hill. We could see caribou everywhere we looked but the land was all open and barren and there was no place to hide to get a close shot. We only managed to kill seven caribou.

"We came a long way to hunt," said my old friend Kaniuekutat who was our *utshimau* on this hunt. "We can't go back with only seven caribou."

"I agree," I replied. "I'm going around that hill to see if I can kill more caribou."

"Be careful, don't get lost!" Kaniuekutat warned me. Barren land was still new to me but I had learned many things from my father. I had borrowed a 22-250 gun from my father-in-law. There were lots of caribou behind the hill and I hit a caribou with every shot. I killed eleven and I would've slaughtered more but I thought that was all we needed. I returned to my old friends and together we went back to haul the eleven caribou to the spot where we'd killed

---

[1] John Poker
[2] Kakushtikuak translates as Dangerous Place

the first seven. We skinned them and removed all the guts. We were just about ready to haul the caribou down to our camp when three more caribou appeared. Kaniuekutat said we should shoot them and then there'd be enough for the three of us. I wondered how we would pull twenty-one caribou with three small skidoos. We hauled the caribou down to our camp and Kaniuekutat suggested we leave the next morning. He said we should pack all the caribou onto our komatiks so we'd be able to leave very early.

We could see caribou heads everywhere all around our camp. White hunters had thrown them away. They'd just cut off the heads and left them behind. The eyes and tongues are very good to eat. The children especially love them. We hated to see all these heads left to waste. We kept some of them along with the seven caribou on each of our komatiks. The spring daylight was long and we made it back to Davis Inlet in one day with our heavy loads.

I always felt perfectly okay when I managed to stay sober. What made me drink again? It wasn't because I had other problems. It was because my whole body needed alcohol. Some alcoholics who have been sober for a while start drinking again because they want to forget things on their minds. Whenever I'd stop drinking it would take me at least a month to forget the things I'd done when I was drunk. For almost thirty years I wasted my life drinking. I could've lived in peace with my parents and my family. Alcohol almost destroyed me but I was able to fight for my life.

In 1976 our third child Nishapet[1] was born. The oldest Gerry was now six years old. We loved our children very much. I didn't think they knew anything about my drinking problems but years later Gerry told me he remembered those years. Our son Pien[2] was born in 1979. Although I'd quit drinking off and on for six or nine months at a time, I was on the booze again and now my wife was also drinking. My drinking was worse than ever. I'd often get sick and end up in the hospital. I couldn't sleep. I just had to keep moving. I couldn't relax at all. I tried to drink water as much as I could but there were times I couldn't even hold the cup. Although it must have been just my

---

[1] Elizabeth
[2] Peter

imagination, every time I tried to close my eyes I'd see someone staring at me. Sometimes I'd talk to myself like I was asking someone for a beer. Sometimes I'd call out the names of my drinking friends. I felt kind of nervous when there was no one else around.

My wife didn't really want to drink but I kept forcing her. Fortunately she wouldn't leave the kids on their own. She'd try to look after them as much as she could. One time in the winter we didn't have any firewood in the house and my children were cold. I grabbed the axe and chopped down a piece of two-by-four from the basement of the house. I was using lumber from my own house to burn as firewood.

Many times my children headed out for school in the morning without breakfast. They'd come home at lunch to no food. They must have expected us to cook something and been often disappointed. Sometimes when there was food in the house we'd cook it up for them before we left to visit our friends but the children would have left for school wondering what they would eat for lunch or supper. Many times they'd say they weren't hungry, probably because they knew we didn't have much food in the house. I was always trying to take charge of my family. If they didn't listen to me I'd get angry. In the evening, Shanut and I would invite our friends to our home for a drink. The children must've felt terrible to see so many people drinking in our house. When I'd make homebrew, my children always seemed to want to help. They'd get the water and pass me the things I needed. I thought my children didn't mind my drinking.

"Daddy, when you were drinking we were really worried about you and at the same time we were afraid of you," one of my little boys told me many years later when he was about 13. "You never noticed anything about what was going on with us because we didn't want to show you that we were afraid." He said they were very happy whenever I quit and they'd hope I'd never start again. It really hurt me to hear this but I was also encouraged to stay sober.

"One day I'm going to stop drinking," I'd say to my wife. But when was that day going to come? My goal was to stay sober and I hoped and prayed I could become a hunter again. If I could stop drinking I could teach my children what my father had taught me. But the day never came for a very long time. I just kept on drinking until five years after our last child was born, but I'm getting ahead of my story now.

At this moment my youngest is sitting beside me at my desk probably wondering why I am writing so many pages. I hope when he's older he'll read these writings and know about my past, about the hunting I did with my father, about my days as an alcoholic. He'll know that if it hadn't been for my children I'd still be a drunk, that two things helped me to stay sober. I finally understood how much my children suffered from my alcoholism and I cared about hunting, fishing and life in *nutshimit*. I wanted to become a hunter again. These thoughts would eventually give me the strength to stay sober.

P INIP[1], AN ELDER, TOLD ME the first band council in Old Davis Inlet was not a real one. Pinip's father Shushepiss[2] and his councilors were handpicked by the priest. Shushepiss was appointed Chief. That council may have received some provincial or federal funding for community services but the priest was the one who handled the money. He may have been the only one who knew how to do it. When I came to Davis Inlet in 1970, Father Frank Peters was still looking after the money but the decisions on how to spend it were made by the Council.

Elections were eventually held in the 1970s. Other middle-aged people were elected as leaders but the elected Chief and councilors were no better than anyone else. The community was not getting any better because these leaders were heavy drinkers. The people all saw what the leaders were doing. We'd stand around and watch chartered helicopters land outside the band council building. The leaders would get off drunk with heavy suitcases and boxes filled with booze. One time I saw a chartered aircraft land with only two German Shepherd dogs and the pilot on board, no passengers.

This was great, according to all the heavy drinkers. We didn't care what happened at meetings. In the 1980s, when young people took over the leadership, the problems got even worse. Most leaders were still drinking. The few people who did not drink could see the waste of band council funding. When I was sober I'd also think it was a waste but if I was drinking I didn't care. When band council elections rolled around it was party time. A person didn't have to be a strong leader to be elected. If he could supply booze to the voters he was guaranteed a successful election. The same people would always get elected and most were related to each other. That made things even worse. Different families were against each other. The family members of the elected leaders would get whatever they wanted from the band council. Others got nothing. One time just before Christmas the band council donated free turkeys to the community. I didn't get one but I didn't care. I didn't know our council had turkey money in its budget. Another time the council ordered

---

[1] Philip Rich
[2] Old Joe Rich

range stoves for the whole community. This was good for all of us, especially the elders.

When a bunch of us were drinking together we'd never discuss anything about life in *nutshimit*. Politics was the one thing we always wanted to talk about. We'd blabber about our leaders and the government people we'd met. We'd argue with each other like a debate to see who'd end up on top. We liked the way alcohol was used to lure us to vote for the candidates. Maybe that was why we talked a lot about politics when we were drunk. We discussed all the things we should do for the community, how we could help the people of Davis Inlet. The next day I'd remember what I'd said. It would really hurt me and I felt shame. The only way I could forget was to drink again.

In those years the leaders had no voice at all. When the government people came to Davis Inlet to meet with our leaders no one knew what was being said at the meeting. We always thought White people knew what was best, even if we couldn't understand what they were saying. What we didn't know was that they were saying things just to keep us quiet. We said nothing and we did everything the government wanted. They controlled our money. They hired their own consulting engineers to work for us. These outsiders would usually bring their own men to work. We didn't know at the time that they were only interested in contracts to build houses or to do studies on water and sewage facilities. We were told many times that Davis Inlet would soon get water and sewage facilities. Many studies were done but nothing ever happened.

No matter who was elected Chief, nothing changed. It was always the same year after year. In the same way that our leaders were powerless in the face of governments, we were powerless against our own leaders. Anyone who tried to voice his or her concerns was the enemy of the council. I wrote many letters to the council about the way the Chief and council were doing their work but my complaints went nowhere because I was an Innu person. If I'd been a White person they would've listened to me. Sometimes when a person went outside of the community to complain the council would offer him a job to buy him off. That would be that, and the complaint would end there.

When the band council came into our lives the government took control of us and part of our culture was lost. We had to follow too many government policies. For forty years I attended many Innu meetings, which the leaders tried to run the way of the *Akaneshau*[1] people. If someone asked a question that

---

[1] White

the leaders didn't like, they'd say the constitution did not allow that question. I'd think to myself, "The hell with the constitution! The Innu have survived thousands of years without ever using any kind of constitution."

The Innu had their own rules to follow but they weren't written down in a book. The elders made the rules and everyone had to follow them. Now elders would speak out at meetings to give advice to the young leaders but the Band Council wouldn't listen at all. They preferred to depend on their *Akaneshau* advisors. Many times a *Akaneshau* would say the same thing as the Innu elder had said and the band council would grab onto the advice. Why had they not listened to the elder in the first place? We thought *Akaneshau* people were the best advisors. We forgot that our Innu elders were the ones to provide advice for our people. The other problem with community meetings was that it was often people who were drunk who did the talking. Or if someone said something important for the community, the leaders would agree with their suggestion but after the meeting everything was forgotten.

In the summer the council would hire students to clean up the community but only the relatives of the councilors would get the jobs. One time my two sons and my friend's grandson weren't hired. I was really upset. My youngest son was crying because other kids his age were working and he had no job. It really hurt me but there was nothing I could do.

People could complain as much as they wanted to but no one would listen and nothing changed. It didn't matter what the leaders did, they'd continue to get re-elected because the majority of voters were related to them. These problems went on into the 1980s and well into the 1990s when things finally began to change a little.

The governments must have known about these problems. They didn't care. They wanted our leaders to continue to drink so that they could easily control them. Governments played all kinds of dirty games with us. Innu people had to follow the direction of these *Akaneshau* officials. We didn't have a real say in anything at all. It would take many years for us to learn that the only solution was for us to heal ourselves. Then people would begin to respect themselves and each other. We'd begin to learn that no one should be left out.

In the late 1970s my friend Kaniuekutat[1] was elected Chief. For many years before and after he was the only Chief elected who was not drinking. He was also an elder. He'd been a drinker before the community had moved from Old Davis Inlet but after his mother drowned he never tasted alcohol again. After he was elected he hired me to be his translator. I wasn't drinking then although before the end of his term I'd once again fallen off the wagon. He didn't fire me and I continued to work for him until the next election.

Kaniuekutat was the first leader to talk about moving the community to another location. He was also the first to get the idea to buy skidoos and sell them at half-price to people who needed them. The money made from the sale went back to the council for other uses. My friend really stood up for the people when he was Chief. He ran again for re-election but lost because he was a non-drinker. He didn't supply any booze to his supporters. He hadn't wanted to call an election but he was forced to call one by the government.

The election wasn't the only way the government meddled in council affairs. It also decided to place the council's funding in a trust fund and would only release money for salaries. Chief Kaniuekutat was very upset. He and his council kept fighting for that money to be released into council hands. The province did not like to see the Chief shouting and standing up to them. They wanted to keep him quiet. They wanted him to follow their orders but Chief Kaniuekutat rejected that plan. He kept fighting for the rights of his people and for what he thought was best for his community, which was why the province wanted to get rid of him.

I was the one who read the letter to Chief Kaniuekutat from the Assistant Deputy Minister of the provincial Department of Rural Development. It said his term as Chief was over and he should call an election. Kaniuekutat had no choice. When the election was finally called, the people with the most booze got elected as Chief and councilors. The money in trust was released to the new Chief because this new council was not against the government. The new Chief was happy to do just what the government wanted. When the Chief and councilors went out to meetings they'd return with a lot of booze. I did that many times too but I was not often a leader.

---

[1] John Poker

Every spring and fall for many years the band councils of both Sheshatshiu and Davis Inlet organized an outpost program that would fly people out in *nutshimit*. The program was very important to people of all ages and it benefited the whole community although some people wouldn't bother with it. They went to nearby bays and hunted on their own without any help from the band council. Although there were serious alcohol problems in Davis Inlet, people were still always on the move. They took their families out to *nutshimit*. There were times when there was hardly anyone left in the community. The school was almost empty. People would stay in *nutshimit* for months at a time.

The Davis Inlet region for as long as I can remember was always a good place to hunt, trap and fish especially in the winter and spring. In the spring most hunters moved out of the community to different places to hunt geese. In the winter, before the caribou migrated to the coast, people traveled as far as one hundred miles west to Border Beacon[1] by skidoos or dog teams. Many hunters from Nain or Rigolet[2] also hunted in the Border Beacon area. One time hunters came from as far south as Black Tickle. They didn't have enough caribou and were looking for someone who might be interested in sharing some of their kill. I had four caribou in my unheated basement so I gave them to these hunters in return for about ten gallons of gas. Black Tickle was a long ways from here so I hated to see the boys go back without any caribou. It was just the way of our community.

The outpost program was very important but the charter aircraft were causing the old ways to fade away. In September the people who wanted to go to *nutshimit* had to register with the Band Council office. People on social assistance would go to the Social Services office to get an advance on their assistance for the fall to buy supplies for *nutshimit*. They wouldn't have to pay back this advance. The people on U.I. would also get three months of assistance but they'd have to pay back the money. When they returned from *nutshimit* after their three months away they'd again claim their U.I. but a certain amount would be deducted from each payment to pay back the advance.

[1] Ashuapun
[2] Uinuat

People flew into *nutshimit* on floatplane. Two trips were needed to haul a family of six or more children and all their gear. A Twin Otter could not carry much of a load because of the heavy float. The cost for charters could be high if there were ten or more families who wanted to go to *nutshimit*. The plane would have to fly from Goose Bay to Davis Inlet, make two or three trips into *nutshimit* and fly back to Goose Bay in the evening.

In the old days Innu didn't have to spend a dollar to travel into *nutshimit*. All they needed was a bit of grub, some ammunition, a gun and a bit of clothing, yet they were able to spend the whole year in *nutshimit*. In the 1970s new machines began to replace aspects of our way of life especially when it came to transportation and tools like chainsaws. Innu began to travel by skidoos, planes or speedboats with outboard motors. The big thing we lost of our culture was the knowledge and ability to travel by foot or dog team. It became easy to get to *nutshimit* and easy to lose parts of our culture. If someone got sick in *nutshimit* he or she would be flown to the hospital in Goose Bay. Our dependency on these planes grew too large. Innu forgot about their traditional medicine. Many White people from Goose Bay began to speak out about how they didn't like us using planes and helicopters to go to *nutshimit*. They said it was a waste of government money and the Innu were getting a free camping trip in the bush.

We also learned that sometimes the machines could do nothing for us. For example, one spring during the 1980s a few families had a camp just south of Daniel's Rattle[1] when a young boy accidentally shot himself in the arm with a 12-gauge shot gun. The wound was real bad. It was during break-up and even though it was only about eleven kilometres away from Davis Inlet there was no way a person could walk on the ice or use a boat. The families were camping on the mainland and Davis Inlet was on an island. It was too dangerous to cross the Rattle because the ice was moving back and forth. There was no radio to call for an emergency chopper. The boy died because he ran out of blood. The people could have saved his life if Davis Inlet had not been on an island. After this, people really began to wonder why the government had settled our community on an island. It was like they had locked us up in a cage to watch us suffer. During spring break-up and fall freeze-up of the ice we couldn't go to the mainland to hunt. We knew now that in a medical emergency we couldn't get back to the community and a young boy was dead.

---

[1] Mishti-shantiss

Our dependency on planes and choppers didn't mean we'd lost our way of life. Even today the outpost program is still very important especially for young people. Although they don't learn the old ways of traveling by foot or by canoe, they do learn a lot about the Innu way of life. We still hunt in the ways of our ancestors. We can still walk long distances in one day. Our elders and some young people still respect the animals. Many aspects of our culture are very much alive. We've taken good care of our culture. Even in the community some people who are not healthy enough to hunt will still often set up their tents outside their houses. They feel more comfortable living in a tent than in a house.

The elders say Innu children used to have their own traditional games but now these have been replaced by *Akaneshau* games, like volleyball, floor hockey, skidoo races and others they learn from the school. This still doesn't replace our culture because another people's culture will not fit into our culture. Our language will be with us for many more years to come. Every child in our community speaks his or her own language. One huge problem is that many of our teachers, the Elders, have passed away. Another problem is that our school does not teach Innu history or language. Does the school have Innu books? As well, I know mixed parents whose children don't often speak *Innu-aimun*. They probably understand the Innu language better than they speak but they find it too hard to speak. We have to be very careful to make sure our language is with us for many generations to come. Once our language is lost it will be gone for good. Nowhere else in the world will we be able to learn how to speak it again.

Another challenge to our culture has been the foreign laws imposed on us to keep us from hunting and fishing. These laws have been a very serious attack on the heart of our culture. The government made our way of life illegal. For many years the RCMP gave the Innu a hard time. People were afraid to hunt while the police were in the community. Now it's also more difficult to get a gun because of new gun laws. Years ago the RCMP came into the community and called a public meeting. They told us that anyone who wanted to buy a gun would first need to get a permit from the police. They said no one would have to pay for this permit but a few years later we had to pay ten dollars. Now we have to pay fifty dollars to renew our permits.

I have no idea whether the RCMP made their own laws. One time I was charged wrongly for impaired driving. I was just trying to start an ATV but it wouldn't go. Someone must've reported me to the police. Whoever it was, he couldn't have been Innu. An RCMP officer came to my house, handed me a summons and told me I was charged with impaired driving. When the court came to Davis Inlet I was happy. I wasn't afraid. When my name was called I stood up and walked over to face the judge.

"You understand the charge?" the judge asked me.

"Yes sir," I said. I didn't call him "Your Honour."

"Do you plead guilty or not guilty?"

"Not guilty."

The judge gave me a date to appear in court again. I thanked him and left. The day the court was leaving I went to the airstrip. I happened to know both the judge and the Crown prosecutor well. Everyone in the building at the airstrip could hear what I said.

"I don't need to call you the 'Crown' since you're outside the courthouse," I told him. "You should drop that charge. My daughter saw what happened and she's going to tell the truth in court. You know you can't win. Besides that, it's not worth me paying $300 for having done nothing wrong."

The judge heard me, looked over to the Crown prosecutor and laughed. Later that summer the charge was dropped.

AROUND 1978 I'D MANAGED to stay sober for a while and was hired to work as director of the Alcohol Program. Not many people had applied for the job. Most people were drinking and I just happened to be sober that year. I didn't care if I didn't get hired because there were always summer jobs available in the community. As part of my job I was invited that August to attend a workshop on alcoholism in Cornwall, Ontario. Every year, also in August, there was the Innu Nikamu music festival in Sept Isles. Since I was the director I decided my bookkeeper and I would leave a week before the workshop in Cornwall to spend a couple of nights at the festival in Sept Isles and then catch a bus to Cornwall. The first night in Sept Isles I started to drink again. I thought I'd only have a couple of drinks but after one I kept going for the next two weeks. The festival lasted only three days.

There were over a hundred Innu from Sheshatshiu at the festival. They'd driven all the way to Esker and taken the train from there. On the Friday when all the people from Sheshatshiu were heading home, I should've gone with them but I was ashamed and afraid of what might happen on the long train ride. I didn't have any money but my sisters would've paid my way. I didn't know what to do after all the people left. I worried about what might happen to me. Where would I sleep that night? Where would my next beer come from? I had many relatives in Sept Isles but they didn't seem like relatives to me. I didn't see them often because we lived too far apart. I ran into an aunt and I was very surprised to hear her call me "Nephew." She was my father's sister, but was she really my aunt? I thought perhaps it had something to do with our culture. When we didn't see our relatives for a long time our relationships faded away.

Anyway, I was able to find many friends who were alcoholics like me. I spent nights with friends and slept any place I could find. Every morning I got up very early and walked back and forth through the community hoping I'd find an unopened bottle of beer. Every time I found one I looked to see if there was any beer left inside and if there was I drank it. At the end of two weeks my body couldn't take it anymore. As soon as the alcohol touched my stomach I started to vomit. I was really hungry but I just couldn't swallow any food.

Someone took me to the hospital. Once the doctor checked my blood pressure I was admitted. He gave me an injection and some Librium. I had an I.V. in my arm. By the next afternoon I felt perfectly okay and I was released.

As soon as I stepped outside the hospital I began to worry about my children. What would happen to them if I lost my job? I tried to forget but everything that had happened to me over the last two weeks kept surfacing in my mind. I wondered how I would get back home. Where would I get the money? I passed by a Department of Indian Affairs office and decided to go see if they could help me out. I talked to the receptionist but she didn't speak any English at all. She told me to sit down and wait. She was gone only a short while when she returned with an Innu worker.

This young woman invited me into her office and asked me what was my problem. I explained the whole story. I was happy to be able to speak in my own language. I asked if the department could pay my way to Goose Bay. I told her my father was a Status Indian[1]. She checked all her files and found out I was also a registered Status Indian. She picked up the phone. I couldn't understand what she was saying in French but I could almost tell she was talking to a travel agent. She got off the phone and handed me a piece of paper to take to the travel agent, who within five minutes of my arrival in her office handed over an airline ticket to Goose Bay, plus a voucher for a night in a hotel in Wabush[2].

On the one hand I was really happy to have this ticket but the truth was only half of me was happy. The other half was sad because of what I'd been through the last two weeks. I spent my last night with my drinking friends. They were drinking and smoking pot but I abstained. I tried to get some sleep but I kept thinking of my children. I told my friends what was on my mind but they were drinking and laughing as always. I knew if I joined them I'd be stuck here longer. I was excited as I thought that in eight hours I'd be out of here.

I was up early the next morning to say goodbye to my friends. I went to see the priest and he gave me a cup of coffee and some breakfast. I was still very weak but at least I wasn't hungover. I borrowed twenty dollars in case I had to pay a taxi from the airport to the hotel in Wabush. My cousin George Pinette drove me to the airport. I spent the night in Wabush and the next day I was very happy to get off the plane in Goose Bay. I didn't have money for a taxi to Sheshatshiu so I took a taxi to a corner store where people from

---

[1] A registered Indian under the federal Indian Act
[2] Uapush translates as rabbit

Sheshatshiu would come to pick up booze. I'd hitchhike from there. My Inuit friend Harvey Mucko from North West River soon drove up in his taxi. He bought beer and asked me if I needed a ride to Sheshatshiu. He offered me a beer. I put it in my pocket but I gave it to someone in Sheshatshiu. That evening I phoned my wife Shanut in Davis Inlet. She seemed happy to hear from me.

"Have you heard anything about my job?" I asked her.

"No, as far as I know no one else has taken your job yet," she said.

The day after I arrived home I was invited to a board meeting. I thought for sure that was the end of my job. I didn't want to defend myself. I told them the whole truth and promised I would pay back any money that I had misspent from the Alcohol Program. The board just told me to go back to work and make sure it never happened again.

During those years I was also one of the church leaders in the community. I'd appointed myself. Anyone could be a church leader, unlike in the old days when the priest ran his own church all by himself. Every once in awhile we held short meetings to discuss who would do the service on Christmas, Easter or a Sunday when the priest was away. If someone was invited to a meeting outside of the community we had to decide who would attend.

One time our church leaders were invited to a retreat in Sept Isles. Five families attended and our priest came along as well. While we were gone the priest received a phone call from Davis Inlet to tell us the Poker family had drowned. Nine of them – a man, his wife and their children – had fallen from a small freighter canoe. Only three survived. They had also gone down but managed to surface and saved themselves by holding onto the capsized canoe.

That was not the first time Innu people had died from an alcohol-related accident. When we got back to Davis Inlet, the Coast Guard divers were searching for the bodies. Most people who had boats also helped. The woman's body was found floating that same day and two of the children were found washed ashore. The others were never found. The man who drowned had been a well-known hunter. My friend Kaniuekutat was his brother. Kaniuekutat's mother had also drowned, and now his brother. It was really a sad day for the whole community but most people just kept right on drinking as if nothing had happened. They didn't want to look at what had happened to Shimun[1] Poker's family.

worked as director of the Alcohol Program right through the 1980s. I managed to stay sober most of the time but once in a while I'd slip up. My job was so overwhelming. Alcohol and children sniffing gas were becoming ever more serious problems in our community. I had no idea how the gas sniffing started. The idea of sniffing must've come from the outside. Maybe a White person told the kids they could get high from sniffing gas. At first we thought gas sniffing was not that serious but later some community members were really concerned about it. No one knew what to do about these children.

Early one morning I was headed for Sango and as I passed by the graveyard I saw a young boy sniffing gas in minus-zero temperatures. I took the gas away from him and told him to go home. He said he'd stop sniffing if I gave him some homebrew. That evening when I got home he was waiting for me to give him a drink. I wasn't drinking so I didn't have any homebrew. I don't know what would've happened if I'd been drinking.

I never trained to work as director of the Alcohol Program but I was an alcoholic and had my own experience of how alcohol affected me and my community. I was able to do counseling by using my own experience. I thought I was able to do my work even with no training at all. Many people who had drinking problems came to see me. I wrote down everything they told me. I guarded these papers and always kept their contents very confidential. My eyes were the only ones to ever see these papers. We held an AA[2] meeting once a week. I wasn't afraid to share my own story with the group.

Sometimes I went to talk to the children in school about the problems with alcohol. I also tried to talk to some of the gas sniffers but they just wouldn't listen to anyone. I felt the need to tell them about my own experience with alcohol but I was never sure whether I was doing the right thing or not. I worried they wouldn't understand, that it might be like I was teaching them to drink. I hoped they heard my message as a warning of what might happen to them if they drank. I know now that I am not an alcohol counselor but if I was

---

[1] Simon
[2] Alcoholics Anonymous

I'd tell young people about who they really are as Innu. I'd tell them about their history and about life in *nutshimit*. I'd explain to them how I wasted my life for over forty years because of alcohol. A counselor should not only talk about the problems of the day. They should mention past, present and future problems as well.

I strongly believed that parents needed to take responsibility for their own children. The parents must have worried about their children but they didn't seem to want to take any responsibility. They were too dependent on alcohol and the dirty politics of the band council. They thought the leaders should do something but no one seemed interested in taking responsibility to save our children. As the years went by, the gas-sniffing problem just got worst. In the 1990s we thought our children needed something to do, like recreation activities. The band council decided to use half of the band council building for a recreation hall. They purchased some video games, pool tables and a television. This was not enough.

No band council who could stay sober had ever been elected, except for Kaniuekutat. He was sober but not his council. Nothing changed; our addictions problems got worse. I thought if only we had a sober leadership other people would follow and sober up as well. I knew that alcohol had the same effect on anyone whether they were Innu, White, Black or any other people throughout the world. I never thought it was a sin to drink as long as the person could handle it, but if you couldn't, the alcohol would control your life. I figured alcohol would always be in our communities but we should be prepared to know how to control it. For people who'd never tasted alcohol I thought they shouldn't bother at all. I knew I had to constantly use all my energy to never touch alcohol again in my life.

D URING THE SUMMER OF 1987 a Sheshatshiu Innu teacher named Kanani[1] was transferred to Davis Inlet for one year and she and her husband moved up that fall. At first they didn't have a place to stay so they decided to set up a tent by the beach down below the mission building. Just as their tent was standing they saw the priest headed their way. They figured he was coming to say hello. Instead he told them to take down their tent because they were not allowed to set it up on church property. The couple didn't argue with the priest and moved their tent over by the airstrip. They thought the priest had the power to tell people where they could set up their tent. The priest maybe thought it was mission property but the church wasn't paying property taxes like it would in a town or city. Who was the church anyway – the priest or the people? Who owned the church? Maybe Kanani and her husband were afraid of the priest. If it was me, I would've explained to the priest this was Innu property, all of this whole land. He was the one who should've moved his house. Innu people had the right to set up their tents wherever they wished.

That same fall after I attended a Native Teacher Training Conference in North West River, the Alcohol Program was also kicked out of a shack owned by the R.C. Mission. The conference was for Native people in Labrador and Newfoundland. An Innu teacher named Shakanin[2] and I talked about education issues in Davis Inlet. I told the people how teachers were abusing Innu students in Davis Inlet. Some teachers wouldn't even let children use the washrooms. I talked about how there was often no water at the school and if it had been a White school it would've been closed down. I spoke out about how the community got no support from the school for its life skills program in which students learned about their Innu culture. Every year we had to fight to get funding for this program. I said some non-Innu teachers did not respect this program and the Innu language was starting to fade in our children.

I talked about how as director of the Alcohol Program I wanted to go to the school to talk about alcohol abuse, gas sniffing and the law. The principal

---

[1] Caroline Andrew
[2] Jaqueline Rich

would only allow me to speak for an hour. I thought this showed a lack of concern and an unwillingness to bend to the needs and concerns of the community. We also mentioned that our teacher aides did not have any training and were being pushed to teach without it. Students would begin school speaking no English and none of the non-Innu teachers spoke *Innu-aimun*. The conference report was released and it made a number of people angry, including the Chief and the priest.

From the first day that priest set foot in Davis Inlet I noticed he was going to be a problem. He was appointed board member for the Alcohol Program and during his first meeting he was already trying to tell us how to run things. I wasn't afraid of him. I was sick and tired of all the *Akaneshau* advisors we'd been listening to for so long. This priest thought he could control the Innu people like the missionaries of the 1940s.

The Sunday after the conference report was released I didn't go to church but I should have. A friend told me what the priest had said about me during his mass. One of the nuns also confirmed this. She said she was deeply hurt when she heard the priest say things about me and that she almost walked out during the service.

A few weeks later the Alcohol Program received a letter from the priest giving us one week's notice to move out of their building. He claimed he needed it for storage but I thought he was angry about the report and he wanted to protect the non-Innu teachers. He shouldn't have put all the blame just on me. There were many other people who had real complaints about him and the way he ran his church. On Sunday mornings when he was about to begin mass he'd lock the door from the inside so no one else could come in after the service had started. I didn't think he supported any of the Innu programs in Davis Inlet.

He must have thought we'd be unable to find another office. We moved into the band council building and the day we moved I called Newfoundland Hydro to disconnect the power. I didn't think we should continue to pay the hydro bills for our old office. One morning one of my sons looked out the window and said to me in a very happy voice that the priest was coming to visit. All my children were glad to see him come but I knew this priest did not like me very much. I wondered if he'd changed his mind and was coming on a friendly visit. I was in the porch ready to greet him when he stormed through the door.

"Hello, what can I do for you?" I asked him.

"Did you ask Hydro to disconnect the lights in your office?" he shouted to me.

"I did," I replied calmly. "We'll no longer be using this building."

"What a stupid thing to do!" he said, still shouting. "Didn't you know I'd still be using that shack?"

"You're the one who's stupid," I said, and now I was shouting too. "You're just trying to take control of the community."

He never made it inside the house. I thought this priest was not fit to work with the Innu people. I called the Bishop. I'd already written him a letter about the priest. I told him I couldn't understand why he'd done nothing about our problems with this priest. I warned him that if he did not get rid of this priest the news would hit the CBC. The Bishop asked me to give him a couple of days to respond. A week later the priest left the community without any explanation. He never got to use his shack and the kids eventually broke the windows and door.

I may have seemed like a bad person to other people but I was a Catholic and respected the Church. I was not being anti-*Akaneshau*, just respecting our way of life. *Akaneshau* who came to our community had to show respect for our culture. They shouldn't make fun of it. The respect we'd shown for *Akaneshau* culture for so many years had brought us no benefits. It was the *Akaneshau* people's turn to show their respect. In 1987 when this priest came to Davis Inlet, the Innu were just about ready to stand up for ourselves.

It took me a long time to figure out that I'm a Catholic and can respect that religion but at the same time I can still use our Innu religion and way of life. I'll continue to believe this for the rest of my life. I don't think the Church meant to destroy the Innu people's culture. The priests must've known that the Innu couldn't be nomadic people forever. They must've thought Innu children should go to school and get a good education so they would be prepared if the government wanted to take away our land. At the same time, governments may have used missionaries to make the Innu give up their land and their rights.

According to the elders, the first Oblate priest to come to Davis Inlet was Father Edward O'Brien, sometime in the 1920s. The Innu named him

Kauapeskuet, or Father Whitehead. Before that the Moravian Church had baptized some Mushuau Innu. Others had been baptized Catholic when they'd traveled south to Sept Isles. My father-in-law Tshenish Pasteen said many Innu in those days were spending time in the Voisey's Bay[1] area in the summer – not only Mushuau Innu but also Innu from as far away as Sept Isles and Fort Chimo. The priests who baptized the Innu at that time kept very poor logbooks. I know because for many years I worked hard to help my people get their old age pensions, spousal allowances and widow's allowances. It was not part of my job but I did it voluntarily. The elders told how Father Whitehead baptized many Innu when he came to Labrador. They would've been born in *nutshimit* and there were no written documents to verify their date of birth. People knew the place names where babies were born as well as where people had died and been buried, but they did not know the dates.

Many elders passed away without ever receiving an old age pension. A number of elders told me they were far older than what Father Whitehead had recorded. I searched through the 1935 and 1945 censuses and discovered that many people were eligible to receive their pension but the people in the Old Age Security office refused to recognize my findings. They preferred to follow Father Whitehead's logbook. I interviewed a number of elders and sent the information I'd gathered from the elders to the Old Age Security people but still nothing happened. They didn't seem to trust our elders although their memories were so clear.

After Father Whitehead made his last trip to Labrador another priest called Father Joseph Cyr followed. He was also a teacher and taught mostly about religion. He was a heavy-looking guy, which must be why the Innu called him Miste-Kaupukuest. He was the first permanent priest in Davis Inlet. Elders say he was a very tough priest both in church and in school. He would not let the last *kakushapatak*[2] sit at the front of the church. He must have thought the *kakushapatak* was worshipping the devil.

After Father Cyr left, Father Frank Peters arrived. He was a Dutch priest and he learned our language very fast. He lived with the Innu for seventeen years. I remembered him from his visits to Sheshatshiu when I was just a young boy. The last priest to come to Davis Inlet in the 1990s was Father Fred McGee. He was a hard-working priest before he got sick. He'd haul, chop and split wood. Whenever I'd make a small *Makushan,* I always invited him to eat

---

[1] Emish
[2] Shaman

with us. He was just like one of us when he came to my house or my tent. He'd always help himself to a cup of tea. That's the way it should be in our culture. You don't have to wait for someone to serve you. You can always help yourself.

Father McGee was a very nice priest who respected everyone in the community, especially the elders. He believed all the things we told him about how the Innu lived in the past. He believed what we said about the *kakushapatak* and our spiritual powers. I really missed Father McGee after he left. I knew he had loved the Innu and our community. He told us after he left there might not be any priest to replace him because of a shortage of priests everywhere around the world. He was right. We no longer had a permanent priest. A priest would now come only every second month or when someone died and he only stayed for a few days.

In September 1993, when I was in *nutshimit* the caribou ran everywhere. Just east of us was another camp that we could contact by bush radio. Every day we'd hear talk about killing caribou. The young hunters at this camp just loved to shoot and didn't care how many caribou they killed. The fall weather was not that cold and there was no way to keep that meat fresh for very long. Drying the meat was the only way to keep it from spoiling. Our elder was very concerned about all these caribou killed but he didn't want to tell the hunters what to do. He wondered whether they'd be able to haul all the caribou meat to their camp. We'd also killed quite a few caribou but we were drying the meat.

The same thing happened in 1996. We hadn't killed too many caribou in our camp, only enough to dry the meat to take home. But a week before we were headed back to Davis Inlet the people from another camp called us on the bush radio to say the boys had killed three caribou that day. Every couple of days we heard reports that they'd killed more caribou. When the plane came to pick us up to go home the pilot told us we had to pick up a sick person at this other camp. We loaded the plane in no time at all and we were soon airborne. I was up front, sitting with the pilot and within five minutes he'd beached the plane. He quickly unhooked his seatbelt, grabbed a rope and walked to the rear of the plane. He opened the door and asked the kids on the beach to turn his plane from behind with the rope. I got off and was shocked to see so many caribou on the beautiful beach extending into deep water. At the far end of the beach I could see another three caribou that had yet to be skinned.

"Are these the three caribou they killed a week ago?" I whispered to my friend.

"Maybe. If the meat has spoiled I guess it won't be our fault." he said.

I wanted to walk over to the three caribou but I didn't want people to think I was investigating anything. I began to understand what the elders had said so many times – that the *Nikatipenimushim*[1] was angry with us because we no longer respected the animals. People were throwing caribou meat away in the dump for the dogs to eat. I'd also often seen the dogs chewing on the caribou bones left lying around. The elders said we had so many terrible problems in our community because the *Nikatipenimushim* was so angry with us. This was why we were suffering from gas sniffing, suicide, family problems and alcohol. In the old days, hunters would bring back their kill and the meat was always shared around the community. Nothing was wasted. Elders talk about how they never saw gas sniffing, suicide and other such problems in those days. People used to drink but not so much. I strongly believed what the elders said – that we must accept some of the blame for our problems because we didn't respect the wild animals. We had to accept some blame for the slow disappearance of our culture. We couldn't blame everything on the Church.

In the past, priests didn't know about Innu life in *nutshimit*. They didn't understand that a *kakushapatak*[2] could communicate with the *Aueshish-utshimaut*[3] and tell his people where to find food, like where they'd find the caribou. The *kakushapatak* and elders had spiritual powers that were part of our Innu religion before the missionaries came to conquer our souls. We know today clearly that the *kakushapatak* was not a bad person but someone who did everything in his power to help his people. He was also a medicine man who could heal the sick. He could perform a shaking tent as well as miracles.

---

[1] Caribou Master
[2] Shaman
[3] Animal Spirit or Master

He could invite the *Aueshish-utshimaut* to his shaking tent and let them speak to the hunters. A *kakushapatak* could also invite a human spirit from another community to enter the shaking tent to share his or her story about the news of their community. The *kakushapatak* was a real *utshimau*[1] and the people respected him. Elders also told of how a person could have *miteu* or *kamiteut*[2] even if he or she couldn't perform the shaking tent.

I have heard some stories about how a *kakushapatak* could attack a *kakushapatak* from another community. This attack would occur not in person but in spirit. Elders say it was very scary to witness a *kakushapatak* use the shaking tent against another *kakushapatak*. It wasn't the *kakushapatak* who did the fighting, but his *Mishtapeu*[3]. When a *kakushapatak* was beaten he'd cry out in pain and call for help.

The person with spiritual powers had many weapons to defend himself from the *kakushapatak*. When the elders spoke of these weapons they didn't mean guns and knives. They may have been talking about the person's dreams. A *Mishtapeu* could come in a dream to tell that person how to make a weapon to help him defend himself. We'll never truly know why there are no longer any *kakushapatak*. We cannot simply blame the Church for their disappearance. We must also blame ourselves because we no longer hunt and trap the way our elders did. We don't respect the animals anymore. We don't handle wild meat properly.

The last *kakushapatak* in Sheshatshiu died in the 1960s. He was a very friendly old man, as was his wife. He'd always make us laugh. He'd call my father "Grandson." He went to church every Sunday with a big cross on his chest. Father Pierson was the priest and he knew this elder was a *kakushapatak*, but he always called him *Mushum*[4]. My brother-in-law Kanatuakueshiss[5] told me this *kakushapatak* performed his last shaking tent on the Kenamu River across the bay from Sheshatshiu. Young people say that if it hadn't been for the church, our own religion would still be alive today. I'm not so sure it's that simple. Priests taught the Innu about the Catholic religion and the Church's rules. They told many scary stories about hell and sinners, stories that made the Innu feel like a useless and bad people. The

---

[1] Leader
[2] Spiritual powers: he or she has the gift of supernatural powers
[3] Spirit Master
[4] Grandfather
[5] Francis Penashue

kakushapatak must have felt left out after he saw some of his people follow the Church.

Now the church has no power over the Innu. We know the church made mistakes. Everyone can see that the church damaged our culture but at the same time it has done many good things for us. I've read many *Akaneshau* books. Every time they talk about the church they make it sound like the missionaries were bad people but the Church did a lot of good for the Innu. They built a small clinic with the help of the International Grenfell Association. I'm also thankful they built schools and invited us to attend. Some of our children finished high school. Some went to university and came back to help our communities.

It's also true that many Innu children were sexually abused in residential schools. All across Canada, priests and Christian brothers have been jailed for this abuse. After the Mount Cashel scandal erupted in Newfoundland, priests and Brothers were charged. Innu in both communities were also charged with sexual abuse. Most of them had been victims of sexual abuse themselves. They'd never wanted to tell anyone what happened to them in the past. It's no wonder so many young people have tried to commit suicide. Some succeeded. They had nowhere to go with their pain, no one to talk to. After we began to hear about what had happened with the priests and Brothers, Innu people were not so ashamed to report their own sexual abuse.

One *Akaneshau* in the community was charged with the sexual abuse of boys but he got away with it in court. Perhaps it was because the judge, the Crown prosecutor and his lawyer stayed at his house when the court came to Davis Inlet. The RCMP were also his very good friends. If he'd been Innu he would have spent many months in jail. The boys who were abused were now young adults and some were married. They were really frustrated and angry. They would have to live with their pain for the rest of their lives. It might take many years for these men to find healing.

Some of these abusers have been our friends. A few years before Father Fred McGee came, another priest was stationed in Davis Inlet. He later returned with the RCMP to face charges for the sexual abuse of boys in Sheshatshiu. He was my good friend and we had often gone hunting together. I couldn't believe my ears when I heard about what he'd done to my nephews, my sister Tshaukuesh's sons. She'd also been friends with this priest. She must have felt terrible because she was very religious. Now she could no longer trust the priest. She continued to do a lot of praying but she wouldn't go to church.

We kept hearing on the news about other priests being charged with sexual abuse but it no longer affected me. I continued to believe what I'd learned from the Church and at the same time I believe in our own spirituality, in Innu values and spiritual powers. I can't be one of those people who no longer trusts the Church. I've seen sick people healed by Innu spiritual powers and I've seen the Church do the same thing.

When I was about twelve years old, a priest abused me in Sheshatshiu. I never wanted to think about it. The image kept creeping back into my mind through the decades but I always felt too much shame to talk about it. I finally told my wife and she also had a story to share about what a priest did to her in Old Davis Inlet. It still pains me to think about the abuse although it happened over fifty years ago. I believe if we are to heal ourselves from abuse we have to learn to forgive. The Church apologized for what they did to the Innu people and we must learn to forgive them. I'm thankful that I learned a little bit of English from the Church. I'm also thankful that my culture is still in me. I have my language and my way of life, both of which I am trying to pass on to my children and grandchildren. It's too bad there are no more *kakushapatak* left, but some elders may still have spiritual powers.

THE NASKAPI MONTAGNAIS Innu Association (NMIA) was set up in 1975 to represent the interests and rights of the Innu of Sheshatshiu and Davis Inlet. During the 1970s and 80s the NMIA was a weak organization. NMIA leaders held many meetings with the Innu from Quebec. The plan was to work together on land rights but the Quebec Innu kept refusing our offer. Elders from Quebec thought it was a good idea because the Innu from Quebec and Labrador had always met each other in *nutshimit* and shared territories for hunting and trapping. But the Innu leaders from Quebec believed that Innu families owned certain territories because their ancestors had trapped and hunted in one territory. They didn't want to share that land. The NMIA agreed with the elders and believed that the Innu from both Quebec and Labrador were a nomadic people free to hunt and trap anywhere on the Labrador and Quebec peninsula. Innu had used this land for thousands of years. The NMIA wanted the Quebec Innu to join us in land rights negotiations but only the Chief from Mingan[1] agreed.

The late Penote Michel[2] was a great leader. He tried to get the Innu from both Quebec and Labrador to work together. When he could see this plan would never work he decided the two Labrador Innu communities would go on our own to negotiate land rights with the governments of Canada and Newfoundland. At first the position of the NMIA was "Why do we have to negotiate with governments about the land? The land has always belonged to us anyway. The government is the one who is claiming the land is theirs." But the governments would never recognize this position so the NMIA had no choice.

The NMIA mandate was always different from that of the band council. Its mandate was to look after land claims and to monitor big development projects like logging, hydro-electric projects, military flight training, the Trans-Labrador Highway or mining.

Another big problem faced by the NMIA was always that even the Innu of Davis Inlet and Sheshatshiu did not know how to work together. We co-

---

[1] Ekuanitshu
[2] Ben Michel. His nickname was Kauitentakusht

operated a bit sometimes but the leaders and residents of Davis Inlet complained because the money received by the NMIA from government was mostly being spent in Sheshatshiu. The Davis Inlet people had a right to be unhappy because the NMIA was meant to represent both communities. Davis Inlet was always trying to separate from the NMIA and form its own organization. This never worked because the leaders were the ones who wanted to separate, not the Innu public.

One time I got elected as vice-president of the NMIA. I didn't drink for the first few months of my term but before the end of it I'd started up again. I was out one time for a meeting of the board of directors. We'd chartered a single Otter aircraft for our return and loaded it with booze. The weather was really bad – too foggy and rainy to be flying. My friend Etien[1] and I were the only two drinking on the plane. The others must have been scared of the weather. We were halfway to Davis Inlet and the pilot didn't want to turn back. I was hoping we'd land somewhere we could spend the night and have a good party. As we flew over Flowers Bay the fog thickened. The pilot had no choice but to turn back a few miles south and then head west. I should have asked him to return to Goose Bay but I was drinking so I wasn't scared. None of us could recognize where we were. The pilot was flying very low because of the fog. We flew some distance and then turned east again. I looked through the window and could see we were in Sango Bay, just west of Davis Inlet. Ten minutes later we landed in the harbour in Davis Inlet. Many people came out to meet us at the beach. We got off the plane and every one of us was showing off with our heavy suitcases and boxes. We weren't thinking about how much damage we were doing to our community.

Another time Innu leaders from Sheshatshiu came on a charter to Davis Inlet for a meeting. I was hoping to hitchhike a ride back to Goose Bay with them. I asked the pilot if he had an extra seat. There was but with no seatbelt. We were six on a Beaver aircraft that normally took about an hour and a half to get to Goose Bay. I was very anxious to land because I wanted to drink so bad. About half an hour from Goose Bay the pilot started to test his landing gears. We knew something was wrong although the pilot never said so. As soon as the plane touched ground at the Goose Bay airport it veered into a snow bank. With no seatbelt I had no way to hang on. I was thrown out of the plane and rolled into the snow. My head missed the broken back wings by

---

[1] Etienne Pastiwet

inches. The pilot must have jumped out before we hit the snow bank and knocked himself out. I could feel pain in my ankle and it had already begun to swell. In a few minutes an ambulance, fire truck and the police were at the scene. One of the Innu leaders from Sheshatshiu Ponus Nuke was cracking jokes.

"What are those guys doing here – the ambulance, fire truck and police? Since when are they worried about us?" he asked foolishly. This was the first time any of us had crash-landed. We were all laughing. I could hardly walk on my foot and was told I had to see someone from Eastern Provincial Airways. I just wanted to go to the club for a drink. As we drove away I looked back at the plane and was very surprised to see that the props, wings and the tail were all damaged. We'd been lucky to survive but after a few drinks I'd already forgotten our adventure that fateful day.

Another time when I was still vice-president of the NMIA I was in Sheshatshiu with no money. My friend and I were drinking that night and we came up with the idea to make a phone call to Natashquan in Quebec. We broke into the band council office and he made his call. Next he showed me where to find the NMIA chequebook. We issued a couple of blank cheques and cashed them the next day. We were soon headed for Goose Bay to pick up booze. Of course we were later arrested and charged for break and enter as well as forgery. We both got a sentence of five months and two weeks. I was only in jail for forty days when I got my parole.

Every time the NMIA or band council talked with government, our words fell on deaf ears. There were many negotiations – about housing, shrimp licenses, water and sewage facilities and many other things that could have benefited our community. The only negotiations that ever worked were over new housing projects. Talks on any other issues went nowhere. Governments would talk about delays and more delays until finally Innu leaders lost interest, like with shrimp licence negotiations. The governments were only playing games with us.

Innu leaders would table a proposal to the governments about many different projects. If the proposal got government approval, our leaders would be really proud but then they'd seem to lose interest in other proposals that might be more important to the people. This was exactly what the government wanted. Our leaders never thought about taking action. They thought negotiating with governments was a better way to make a deal than protests. We didn't know the government was just shoving a few dollars into our mouths to keep us quiet.

In 1985 I was appointed by the NMIA to be on the board of directors of the Northern Innu Health Council. The Health Council received a few dollars from the federal government. We were supposed to look after health issues in our communities. When people had concerns about the clinic, the nurses or anything else relating to health, they'd come to us. Sometimes we'd pay the transportation costs for a sick person and an escort to travel to a St. John's hospital. The first year we also successfully lobbied for funding for the outpost program to help people go to *nutshimit* that spring. For some reason the band councils did not fund the program that year. We thought this was a health issue because our people are so much healthier when they are in *nutshimit*. The Health Council also got involved in the Innu campaign against low-level flying. Innu people living in camps in *nutshimit* were having problems with NATO jets flying over their camps. We also thought this was a health problem. The Canadian Public Health Association agreed with us and published a report about it.

The federal government did not agree with us that the outpost program or low-level flying had anything to do with Innu health. They just wanted the Health Council to negotiate with them for non-insured health benefits. Non-insured benefits involved getting funding to cover medical expenses that the provincial medical insurance (MCP) didn't cover, such as travel to hospitals to see a specialist, or to pay for glasses or a dentist. At the time the federal and provincial governments were not paying much attention to the Innu. We weren't registered as Status Indians. Although I was registered, my status card was useless in Labrador and I couldn't get any of the benefits that registered Indians received anywhere else in Canada. One time the Health Council went to Ottawa for a meeting about non-insured benefits. We'd been told many times that the Innu didn't have to be registered to receive non-insured benefits, but for two years nothing happened with our negotiations.

I was still working as Director of the Alcohol Program at the time. Many people would come to see me to help them stop drinking. I knew they needed medical treatment first. They needed hospitalization and medication to help them dry up those first few days. I'd asked the nurses three or four times to send this person out to the hospital but they'd always said no. They said if the people really wanted to stop drinking, they could do it on their own. I complained about these nurses to the Innu Health Council, which then officially complained to the Grenfell Regional Health Service.

THE LATE KANIKUEN PENASHUE[1] was the first president of the NMIA to take action against the military low-level flying. For ten to fifteen the NMIA did its best to save the environment and the animals. Kanikuen was not well-educated in English but he was very well educated in his own culture. He knew a lot about life in *nutshimit* and how Innu lived in the past. He wasn't that old but he'd heard a lot of stories from his father and his grandfather.

During Kanikuen's reign in the 1980s, the Sheshatshiu Innu began to lead a strong protest against NATO low-level flying in Labrador. Military jets were flying low-level over Innu families in *nutshimit*. I was overflown a couple of times – one time when I was with my son who was about 10 years old. As we walked in the open barrens three jets flew over us suddenly without warning. My son started running back to where we'd come from and I had to call him to let him know that it was military planes. I discovered first-hand how that level of noise from those planes was very dangerous for small children.

The Innu never gave permission to other countries to practise war over our land *Nitassinan*. The pilots were learning to fly very low so they couldn't be detected by enemy radar. NATO was using Innu land to practise how to protect their own countries and kill their enemies. The Government of Canada was leasing out Innu land and only cared about the money, money, money. They didn't care if they polluted our land, if they scared or killed the animals, if they freaked out our children and elders.

Tshikauinu Assin[2] feeds all the animals and birds. What happens if the land and the lakes are polluted? The wildlife and fish have nothing good to eat. The government will certainly not provide food for the wildlife like people do for dogs and cats. In grocery stores everywhere in Canada you'll find food for dogs and cats. Farmers have to store feed for their cattle in the winter. But wildlife has to find its own food year round. This is why the Innu always wanted to protect the land and the animals.

---

[1] Greg Penashue
[2] Mother Earth

Low-level flying was a very hot issue for the Innu of Sheshatshiu and the Quebec Innu communities. The Innu from Davis Inlet didn't join in this protest because the two communities didn't know how to work together. Davis Inlet Innu hadn't found their voice yet at all. Maybe Davis Inlet leaders thought it would be better to talk with the military rather than protest. They preferred negotiation to taking action. They didn't know any better.

In the late 1980s the protest against low-level flying began to really heat up for the Sheshatshiu Innu. The government was talking about setting up a NATO military flight training superbase with 40,000 flights per year and even a bombing range using live ammunition. The existing 6,000 flights were 6,000 flights too many. The Innu were very concerned about what would happen if this base went ahead, so hundreds of Innu decided to protest and set up camp at the east end of the air base in Goose Bay. Many times, over and over, the Innu protesters broke through the security fence and walked onto the runways to stop the military jets from taking off. It was something to see: women with babies, men, children and elders. Sometimes they sang hymns. Over 250 Innu were arrested for their civil disobedience and some spent long periods of time in jail. Innu support groups spread the news about what was happening to the Innu throughout the world. Elders and leaders from both Sheshatshiu and the Quebec communities traveled as far as Europe a number of times to spread the news. Etuet and Akat Piwas from Davis Inlet were one couple invited on one of these lobbying trips to Europe.

In Goose Bay a local committee called the Mokami Project Group (MPG) was lobbying hard to get this NATO base. They were in favour of low-level flying and very much opposed the Innu protests. One time they took a CBC crew out in *nutshimit* to take pictures of an Innu campsite. CBC filmed the site, especially the garbage they found nearby. That news story aired with the message that the Innu were ruining the land with their way of life. The MPG did everything they could to make the Innu look bad to the Canadian public. The MPG should've taken the CBC out to Churchill Falls and shown them how much land was flooded by their government. CBC should've taken pictures of the forests along the Churchill Road near Goose Bay where many thousands of cords of wood were left to rot. They should've visited the open pit mines in Labrador City and Schefferville[1]. They should've landed on the bombing range near Minipi Lake[2] to see real destruction of the land.

I happened to be around one time when the Sheshatshiu Innu were camping at the end of the airport runway in Goose Bay. They'd decided to protest and walk onto the runway one more time. Two military police officers sat in their trucks, one on each side of our campsite. They were keeping an eye on us to make sure no one would get inside the fence. It was a wooden fence before they replaced it with one rimmed with barbed wire along the top. As people planned the event someone suggested only the women would go onto the runway. I wondered how anyone would get beyond the fence without breaking it down. I stood near the fence with some of the women but I never even noticed when two young adults broke off two or three fence boards. The women walked through the hole one by one and marched towards the runway. The military police never tried to stop them but every one of us knew they had called the RCMP.

We watched the women walk to the main runway but we were too far away to see what happened when the police arrested them. I don't know if they walked to the police car of their own free will but protesters told me they all sat on the ground and had to be carried one by one to the police car or bus. The police had a bit of work cut out for them. All the women arrested were taken to the police detachment where they had their fingerprints and pictures taken. Most of them were released that day but a couple of them were kept in the lock-up. They'd already been arrested and signed undertakings swearing they wouldn't participate in any more protests on the runway. Here they were at it again. Other women were already in jail. The plan was to see how many women would get arrested to join those who were locked up to keep them company.

I was staying in my sister Tshaukuesh's tent at the protest camp. An elder, Miste-Manimatenin[3] , was also staying with us and told us stories about her younger days. She must have been very surprised to see what was now

---

[1] Matamekush translates as little trout

[2] Minai-nipi

[3] Mary Madeline Michel

happening with her people. She'd never had that kind of experience before in her life. I asked this old woman if she knew why the protest was taking place. She said she was taking action to save the environment and the animals.

That evening I went to Happy Valley to shop. On my way back to the camp I bought a six-pack of beers for that elder. I was drinking off and on that year. The elder didn't like to drink alone so my sister and I each drank one can of beer. The next morning I was up early to visit friends before heading home. After four days at the protest camp it was time for me to go back to Davis Inlet. I was feeling very frustrated because many people had asked me the same question during my stay at the protest camp.

"Why don't the *Utshimassiu*[1] leaders join this protest? Are they afraid to be arrested?" they asked.

"I have no idea," was my lame response. There was a northern training zone for low-level flying and the jets screaming low over our hunting grounds in that zone were affecting every hunter in Davis Inlet. I agreed that the *Utshimassiu* leaders may have been afraid to be arrested but I also thought they were not involved because the relationship between the NMIA and the *Utshimassiu* band council was not good. The council was interested in the shrimp fishery and the leaders thought the former minister of fisheries, John Crosbie, would issue a shrimp licence to them. A leader had told us that the government officials had said the Council had to support low-level flying if it wanted that shrimp licence.

Later that year the Innu of Labrador finally received non-insured health benefits. Supporters from across Canada had put a lot of pressure on the federal government. They may have thought these benefits would keep the Innu quiet but the protests in Goose Bay continued.

I was in Sheshatshiu when another protest was organized. Once again the *Utshimassiu* leaders were invited but declined. I was happy to participate. This time the plan was to enter the airport runways from the gate off Loring Drive. There were many of us but I was the only one from Davis Inlet. We never made it on to the runways. Many RCMP and military police arrived and told us we were not even allowed onto the base. When we heard this we unloaded our tents and stoves and just walked right past them through the gate. Just as we were setting up camp a bus arrived. Three Mounties approached us and told us we were under arrest. We walked voluntarily to the bus. Each of us was asked our name. Some Innu were hauled into RCMP vehicles and the rest of

---

[1] Davis Inlet

us were put on the bus. We arrived at the police station and we all had to give our fingerprints and have our pictures taken. First we had to look straight into the camera and then they took a sideways shot. That made us feel like real criminals. They were treating us like murderers although we had only been involved in a non-violent protest.

When it was my turn to be fingerprinted the officer asked me my name. After they'd taken my picture he told me there was no room in the cell for me. He said he'd let me go but I had to sign an undertaking to promise I wouldn't participate in any more protests. I waited for them to bring the paper for me to sign but then another officer called out to his buddy.

"Where is that guy from?" he asked, referring to me.

"I'm from Davis Inlet," I said.

"Davis Inlet stays," I heard another officer call out. I was taken to another room where they asked me to empty all my pockets and take off my shoes. There were nine of us in a small cell with only two steel bunk beds. They gave us a couple of extra mattresses so we could sleep on the floor. Jim Roche, a priest at that time, was in the cell with us. I guess we all felt the same way. There were no guilty feelings because we'd done nothing wrong. We'd only protested to protect our land and the animals. Many elders joined in the protest but none of them were locked up. It was not possible for the RCMP to keep the elders in jail because it would have been too shameful. When I was released I was given a summons with the date of my court appearance.

After many protests at the Goose Bay airport, my two sisters landed in jail with a number of other women from Sheshatshiu. They were transferred to the Women's Correctional Centre in Stephenville, Newfoundland. Some were there for over two months. Some Innu leaders were also jailed for their involvement in the protests.

That summer the federal minister of defense, Bill McKnight, came to Sheshatshiu to meet with the Innu. Once again I was the only person from Davis Inlet at that meeting. Many Innu people made presentations to Minister McKnight. I sat behind the elders and listened closely to what they had to say. Some of them were very good speakers with strong words. The late Kanikuen Penashue, then president of the NMIA, was sitting with the minister and the late Tanien Ashini who was serving as interpreter. Many Innu questioned the minister, hoping he would provide some answers.

Every elder who spoke said almost the same thing – that Innu people were being jailed because they wanted to protect the land, the animals, the lakes, mountains and rivers. They said if the land was all destroyed there'd be no future for our children. They said they believed there'd be nothing left for us after a land claims settlement. But the saddest moment at this meeting was when the children read out their presentations with tears in their eyes. They were crying because their mothers were still in jail. They asked the minister to release their mothers. They said the women were not criminals. They'd protested against low-level flying to protect the environment and for the safety of their own people.

After everyone else had made their presentation it was my turn. When I finished, the minister just left without answering a single question. He said he'd run out of time. It seemed he hadn't listened to a word we said. He'd only come to Labrador to hear what the military had to say. Funnily enough, he left and spent a half-hour outside responding to the questions of the reporters. Maybe he laughed all the way back to Ottawa.

About a month later I got a call in Davis Inlet to tell me the protesters were due in court early the next week. I was supposed to appear with the others. I traveled to Sheshatshiu and we arrived in Goose Bay early on the morning of the hearing. Many Sheshatshiu Innu were already at the courthouse. A few minutes before court was to start, two RCMP vehicles arrived carrying the women prisoners from Stephenville, including my sister Tshaukuesh and my niece Manimat[1], four RCMP officers, the late Tanien Ashini[2], Tapit Nuke[3] and others. The RCMP escorted the Innu prisoners into the courthouse. A bunch of us were standing outside the building. I knew exactly how they felt when they saw their children in the courthouse. The RCMP moved them along so they could not stop to talk to their own children. Everyone could tell how they felt from the tears in their eyes. They actually allowed my sister Tshaukuesh to talk to the media for a few minutes.

"Here we are! Look at us now," she said to the government, using the media to speak to them. "You people are having good times while we sit behind bars for trying to protect the environment and the wildlife. Look at our children. They're the ones who suffer the most. How would you feel if you were in jail and had to leave your children behind? We're in jail because we're protesting against low-level flying. We'll continue to do this for the sake of every Innu, Inuit and White person so that we'll all be able to use this land for many generations to come."

---

[1] Mary Martha Hurley
[2] Daniel Ashini
[3] David Nuke

Innu people packed the courtroom. When the judge walked in, the RCMP rose to stand but no one else stood. The Innu defendants did not have a lawyer. Penote Michel was chosen to speak for them. A young woman was called to the witness stand. The Crown prosecutor asked her a question and she responded in her own language – *Innu-aimun*. The judge seemed embarrassed. Other names were called as witnesses but again everyone spoke in *Innu-aimun*. No one would speak English. One of the officers stood to say they'd been unable to find an interpreter for the hearing. The judge left the bench. We were all still in the courtroom. I left to go home that afternoon. Later my niece told me they'd also called my name but they'd only just gone through the motions of calling out all the names.

After so many protests the RCMP could no longer keep Innu people in jail. There was no room in the jails for all the protesters and the governments of Newfoundland and Canada must have been ashamed of what they were doing to the Innu. I was glad to return to Happy Valley when the court was held again. The protesters were facing the same charges. This time the RCMP had found an interpreter – an Innu person from Sept Isles. We were very disappointed but Pentenimi[1], an Innu Nation worker responsible for justice issues, talked to the guy.

"You are like Judas who betrayed Jesus," Pentenimi told this man. "This is what you're doing to us by helping the police." That afternoon the Innu interpreter changed his mind and decided not to help the police.

Later that year all the charges were dropped, including mine. There were other outstanding charges to be heard but the RCMP could not find an interpreter. How could they hold a fair trial if the defendants could not be understood? This is a basic premise of the foreign Canadian law.

Low-level flying wasn't the only issue over which the Innu decided to organize a protest. The Sheshatshiu Innu were fed up with wildlife laws and regulations. During the winter of 1987 they invited the Innu of Davis Inlet to join them in a caribou hunt in the Mealy Mountains, just across the Bay from Sheshatshiu. Seven or eight of us joined the people of Sheshatshiu in their

---

[1] Bart Jack

hunt, including Tshatsh[1] Rich, Prote Proker, Shuashem Nui and me. The day we arrived in Goose Bay I had the feeling many White residents knew why we were there. We took a taxi to Sheshatshiu.

Some people had already set up camp along the Kenamu River. I went to visit Penote Michel's father Shimun[2] Michel, one of the respected elders in Sheshatshiu. He was happy to see me and asked me how many of us had come from Davis Inlet. His son-in-law had left that morning to join the protest but would return to pick up him and his wife. Shimun told me the story of what had happened to the caribou herd in the Mealy Mountains after the Americans set up their base in Goose Bay. When the herd was open to all hunters, White or Innu, the American military would always go caribou hunting in that area. They used machine guns to hunt so it was easy to imagine how many caribou they killed. Shimun said it was no wonder the caribou population had gone so frighteningly low. I just sat in the chair and listened carefully. He never used the word "machine gun." We have no word in *Innu-aimun* for this type of gun. I remembered watching war movies when I was young and we called machine guns "rat-tat-tats." Shimun said the military had used rat-tat-tats to kill so many caribou. I almost laughed when he said this because it reminded me of my childhood. But I knew what he was saying was very serious, especially for the Innu. When he'd finished, I stood up to leave and told him I'd see him in the camp that evening.

I went to ask my friend Shamani[3] Andrew if I could use his skidoo. He said I could if I'd drive his mother Kanani out to the camp. She'd packed all her stuff and was smoking while she waited for someone to pick her up. Her daughter Manishuni[4] accompanied her. My mind was full of worries. I knew it would be a rough ride and wondered how she'd be able to sit in the komatik because of her age. I asked her if she knew why the Innu were hunting caribou in the Mealy Mountains at this time.

"I want to support the young leaders," she said to me in *Innu-aimun*. "Besides that I will be very happy to get a taste of caribou meat." She sat in the komatik with Manishuni and I drove slowly down the hill from her house to the beach. As I tried to cross the beach road the komatik slipped and tipped over. My two passengers fell out. I was lucky I hadn't been driving fast. I stopped and asked my aunt if she was hurt.

---

[1] George
[2] Simon
[3] John
[4] Julianna

"I'm too tough to be hurt," she said in a joking way.

It was kind of a cold day and I could see she was not dressed that warmly. The trip would take us a little over an hour and my only thought the whole time was about the comfort of this elder in my komatik. In her life she'd walked from Sept Isles, Quebec, all the way to Sheshatshiu and many other different places in Labrador. I wondered how she felt about riding on the skidoo. She couldn't have known in her younger days how these machines would change our lives. Her means of transportation were her two feet. I'd heard many elders use this expression. If a young person asked them how they'd traveled from place to place, they'd say, "with my two feet."

Finally we reached the camp at Kenemich River[1] where the banks on both sides were high. The tents sat on the top of one bank so I couldn't drive all the way. I had to ask my passengers to walk over to the bank and I helped my aunt walk up the hill. People were happy to see me and asked how many of us had come from Davis Inlet. I could see caribou lying outside the tents. The people were really serious about taking the caribou from this protected area. They weren't afraid. They were working together as one. Plans for this hunt had been made with elders who said the herd could support a kill of about seventy animals. The next morning I joined the caribou hunt. We killed six caribou and returned to the camp right away. Wildlife officers were patrolling the area with a chopper.

The next day we were told the RCMP and wildlife officers were coming to raid our camp. Everyone in the camp just waited and the officials arrived on skidoo about noon. All our tents had been set up close together. Four RCMP left their skidoos down river and walked up to the camp. The wildlife officers waited down below. There were about twenty caribou just outside the camp. The Mounties wanted to talk to a leader. They asked for Tanien Ashini or Kanikuen Penashue. Everyone was shouting at the Mounties. One officer asked the priest, Jim Roche, if he had eaten any caribou meat. Father Jim said they'd have to open him up to get the meat.

One elder talked to the police through a translator. Every word he said was translated into English but soon he also began to speak in English. He must have been so upset he never realized he was speaking English or maybe he didn't trust his translator. The RCMP officers could do nothing. They couldn't arrest anyone or take the meat because the women and children were

---

[229] Tshenuamiu-shipiss

sitting on the carcasses. The wildlife officers were too afraid to come up to the camp. Maybe they were too ashamed to face the Innu people. There was no violence. The RCMP walked back over the riverbank and left in peace. Over the next few days they'd often fly their chopper over the camp but they never landed. More than sixty caribou were killed during the hunt. Hunters traveled to the community at night to bring meat to their family members who had not joined the protest. As far as I know, no one was charged on this hunt.

I N 1993 MY OLD FRIEND KANIUEKUTAT[1] was chosen to be in a film and I served as his interpreter. We were flown to *nutshimit* to Ushpuakaniss, a lake to the west of Nutakuan Lake, with the filmmakers James Wilson and his British crew. I'd never before seen Innu filmed living in *nutshimit*. Kaniuekutat had no experience in this kind of film work. His experience was life in *nutshimit* and he found it very difficult to be filmed while he was going about his business. I too found it very difficult to work with the crew. Kaniuekutat didn't like to do things over and over again. He got tired easily. The cameraman would tell me to tell Kaniuekutat to walk back from a distance away. If a small mistake was made, he had to do it again. I hated to tell Kaniuekutat he had to try again. But we managed to finish the film during the four weeks in *nutshimit*. The film is called *The Two Worlds of the Innu*.

The following October, Kaniuekutat passed away. His death was a great loss to the community. I gave the homily at his funeral. I thanked everyone for coming to pay their last respects. I told people that a great leader had passed away. For over twenty years Kaniuekutat and I had been close friends. We'd gone hunting many times together in both winter and summer.

I believe Kaniuekutat had spiritual powers. One day he'd come to our house and told me I should go to Caribou Hill[2]. He thought I might find caribou there. I didn't know how to respond but I respected what he had to say and kept it in my heart. I thought about it that night and figured he might be right. The next day I went to see another friend and told him what Kaniuekutat had said. We went to Kaniuekutat and he explained to us all the traveling routes to Caribou Hill. We headed out the next day and killed twelve caribou. I was very surprised and wondered how Kaniuekutat had known that there would be caribou in this place.

Years earlier when I was still drinking, Kaniuekutat had continued to visit me as usual. He never gave up hope that I would quit. I felt his respect even though I was drinking. He told me I'd one day be able to help myself and deal with my drinking problems. I'd never told this to anyone before I said it out

---

[1] John Poker
[2] Atiku-uapishkuss

116

loud in my homily. I wondered who had helped to give me the strength to stop drinking? Kaniuekutat helped me in many ways and I respected him so much as a leader and as a friend. I never heard Kaniuekutat use any angry words all the many times we hunted together. He always seemed happy to be out of the community. Sometimes after we set up our tent he talked about his vast experience of hunting, about all the places he traveled to and how he survived off the land. I would especially enjoy his stories about his late father and mother. I could almost see and feel how much respect he had for his parents.

I often used what I learned from Kaniuekutat. Whenever I went hunting I would always share part of my kill with him. The last time he went hunting he invited me along but I couldn't go because we didn't have enough food in our house and I had no money to buy any. I told him I'd join him later after I got paid. I asked him to wait for me at Kutshinapess. He was going to Nutakuan River and a place called Takuatuepan. Before he left I invited him over to my house to share a meal with my family. I'd made a *Makushan* the night before. He told me I could use his boat. Later that fall he invited me once again to join him in *nutshimit*. The Band Council had no funding to fly people into *nutshimit* but Kaniuekutat told me we would try again next fall.

The day he died we were in Natuashish, which is on Sango Pond, before our community was relocated to this site. I found out about my friend's death when I got back home. James Wilson from Europe was visiting us that month. He was the fellow who'd spent some time in *nutshimit* with us making the BBC film. James was very sad to hear the news. He told me how sad he felt for Kaniuekutat's grandchildren and his daughter Katnin[1]. James wanted to know what he could do for the family to show how much respect he had for Kaniuekutat as a friend. I told him he should stay to attend the funeral.

Kaniuekutat was our next-door neighbor for many years after Shanut and I moved out of her parents' house and got our own home. He visited us every morning. Whenever I went out for meetings or every time I went out hunting he would visit right away on my return to get my news. When I hunted I shared some of my kill with him. He must've known how much respect I had for him. Whenever I needed anything from him he always gave it to me. When I asked him to do something he never refused. Sometimes when he got his pension cheque he gave me money to buy myself cigarettes.

When people were in *nutshimit,* Kaniuekutat would always leave his bush radio on in the community even through the night so he'd be able to hear

---

[1] Kathleen

people calling in case of an emergency. He often used his radio to contact people in *nutshimit*. When someone was sick in *nutshimit* he'd pass the message on to the band council.

Kaniuekutat had so many friends in both communities and from away. One of his dear friends was the late anthropologist Georg Henricksen from Norway. Georg had come to live with the Mushuau Innu in the 1960s. I called Georg after Kaniuekutat died to tell him the bad news. Georg was very sad to hear this news. Georg was working on a book about Kaniuekutat's life. I was the translator for that book. Georg said the book was advancing but unfortunately Kaniuekutat would never see the finished product.

My children also had a lot of respect for Kaniuekutat. He was a great teacher, not in the ways of White education but in Innu education about our traditional way of life. Many times when we'd plan to go in *nutshimit* my children would ask me if he was coming along. When I got back from the funeral one of my little boys asked me if Kaniuekutat was also coming home. He didn't want to believe that our old friend was gone. On the Sunday before Kaniuekutat died he was in hospital. I'd prepared a *Makushan* from four caribou. I invited my father-in-law and I asked my son to go invite other people to come. When I listed the names, my son asked me why I was not inviting Kaniuekutat. Before I could answer his grandfather told him that Kaniuekutat was not very well.

Kaniuekutat really respected the teachings of the Church and at the same time he believed in the *Aueshish-utshimaut*. Innu people also call these spirits "Outside Spirits." When he died I wanted to always follow what my friend believed because he was such a great leader. I didn't want to try to replace him but I wanted to believe what he believed. He left so much knowledge behind for us to use and I wanted to make sure our children would follow his ways.

The church was packed for Kaniuekutat's funeral, standing room only. As I stood there with my microphone it was difficult for me to go on as I watched people with tears in their eyes. I had to use all my energy to hold back my own tears.

To become a good hunter the Innu have to learn many skills and they must have a good memory. I watched *Nutaui*[1]: how he shot the animals, cleaned them, set traps for mink, otter, marten or beaver. I learned that for otter and beaver, the trap sometimes has to be underwater but it can also be on dry land. It doesn't really matter as long as the person knows how to set it. In the water the trap has to be in shallow water because both beaver and otter have short legs. A couple of sticks are set on each side and the trap has to be placed over to one side, either the right or the left, because both beaver and otter use both front legs to walk as soon as they touch the bottom. Also, you have to tie a five-pound rock with a rope onto the trap. When the beaver or otter is trapped it will pull the rock into deep water and drown. Beaver castor is used for bait. The animals won't eat the castor but the smell will attract many different kinds of animals.

Hunting caribou is different again. When Nutaui hunted caribou he shot the leader first. A herd's leader can easily be recognized because she's always in the front. After Nutaui shot the leader, the other caribou just stayed in one place. If another one wanted to take the lead, Nutaui would shoot it. Sometimes after the leader was killed others would run towards you and you could easily kill them all.

One thing Nutaui told me – but I never witnessed – was what to do when someone finds a black bear in a den. The person has to talk to the bear and ask him to come out of his own free will. Nutaui said the bear understands when a person talks to him so he'll follow instructions. If I ever found a black bear in the winter I wouldn't know what to do but I guess I'd try what Nutaui told me. In the fall, black bears are very wild and they can easily hear a tiny noise from a long distance. If a person sees a black bear in the fall he must take off his boots or moccasins to get close enough to shoot the bear. He'll make less noise if he walks with only socks. Even the crack of a small stick can be heard by the bear. My father was not talking about bears in a zoo or a dump but about wild bears that eat only berries.

Young people can learn hunting skills on their own but they'll miss many things. Parents have to teach their children about hunting skills and life in

[1] My father

119

nutshimit. A hunter has to learn what gear to take. If he decides to go for a couple of days he must not forget to bring matches, an axe, ammunition and a kettle. He must also bring a gun and a little bit of grub. I didn't learn to hunt on my own. Nutaui taught me how to protect myself from dangers such as cold and stormy weather. A winter storm can hit in a matter of minutes and last anywhere from half an hour to twenty-four hours. A hunter must always be prepared. In the barrens he has to know where there are wooded areas. He doesn't have to worry so much when he's in the woods. He can survive outside as long as he has matches no matter how cold it is.

Nutaui also taught me how to walk safely on bad ice. In *nutshimit* it often snows the day after the first night of freeze-up, making it hard for the ice to thicken. The snow falls and warms up the ice. If there is no snow for two or three days after freeze-up, and if it's cold enough, the lakes will be safe to walk on the ice. In the fall some lakes freeze up early. By the middle of November the ice can be eight or ten inches thick but there's always one bad spot on those lakes that's hard to notice when it's covered with snow. It could be in the middle of the lake or close to shore. We call it *nipinamushiu* or "summer water or water that never freezes along the lake or river shore." It could be only a small area but it stays unfrozen all winter. My father showed me how to use a long stick to test the ice whenever I walk on a newly frozen lake.

Nutaui also taught me how to use a gun safely. When I go out hunting I make sure the gun isn't loaded and when I return I again check my gun to make sure it's not loaded. I also learned never to point a gun at anyone even if the gun isn't loaded. I always place bullets in a safe place. I never let my children play with the gun or cartridges. My father always told me that if there were two of us hunting I should never load my gun until I was ready to shoot. He also taught me never to waste any bullets practicing because ammunition was needed to kill animals to feed the family. Even just four or five bullets could save you from hunger. If you killed three caribou out of your five remaining bullets you had wild meat for a long while.

"Never shoot more animals than you need," Nutaui used to say to us. "If you don't respect the animals the *Aueshish-utshimaut*[1] will not forget you. You'll have a hard time to find the animals you're looking for."

All the different animals, both large and small, have their own *Aueshish-utshimaut*. The otter, the beaver, fish, mink and seals, all the animals that live

---

[1] Animal Spirit or Master

in water have their own *Aueshish-utshimaut*, as well as the animals who live on the land. To be a successful hunter you must follow Innu hunting rules created by the *Aueshish-utshimaut*. Elders can communicate with these *Aueshish-utshimaut* and pass on their instructions to hunters and women too. The spirit of any animal or thing who attends a shaking tent comes to life and talks. As a boy, Nutaui told me to get dressed every morning before daylight. He said the *Aueshish-utshimaut* usually visited the Innu before daylight to see if all the young boys were dressed. When it saw the boy was dressed the spirit would be satisfied.

An Innu hunter has to believe what his dreams tell him, not when he's in the community but dreams in *nutshimit* have to be taken seriously. He or she doesn't have to dream directly about the caribou or any other kind of animal. A man might dream about making love to an Innu or a *Akaneshau* woman. This dream will really be telling him what he should do the next day. He might also dream about different things that belong to him, such as a gun, an axe or a knife. If he dreams that the barrel of his gun is blocked, it would be better not to use the gun the next day but to give it to a friend to use. An accident could happen if he used it.

The hunter might also dream about an old man or woman telling him what to do the next day. If a person understands his dream he doesn't have to tell anyone about it. The dream is like an outside spirit telling him what will happen the next day. The spirit doesn't speak directly about what he will see or what he should hunt. The spirit will use a parable but the person who dreams will understand with the support of the spirits. A hunter has to respect his dreams and at the same time he has to be careful. Some dreams provide warnings, some dreams tell you what kind of animal you'll kill and others tell you where you should go hunt the next day. I can't speak on behalf of women but they may have the same understanding as men.

To become a successful hunter I learned to respect all the animals I killed, small and large. I learned to follow the hunting rules, to respect the lakes, ponds, rivers, brooks, mountains, hills, trees – everything that grows on earth. To respect these things I have to feel I'm not alone, that the ponds, the trees, rocks, mountains and rivers are there with me. The elders passed on to me their belief that everything that grows on earth has its own spirit like a human being, even a stump. The spirit of the snow can speak to us in a shaking tent ceremony. A hunter has to prove that he loves the land and the animals by hunting every day.

"If you want to be a hunter, don't let the bad weather stop you," Nutaui explained to me. "*Tshishiku-napeu*[1] likes anyone who loves to hunt and will give you fine weather." He told me how a real hunter doesn't care about the weather. When I was in *nutshimit* with my parents the weather could be really bad sometimes for two or three days. My father just grabbed his gun and snowshoes and headed out. An hour later the weather would have cleared up. I didn't care to go out in bad weather. I wanted it to change before leaving.

One winter I took my whole family out camping about twenty-five kilometres outside of Davis Inlet. A couple of days later the weather turned bad and the snow began to fall very hard.

"I'm going hunting anyway," I said to my wife. "On my way back I'll check our rabbit snares."

"In an hour you'll see the sun," I said to my daughter Nishapet just before I left. I was only joking but in a couple of hours it stopped snowing and the sun poked its head through the clouds. By afternoon the sky had totally cleared.

A hunter has to believe what the elders tell him about the Spirits.

---

[1] Sky Spirit

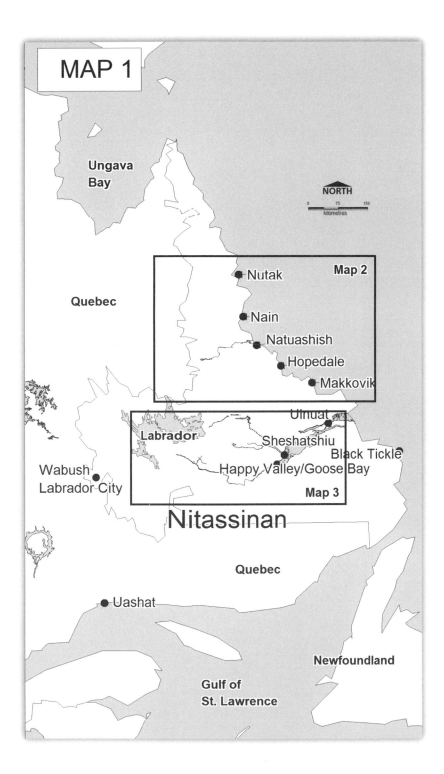

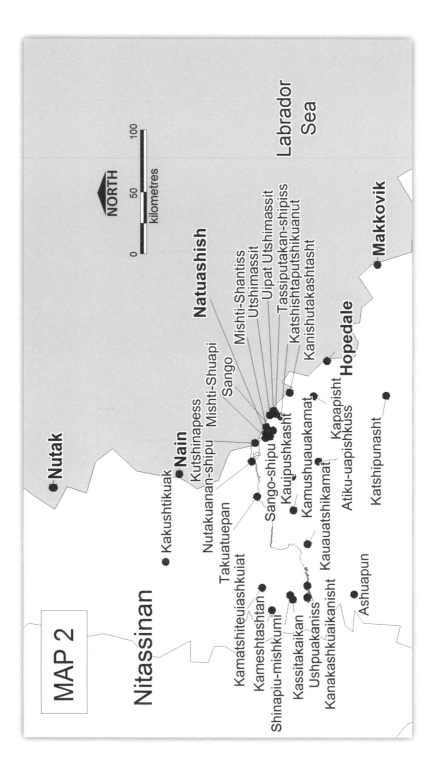

MAP 2

Nitassinan

Nutak

● Kakushtikuak

Nain

Kutshinapess

Nutakuanan-shipu   Mishti-Shuapi

Takuatuepan

Kamatshiteuiashkuiat

Kameshtashtan

Shinapiu-mishkumi

Kassitakaikan

Ushpuakaniss

Kanakashkuaikanisht   Kauauatshikamat

Ashuapun

Kamushuauakamat

Atiku-uapishkuss

Kapapisht

Katshipunasht

Mishti-Shantiss

Utshimassit

Uipat Utshimassit

Tassiputakan-shipiss

Katshishtaputshikuanut

Kanishutakashtasht

Natuashish

Sango

Mishti-Shuapi

Sango-shipu

Kaupushkasht

Hopedale

Makkovik

NORTH

0   50   100
kilometres

Labrador
Sea

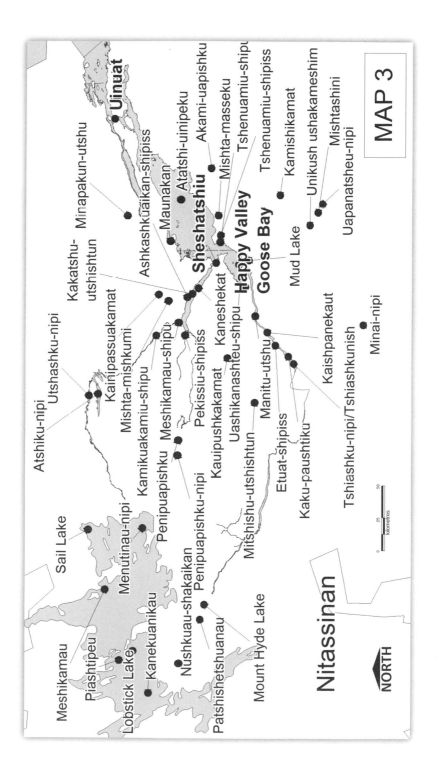

Uinuat

Minapakun-utshu

Ashkashkuaikan-shipiss

Kakatshu-
utshishtun

Kainipassuakamat

Atshiku-nipi
Utshashku-nipi

Mishta-mishkumi

Kamikuakamiu-shipu

Penipuapishku

Penipuapishku-nipi

Meshikamau-shipu

Pekissiu-shipiss

Kauipushkakamat

Uashikanashieu-shipu

Mitshishu-utshishtun

Etuat-shipiss

Kaku-paushtiku

Maunakan

Atatshi-uinipeku

Akami-uapishku

Mishta-masseku

Tshenuamiu-shipu

Tshenuamiu-shipiss

Kamishikamat

Unikush ushakameshim

Mishtashini

Uapanatsheu-nipi

Sheshatshiu

Happy Valley

Goose Bay

Kaneshekat

Manitu-utshu

Mud Lake

Kaishpanekaut

Tshiashku-nipi/Tshiashkunish

Minai-nipi

Sail Lake

Meshikamau

Piashtipeu

Menutinau-nipi

Lobstick Lake

Kanekuanikau

Nushkuau-shakaikan

Patshishetshuanau

Mount Hyde Lake

Nitassinan

NORTH

0   25   50
kilometres

MAP 3

Camp at Ushpuakaniss where Shuash hunted with Kaniukutat and Prote Poker.

Shuash (George) and Shanut with some of their grandchildren outside their house in Natuashish, 2005. Photo by Marie Wadden

Shuash's sons and granddaughter: Napess, Anishan and Gerry Andrew.

Shuash's brother-in-law Shuashem Nui, 1992. Photo by Camille Fouillard

Shuash's sister Tshaukuesh trekking in the Mealy Mountains.

Kaniuekutat at Natuashish gathering,
1992. Photo by Camille Fouillard

Shuash conducting an interview during the Davis Inlet People's Inquiry, 1992. With Shuash are Akat Rich, Katnen Benuen and Shinipest Andrew.
Photo by Camille Fouillard

Shuash. Photo Prote Poker

Shuash with his friend Apenan Pone.

Shuash with Kaniuekutat, with a canoe under construction. Photo by Pat Kelsall

Shuash at Natuashish gathering, 1992.
Photo by Camille Fouillard

Elder Tuamish playing the Innu drum with Prote Poker.

On a canoe trip down the Mishta-shipu (Churchill River) with Shuash's sister Tshaukuesh.

In 2001 George travelled on the Churchill River to a salmon fishing camp at the mouth of the Kenamu River. This trip was part of an Innu Nation study assessing the changes to the river should the Muskrat Falls hydro development proceed. He was accompanied by Sheshatshiu Innu George Nuna, Tapit Nuk and Simon Andrew. Photo by Annette Lutterman

Family photo. Bottom left to right: Nishapet, Shanut, Shuash, Shakanin.
Top left to right: Gerry Andrew, Napess, Gerry, Peter, Jonah.

Shanut and Napess with meat drying over the stove.

Shuash on a hunting trip with his son Napess and friends Sepastien and Desmond Piwas.

Shanut cleaning a porcupine with grandchild Maniten.

Davis Inlet, or Utshimassit, Place of the Boss, as it is known to the Innu, 1989. Photo by Camille Fouillard

Shuash's parents-in-law, Meneshkuesh and Tshenish Pasteen taken at a
makushan in Natuashish, 1992. Photo by Camille Fouillard

Tshenish Pasteen speaking at a land rights meetings at North West Point
(Ushunaiat), 1990. Photo by Camille Fouillard

Tanien Ashini speaking at an Innu protest against NATO military flight training on the base at Goose Bay, 1989. Photo by Bob Bartel

Sam Napeu with Kanikuen Penashue at land rights meeting, 1990.
Photo by Camille Fouillard

Shuash's eldest son, Gerry, 1992.　　Shuash's sister Nush, 1990.

A meeting to discuss relocation held on a hilltop overlooking Natuashish during the People's Inquiry. From left to right: Tanien Poker, Pinip Rich, Tshimi Nui, Manishan Nui and Prote Poker, 1992. Photo by Camille Fouilalrd

Tents along the Sheshatshiu shore, before houses were built. Circa around 1957.

The frame of a sweat lodge set up outside of Davis Inlet.
Photo by Camille Fouillard

Kaniuekutat.
Photo by G. Henriksen, 1966

Matshitu-napeu.
Photo by G. Henriksen, 1966

Shuash as a young man, taken with his father Shimun and sister Maniaten.

Shuash's son Jonah at a camp between Daniel's Rattle (Mishti-shantiss) and Davis Inlet (Utshimassit).

Shuash and grandson Mario in the Lobstick area, 2000.

IN 1989, WHEN CLYDE WELLS was first elected Premier of Newfoundland, he said his government would settle land claims within two years. Where did all his land claims talks go? Whenever the Innu held a protest, Premier Wells would suspend land claims negotiations. Talks were going nowhere anyway. They were moving forward so slowly it didn't seem like the governments would ever agree with the Innu. The federal and provincial governments couldn't even agree with each other about the price they should have to pay the Innu for their land in a final settlement.

The money for the Innu to participate in land claims negotiations came from the federal government but it was just a loan that we had to pay back. Many non-Innu complained about the money we received from government. They said we were wasting the taxpayers' money and complained that we didn't pay any taxes. This isn't true. The Innu always paid taxes like everyone else in the province until only a few years ago.

For a long time the Innu were against low-level flying, mining, forestry, the Trans-Labrador Highway or any other developments that would destroy the land. We believed that no development should go ahead while land claims talks continued. At the rate negotiations were progressing there would be nothing left for us to claim by the time we reached a final settlement. The land would be polluted and the animals would've disappeared. Hydro would flood the land and pollution from mining would destroy our waters. For years governments thought we wanted to stop all developments in *Nitassinan,* but this was not our plan. We understood that *Akaneshau* people needed jobs to survive but our goal was to protect the land. We wanted to reach a land claims settlement so that we could then sit down with governments to negotiate which developments should go ahead and make sure all parties could benefit.

No matter the costs, we want studies done before any development is approved. These studies should look at water, rivers, forests and the feeding grounds for small and large animals. The most important thing to look at is fish. In the fall, saltwater fish like char and salmon migrate to the rivers and into freshwater lakes. Some fish spend a whole winter in freshwater before they migrate back to the ocean in the spring. We must protect freshwater lakes because they are home to the fish. Polluted lakes will poison the fish and other small animals that feed on them. If a lake is polluted the fish can't escape. Fish can't walk on land. In the Voisey's Bay mining area, how good were the studies about the tailings pond, about where they'd dump the waste? Were there any fish in that pond? Will that pond ever flood?

Governments argue that Labrador is a big land with a small population. They see *Nitassinan* as a good territory for any kind of development. But they don't know about the life of the many different animals we live with in our homeland. Governments don't care about the animals. We Innu want to protect the land for the animals and our future generations.

Land claims talks never went anywhere for so many years because the Innu had to find their voice. For decades Davis Inlet had no voice at all. Part of the problem was that the band council and NMIA leaders were not educated. First the priest controlled the council and then outsiders took over. We thought *Akaneshau* advisers were the best, but if we'd known that *Akaneshau* only wanted or knew how to follow government rules we'd never have invited them to help us. I'm not saying *Akaneshau* are bad. Many really support the Innu people but they don't tell us what to do. Some work very closely with us. They understand and respect our culture. They know their culture and the Innu culture don't fit together and can't be mixed.

My question to our *Akaneshau* legal advisors is always, "How well do you know the Innu culture?" They learn a lot from Innu leaders but not enough. They should spend time in *nutshimit*, maybe for a month every year to learn about our culture and better understand how we live in *nutshimit*. They wouldn't necessarily be better advisors but they'd have better answers to respond to the governments' questions. We continue to have to teach the *Akaneshau* who work with us that they're not here to take control. When we hire *Akaneshau* we should be in charge. For a long time we were brainwashed by *Akaneshau* but eventually we managed to stand on our own two feet. Now we need to learn how to work together as communities. How can we stand up to governments if we don't work together?

In 1990 the NMIA changed its name to the Innu Nation. Naskapi and Montagnais are words that were never recognized by the Innu. We never gave ourselves the names of tribes. We don't know where those names came from. It might be *Akaneshau* fur traders or missionaries that gave us those tribal names.

Peter Penashue was elected president of the Innu Nation in 1990 and Tshatsh Rich from Davis Inlet was elected vice-president. These two leaders were sober. Young Prote Poker who was elected Chief in Davis Inlet was also not drinking. I was hired to work with the council and I was very pleased to work with a sober Chief. The council didn't get much funding from the government but Prote was still doing his best to make improvements. His main goal was to make the community dry. He also wanted young people to learn more about our culture. He would've done a great job if some of his councilors hadn't been drinking. After about a year and a half he called an early election because he'd become more interested in hunting.

Kiti Rich[1] ran in the election and was the first woman elected Chief in Davis Inlet. She was well educated and she also didn't drink. Other people had stopped drinking in the community but alcohol still hit our community again in the most terrible way one night in February 1992. It was Valentine's Day and I was in the hospital in Goose Bay. Around 7:00 that morning I heard a small girl crying. I asked the nurse who this girl was and she said her last name was Rich. She said a house had caught on fire the night before in Davis Inlet and six children had died.

I phoned home to find out more. My wife could hardly talk to me through her tears as she tried to tell me the names of the children who'd died in the fire. Those houses were poorly insulated. There was no furnace or electric heat, only wood stoves. Without firewood there was no way to heat the house. After the investigation on how the fire started we learned that the children may have been using a hotplate to heat one of the bedrooms. The fire must have started when a blanket accidentally touched the hotplate. The children were probably sleeping on the floor and they'd plugged in the hotplate too close to where they slept. One child's remains were found under the bed. He may have tried to escape from the fire.

I knew one of the boys very well. He was about five years old. His grandparents had adopted him and named him Tshakapesh. His grandfather was my best friend. The boy spent most nights with his grandparents but he must have been sleeping over with his sisters when the fire broke out. I really missed this boy who was so cute and talked like an adult.

---

[1] Katie Rich

The fire occurred during one of the coldest months of the year and there was no fire equipment in the community. Even with a fire truck, where would they have gotten water? With no road they could never have reached the house in time. People just watched helplessly as the house burned down. The police were going to charge the parents for abandoning their children but the leaders and the community spoke up on their behalf. We felt that the parents had suffered enough after losing all their children. If the police took them to court everyone knew they'd suffer more and needlessly.

After the fire, news spread all over Canada and Europe about our plight in Davis Inlet. Innu Nation President Peter Penashue asked the Indian Affairs Minister, Tom Siddon, to hold a public inquiry into the living conditions in Davis Inlet to find out why these kinds of tragedies were happening in our community. Why had people been moved onto this island and why had we been given such poor housing?

The minister said the federal government would not fund such an inquiry. The Innu Nation decided to use money from the Innu Defense Fund to hold our own People's Inquiry. The band council and the Innu Nation worked very closely together on this Inquiry. I was hired as one of the inquiry's commissioners along with Manteskueu[1], Epha[2] and Etien Pastiwet. It took us five weeks to carry out the work of talking to people.

We asked the people many questions. We asked about what life was like before the missionaries came to Labrador. People told us about who had made the decisions to move the Innu to Nutak in 1948 and to Davis Inlet in the 1960s. They told us about how often the Newfoundland Rangers used to come to old Davis Inlet. Did the government ever talk about water and sewage at the new Davis Inlet? How did the people feel about the RCMP presence at Davis Inlet? How was life in *nutshimit* compared to life in the community today? Was there a lot of drinking in old Davis Inlet compared to today? People told us how there were no band council elections in old Davis Inlet and it was just the priest who appointed the Chief. We asked the people about all the different institutions – the church, the school, the government, social services, the police and the store – and how they had changed our lives. The people we talked to shared a lot of stories about all the changes that happened to us.

The co-ordinator of the Inquiry, Camille Fouillard, did a tremendous job. She typed up all the responses we collected from the people. Camille is well-

---

[1] Mary Georgette Mistenapeo
[2] Nympha Byrne

known in both Labrador Innu communities. When the Innu have needed her to do some work she never refuses. She's been one of our best supporters. All the responses from the inquiry were put together in a report called *Gathering Voices: Finding the Strength to Help Our Children* and published in a book.

Before this tragedy happened we were already talking about relocation to a new community. The late Kaniuekutat[1] was the first elder to speak about relocation. He believed it would be safer for us to hunt from the mainland rather than an island because of the ice in the spring and fall. The Inquiry report also listed good reasons for relocation. There was no water and poor housing in our community. The land to build new houses was too small. The mountains surrounding the community made expansion impossible. Although the island was 40 kilometres long it was mostly sandy and marshland.

In December 1993, another very important event happened in our community after Kiti Rich was elected Chief. The provincial court had come to Davis Inlet on its regular circuit. Kiti must've felt sorry to see her people facing the judge, being found guilty, getting convicted and taken away to the lock-up. I can't describe exactly what happened because I was in Goose Bay. Prote Poker got a call from Kiti who told him a group of women, including herself, had kicked the judge and the RCMP out of the community. Everyone was so happy to hear this news. No Chief had ever done such a thing anywhere else in Canada. After we got back to Davis Inlet a videotape of what happened was shown on the community channel. We saw how the RCMP could do nothing. The tribal police could also do nothing but there was no violence. It was a peaceful protest. The judge, his court and the RCMP just accepted the women's request and left the community with no argument.

The next summer, when the Newfoundland government decided it was time for the court circuit to pay us a visit again, it decided to close down the airstrip to any other flights. They probably didn't want any media people to fly to Davis Inlet but there was no way to stop them. Some media people chartered a plane to Sango Bay and we went to pick them up by boat. As well, after we heard the government had shut down the airstrip we decided to block

---

[1] John Poker

the runway. We placed lumber, oil drums and a truck across the runway. The RCMP plane came but couldn't land. We heard there were a hundred RCMP officers standing by in Goose Bay. Newfoundland was planning to use the military and their choppers to bring them in. People from Sheshatshiu came to join us. The mail plane had to land in water to deliver the mail.

We agreed there'd be no violence but we were worried about our kids. The young people were so angry they vandalized the RCMP building. The band council held a public meeting so everyone would understand that there should be no violence. I asked my son not to get involved in the protest. He asked me why I wanted to stop him and reminded me I'd be there. The justice minister was trying to scare us by sending in all these RCMP and military police but we weren't afraid. We were prepared to go to jail with our children. No Mounties landed in Davis Inlet. The Newfoundland government must've changed its minds when it found out media people were in the community.

Later, negotiations began with Justice officials, the Innu Nation and the Mushuau Innu Band Council. We heard that Kanikuen and Akat[1] Rich would be charged for having left their children in the house that burnt down. Everyone in the community was affected by this decision. We knew the couple had already suffered enough. I don't like to talk about this tragedy that I will never forget.

In 1994, Simeon Tshakapesh replaced Kiti Rich as Chief. Simeon also did his best to solve the alcohol and sniffing problems. The use of alcohol had really been going down over the last three years. Many adults had quit drinking but gas sniffing was still a big problem. A Safe House was built for the children and also served as an office for the Health Commission. The new Chief was focused on our healing. The long-term plan of the band council was to try to solve the social problems here in Davis Inlet so that we wouldn't take them with us when the community was relocated to Natuashish (Little Sango Pond).

Simeon was a tribal police officer before the election. The courts and policing were still a hot issue in Davis Inlet. Simeon was well prepared and kept his people informed when something came up regarding the government's plans. The Chief and council, along with the Innu Nation, managed to negotiate a policing agreement with the Justice Department. After many meetings an agreement was finally reached. The court came back to Davis Inlet almost before the ink had dried from their signatures.

---

[1] Gregory and Agathe

It was around this time that the Innu Nation and the band council decided that training might help to solve addictions problems. They invited the Nechi Institute from Alberta to provide training for about twenty people from the community. People from Sheshatshiu also participated. I took about a week of training before I decided it wouldn't work for me. I was learning about a number of drugs that I'd never even heard of so I quit.

My son Pien had a dream in which he saw his grandfather Tshenish crucified on a cross as he was walking by the school. The crucifixion was just like the one Jesus went through as described in the Bible. In his dream Pien ran to his grandmother's house to tell her. She came out and saw her husband crucified on the cross over the big rock just outside their house. Pien dreamt that the Nechi trainers and some trainees threw a traditional *teueikan*[1] at Tshenish. They told him he was not a traditional singer and his songs were useless. Pien and other young people took their grandfather's body off the cross. At this point in his dream Pien woke up. Since dreams are very important in Innu culture, I thought to myself that this Nechi training would cause more problems for us.

After a year of training, Nechi trainees were hired to work as alcohol counselors. The idea was to send people out for treatment to the Poundmakers Lodge in Alberta. They sent many people there, both parents and their children. Some would return from their treatment and do well but others went back to drinking and kids started sniffing gas again. Innu counselors also held the first mobile treatment program, where they took people outside the community into *nutshimit* for addictions treatment. They brought in resource people from the outside, including some elders. At least the leaders were doing their best to heal the people, although it wasn't working very well.

These healing services looked good at first with their healing circles and sweat lodges. Because the sweat lodge was very dark and hot inside, everyone felt free to talk about his or her own problems. The sweat lodge was like an AA[2] meeting. What was heard in the sweat lodge stayed there. Everything was confidential. Nothing in the sweat lodge was ever to be repeated to anyone ever again. With this aspect of our healing, the sweat lodge was reborn in our culture.

The Nechi elders from the outside taught our young people how to use a sweat lodge. I wondered why the young people didn't ask their own elders to learn how to use the sweat lodge. Some Innu elders were against the sweat

---

[1] Innu drum
[2] Alcoholics Anonymous, an addictions self help program

lodge because they thought some young Innu were making fun of our traditional way of life. They pointed out that this kind of sweat lodge was built a different way than the traditional Innu *matutishanitshuap*, which was used only when someone was sick or elders were very tired. The Innu lodge was built the same way except that sometimes the Innu would leave a hole open at the top. The hole would be covered during the sweat. I'd heard elders sing inside the Innu *matutishanitshuap*. When the sweat was over, the elder would ask someone to open the top and pour water onto the hot rocks. They would let the hot steam out of the top and then talk to the rocks. I'd seen a *matutishanitshuap* built inside a tent during wintertime.

Millions of dollars were spent to send people to Poundmakers Lodge for treatment and to bring Native elders to our community. Some people thought the money would have been enough to build our own treatment centre outside the community. Some people blamed the Nechi training for some of the things happening in the community. Many young couples were deciding to separate in both communities. Those who'd gone through the Nechi training were still having the same family problems as the others. There was still a lot of gas sniffing and suicides.

A mobile treatment program for both Davis Inlet and Sheshatshiu was held in Ashuapun, south of Border Beacon. This was the first time the Innu were running their own treatment program. This was one good thing that came out of the training. The Band Councils provided ground and air transportation. Innu elders from both communities were hired to work with the young people. Both Sheshatshiu and Davis Inlet couples attended the treatment. Thousands of caribou were swarming the area at that time.

When the treatment program ended, a very interesting report was released to the two band councils and the Innu Nation. The report said the treatment had been very successful but only months later some of the participants were on the booze again. Some people were doing okay but others not so well, especially some of the kids. They were still sniffing gas and had been picked up by the tribal police to be sent to the group home in Sheshatshiu. We couldn't complain about the treatment program because this had been our first try. Maybe next time the program would be better.

One beautiful day I went to visit an elder at Daniel's Rattle, a few kilometres outside of Davis Inlet. When I arrived at the camp the elder was sitting on his komatik outside his tent. I walked over and sat on the komatik too.

"The ice is getting bad so fast," he said to me.

"True. There's a lot of deep water in some places I just came from." As we continued to talk, a Twin Otter flew over headed west.

"I wonder where that plane's going?" I said.

"I heard on my bush radio that they're taking ATVs to Border Beacon and it's probably for the mobile treatment program," the elder said.

"I don't know anything about that," I said. "I don't know why they need ATVs to run the mobile treatment program."

"I heard they're taking lumber and plywood to build cabins at Border Beacon. They say it's too far for them to get fresh boughs every week. Who's paying for all this?" the elder asked.

"The band council is paying for most of the transportation but for other things – like the satellite dish, radio, telephone and food – the Health Commission is paying for that."

"It must be very expensive," he said. "Why didn't the Health Commission consult with the elders before deciding on Border Beacon? It would've been better to have the program nearer to Davis Inlet. They could hire local people for ground transportation. People have their own skidoos and they need the money. We, as elders, have some ideas but the young leaders don't need us anymore."

The elder said the mobile treatment program was not going to work unless Innu elders were involved. People from the outside would not solve our problems. He thought Innu children should first be taught their traditional way of life out in *nutshimit* before being sent out for treatment. He wanted to see the children taught how to make homemade tools or snowshoes, how to use these tools to travel in the winter by foot, to haul a sled, to canoe and portage, rather than being too dependent on machines such as speedboats, skidoos and chainsaws. He thought the children would be so proud to learn these things. They would then be able to make their own choices about whether they wanted to go out for treatment afterwards.

He continued to tell me a story about the mobile treatment program he'd attended where there were many Native elders from Western Canada. A few local elders were also hired.

"They didn't like me to be there at the healing camp," he said to me about those outside elders. "I didn't care because this healing gathering was happening on my very own land. I was not even invited to have a sweat with them." He thought the mobile treatment program was not well organized. Some people who attended stayed sober for a few months and then went back to drinking. This happened so many times. There had to be a better way to help our people heal. As a band councilor I couldn't answer his questions. He was an elder and knew better than me.

"I was an alcoholic and didn't need treatment programs," I said. "I made my own decision to quit and it's been sixteen months since I've been dry."

"In our culture, when a person wants to do something the decision has to come from their hearts not from an outsider, " the elder told me. "It has to be an elder from the community who runs the treatment program rather than young alcohol counselors. We must spend the money wisely. All the things we have today like skidoos, outboard motors, chainsaws and money are new. Sure they make our lives easier but young people don't know we're leaving our culture behind. Four years of treatment programs and still nothing has happened because the programs are coming from another culture."

I didn't say another word. I would've liked to stay longer but it was time for Shanut and I to go back to Davis Inlet. On the way, I kept thinking about what the elder had said about taking from other people's culture. Maybe he was talking about how Innu counselors should use our own culture to help people heal. We arrived home safely. I hoped to visit the elder again before the ice broke up.

In 1994, just before Christmas, we heard about the discovery of nickel, copper and cobalt at Voisey's Bay. The Innu name for that place is Emish. Chief Simeon Tshakapesh called a public meeting about Voisey's Bay and land claims. In the 1960s no Innu were consulted about the hydro project at Churchill Falls and the government was now thinking it could get away with using our land without our consent. It was hard for us to believe what was happening. The news of the discovery spread all over Canada and Europe. When mining companies heard the news their eyes lit up with dollar signs. The Innu were left out of the story.

After the discovery at Voisey's Bay, the exploration company Archaen Resources began doing more drilling at the site without any consultation with the Innu Nation or the LIA[1]. The mining rights to the area were bought up by Diamond Field Resources and later scooped up by Voisey's Bay Nickel Company (VBNC), a subsidiary of Inco. Some Inuit were employed early on with Archaen Resources.

In the meantime, the Innu Nation and the Mushuau Innu Band Council organized a protest at the exploration site at Voisey's Bay. Chief Simeon, his councilors and Tanien Ashini from Sheshatshiu traveled to the site on skidoo to meet with Archaen Resources. They brought along a video camera to film the site. A few days later a couple of guys came back to show the videotapes on the community channel. These leaders were well organized. They announced on the radio the time the tapes would be aired so everyone in the community was watching.

I was lying in my bed listening to country music from my tape recorder when my wife came to tell me the Voisey's Bay videotapes were on television. In *Innu-aimun,* Chief Simeon invited all Innu to join the protest. Anyone with a skidoo could obtain fifteen gallons of gas from the Council. If they didn't have a skidoo the council would pay for their transportation.

Shanut and I decided to go with our sons, Pien, Napeu and Jonah. I didn't waste any time and collected my gas. The next afternoon we left with Shushep[2] Gregoire and his family. Some people had already left and others followed. It was dark by the time we reached the Bay. We had to travel through a lot of salt water and it took an extra couple of hours to reach the camp. When we arrived around 9:30 all the tents were full of people so we had to set up our own. It wasn't easy to set up in the dark but we had no choice. Our children needed a warm place to sleep. Pien and Shushep's son Mike did a good job getting the wood.

The next morning was very cold and windy. The RCMP had already arrived. Chief Simeon suggested we move our tents closer to the drill-site. More RCMP landed at the camp and there were now 50 or 60 of them. Every night three or four of them would patrol the drill-site. They built a big fire to keep warm. I asked one why they had to be there all night? He said it had nothing to do with protecting the drill. They were just doing what they were told. I felt sorry for them but I was also frustrated. This was a non-violent protest. I

---

[1] Labrador Inuit Association, now the Nunatsiavut Government
[2] Joseph Mark

wondered why the government had to send so many RCMP like we were animals. They should've known better. We weren't there to harm anyone or to pull the drills down. We were there to protect the environment and the animals. We were doing the right thing for our children's future.

I thought the Innu Nation and the LIA would've had a stronger voice if the LIA had joined us in our protest. Both the Innu and Inuit had used that land for longer than we could remember. The Innu Nation and the LIA had an overlap claim on the land at Voisey's Bay. Why didn't the LIA join our protest? Like some people said, maybe it was because very few true Inuit were working with the LIA. Most people who ran that organization were Settlers.

Ed Roberts was the justice minister in the Wells government. He didn't recognize our Aboriginal rights. Like Joey Smallwood, the first premier of the province, Roberts and Wells thought all the people living in Newfoundland and Labrador were all Newfoundlanders. How many times did we hear Ed Roberts repeat, "The law is the law and everyone should follow it?" If that was the case, why did Newfoundland give permission to Diamond Fields to do exploration work at Voisey's Bay when they hadn't consulted with the LIA and Innu Nation? The Canadian Constitution recognized our rights but the provincial government was ignoring this law. They were stealing the land from the Innu and Inuit. The government of Newfoundland was also breaking environmental protection laws. They hadn't asked the company to do any environmental impact study of Voisey's Bay before starting their exploration work. How could Ed Roberts, the justice minister, not know he was breaking his own law?

Our first protest lasted about two weeks before we shut everything down. The second time we went to protest at Voisey's Bay the drill had been moved a few metres away and ran a full twenty-four hours a day. There was nothing we could do. My sister Tshaukuesh from Sheshatshiu was there along with Penote Michel and his family. Two women were arrested but an hour later they were released. About a week after the protest began, LIA leaders came to meet with the Innu Nation but the meeting went nowhere. A few days later we got a fax from the president of the Innu Nation saying the company was willing to meet with us in Sheshatshiu.

In the end nothing really happened. The protest was over and negotiations with the company continued. We all headed back to Davis Inlet. On our return we saw a lot of caribou just before we got to Zoar. I stopped my skidoo to watch the caribou cross the bay. I wondered whether they would still be in the area after the mining started.

Back in Davis Inlet my sister said she wished we'd all stayed a little longer at the protest camp. She felt the same way about the caribou and the pollution that a mine would create at Voisey's Bay. She thought it would've been hard for the province to keep so many RCMP there for a long period of time. Months later the government released information about how it had spent over a million dollars during the protest at Voisey's Bay.

The day we got back from the protest some of us left for Goose Bay to meet with the company. The Innu Nation asked the company to recognize Innu rights but the company refused. Their people said it was up to the government to give them permission to do this exploration work and build their mine. We should have stayed in Voisey's Bay and continued our protest instead of coming to this useless meeting. The problem was that we didn't have any media people at our protest.

In the middle of our two protests the Innu Nation presented a proposal to Diamond Field Resources. I was at the meeting in St. John's when our President Peter Penashue handed the proposal over to Herb Clark, one of the company's chief negotiators. He looked at it and handed copies to the others. They excused themselves from the table. They must have felt they needed a short caucus to discuss the proposal by themselves.

The proposal wasn't new and had been shuffled back and forth between the Innu Nation and the company for weeks. Many changes had already been made, especially over wording. This was meant to be the final draft. We were certain both parties would agree to it. About a half hour later Herb Clark came back to tell us they'd approved our budget for half a million dollars. This was nothing to get excited about. We knew this was money coming from our land. Part of that money would be used for a Task Force on mining activities, including a community consultation to find out how people felt about all this mining exploration on our land.

Four Innu commissioners were hired from each community, along with a co-ordinator, Camille Fouillard. The commissioners interviewed almost 300 people in Davis Inlet and Sheshatshiu, both men and women and people of all ages. Eight weeks later the research report of the task force entitled *Between a Rock and a Hard Place* was released with twenty-four recommendations for immediate response. The report stated that the people were giving the Innu Nation a mandate to go ahead with great caution to try to negotiate an IBA[1] with the company.

Exploration was a very big issue for me. The Innu had always traveled in *nutshimit* looking for food or a place to camp but they didn't damage the land. Mining exploration at Voisey's Bay was like the company looking for a place to destroy. In our language the word for "exploration" means "damage." The worst yet to come was the mine development. They would destroy and pollute the whole area. Many lakes would be contaminated. Fish would die. Animals, big or small, would move away. Waterfowl would no longer use that area for nesting grounds.

Even if the company did not build their smelter in Nitassinan there would still be many problems. We worried the company might build a mining town that would bring an increase in alcoholism and drugs in our community. There would be boat and skidoo accidents. People would travel in rough water and bad ice trying to get to the Voisey's Bay town. There would be many new roads, and outsiders would build their own cabins on every lake and river in the area. Innu and Inuit would no longer be able to hunt and trap and there might not be any animals. Mark my words. I knew that in 20 years the beautiful waters and land of Voisey's Bay would be a wasteland.

All kinds of jobs would be available at Voisey's Bay: heavy equipment operators, linemen, hydro operators, office jobs like bookkeeping and secretary, janitors, maintenance, plane ticket agents, airstrip operators, store clerks, managers, plumbers for water and sewage, people who would work at the dock, just to name some of them. But people had to be qualified to get those jobs. Well-paid jobs would go to the outsiders. It was possible there'd be only short-term jobs for Innu people. Innu would first have to take some training before they could be hired. The people who'd suffer the most were the hunters and trappers.

I worried about what would happen if a young person got a permanent job. He'd lose his way of life forever. An 18-year-old man who'd just started to learn his traditional way of life but never completed this education would have his culture in his right hand and in his left hand he'd be qualified to get a good permanent job at Voisey's Bay. He'd set aside his own culture, thinking he'd come back to it later and he'd choose to live like a non-Innu. I didn't want to see

---

[1] Impact Benefit Agreement

our culture disappear. I thought if any Innu worked permanently at Voisey's Bay they should ask for at least two months of cultural leave with pay every year.

When the iron mine in Schefferville closed down, everyone – Innu and non-Innu – in the town were affected. Most people were laid off. The land once used by the Innu to hunt and trap had become a wasteland and a man-made barrens. Schefferville had been a good place for caribou, part of their main migration route.

What choice did we have to protest or negotiate? We were trying to protect the land and the animals. No matter where we stood it was like giving away our land. If we protested, how long could we actually stay at the site? People would get tired and feel helpless because the development would go ahead anyway. If we didn't negotiate, what benefits would we get? Nothing. We would just watch our land being destroyed. I thought we should continue to negotiate with Diamond Fields but make sure we got what we wanted. In our negotiations with the company we never agreed to stop our protests. We kept the option to protest if we had to.

I would have preferred if land claims had been settled before any development was allowed to go ahead. Chief Kiti Rich was really against the mining development and didn't believe in IBA negotiations. Many people from Davis Inlet agreed with her. Part of me as councilor thought it was time young people put away the booze and went back to school for training if they were interested in getting a job. I thought if IBA negotiations went nowhere, young people would be the most affected. I hoped young people were still strong believers in their own culture and would continue to use the land for hunting and trapping.

In the meantime a mining fever spread all over Labrador. By June of 1996 more than 280,000 stakes had been claimed for mineral exploration in Nitassinan. The media seemed very happy to report about how easy it was to stake a claim on Innu land.

IN MARCH 1995, CHIEF SIMEON Tshakapesh called an early election. Maybe he felt too much pressure from the community. He'd been doing a good job but some people were complaining about his leadership. I wasn't surprised. No matter who the Chief was there were always complaints.

Etien Pastiwet and Kiti Rich ran for Chief in the election. One candidate used alcohol to try to get elected and he came very close to succeeding. I was pretty sure Kiti would win easily. The votes were counted that night and the results were posted on the community channel. I anxiously waited to see who would win. At first Kiti was way ahead but Etiene managed to catch up by the time they'd counted about half the votes. In the end, Kiti won by only six votes and I was elected councilor.

We all went over to congratulate Etien for having come such a close second. If he had not used alcohol he would have been elected. We promised him a job as outpost coordinator. He told us he'd sell us his house to use for the Safe House we wanted to set up for children who were in crisis. He asked for a skidoo in exchange. This later turned into a problem between him and his wife.

Over the summer most people in Davis Inlet were working. We managed to hire twenty-five students. A life skills project was set up to teach them how to make snowshoes, moccasins and other homemade tools used in the old days. Both men and women were hired on to do housing repairs. Other jobs included maintenance work, garbage collection, getting wood for the sick and elderly and home care. A number of women working in home care were trained in Goose Bay at the Paddon Home on how to look after the old people and the sick.

Chief Kiti Rich was doing her best to make the community a better place to live. Gas sniffing and alcohol were still our main problems. A former Chief was hired as healing co-ordinator. I thought he'd do a good job if he could get enough support from the community. A report with a seven-point plan for recovery and healing was prepared by the band council and presented to governments. Entitled *Hearing the Voices,* it was a follow-up to the earlier report on the People's Inquiry, *Gathering Voices.* The plan was asking: 1) for the relocation of Davis Inlet, 2) to send gas sniffers to a treatment lodge in Alberta, 3) to set up a team of Innu counselors to deal with the children when they came back home, 4) to set up a family treatment program, 5) for Canada to accept its responsibilities towards the Innu, 6) that governments meet with Innu leaders and 7) that governments recognize Innu rights.

It took years of negotiations with governments to get a commitment from them to relocate the Innu of Davis Inlet to Natuashish. The Newfoundland Government said they would give us the land for relocation but they wanted the federal government to fund it. It was ridiculous for us to hear Newfoundland say it didn't recognize that the land already belonged to the Innu. We didn't recognize Newfoundland's claim of ownership.

After four years of fighting, the federal cabinet finally approved our request for relocation. Everyone in the community was really excited, especially the elders. When I saw the agreement signed on November 13, 1996, it brought back a lot of memories of my old friend Kaniuekutat, the elder who had really pushed for relocation. He would've been very happy. After the ceremony some elders played the *teueikan*[1]. People started to dance. Even the minister of Indian Affairs joined us along with Premier Wells of Newfoundland.

A few months later Kiti called another election. I have no idea why. She'd received a few letters of complaint. Maybe she was tired after having worked so hard to get approval for relocation although she hadn't been alone. The Mushuau Innu Renewal Committee (MIRC) made up of Innu elders and other community members was set up and was working hard with a consultant hired to manage the whole relocation project. He was the one to contact government officials for us but he was not making the decisions. He was working for the band council and the MIRC. That's how it worked at the beginning.

Prote Poker ran again in this election and won. Once again we had a Chief who didn't drink. A few months later there was an Innu Nation election and Kiti Rich was elected the first woman president. This was also the first time the president was elected from Davis Inlet. Tanien Ashini from Sheshatshiu was elected vice-president. There'd been a lot of fighting between the two communities. I was afraid the Innu Nation was going to split up and Davis Inlet was going to pull out, but after Kiti won everything calmed down.

The new band council was also doing well. We were seeing a new kind of Chief in our community. Prote held many public meetings mostly about relocation. A lot of people were employed and there would be more jobs at

---

[1] Innu drum

the relocation site. The band council had organized training programs to make sure that both men and women would be trained for these jobs. For almost ten years every Chief had done a good job for the community. Prote had gone back to school to complete his Adult Basic Education. Even more important he was well educated in our way of life and had learned many things from the elders. Kiti Rich was also well educated in the *Akaneshau* system, as well as in our way of life. *Akaneshau* education was very important in politics but Innu education was far more important and could be used in many ways. A leader had to know how to survive in *nutshimit*. He or she had to be a trapper or hunter who strongly believed in his or her own way of life and in the *Aueshish-utshimaut*[1].

After Prote was elected it was hard to satisfy everyone and some people still complained about the band council. It wasn't easy for a Chief to be in that position and hear complaints every day. At the same time he had many serious decisions to make that would affect our people for generations to come.

Just before Christmas of 1996 I went to Ottawa with some elders. Before I left I went to visit my friend Pinip Rich who was very sick. Pinip was Kiti's father. He was supposed to come with us to Ottawa but was too sick. I didn't know if he recognized me that morning. I didn't try to talk to him. I just left and waved goodbye. We were about to board a plane in Goose Bay when our lawyer, John Olthuis, called me to say Pinip had passed away. All the way to Ottawa he was the only thing on my mind. He was another one of my best friends. Why were all my friends dying? First it was Mishen, then Kaniuekutat[2], Napeu and now Pinip Rich.[3]

My personal belief is that they were killed by *kakushapatak*[4] from away. Before Pinip died I dreamt that I was outside my house and saw a wounded caribou crying like a human being. I told Shanut something was going to happen in the next couple of days. And Pinip died. Pinip Rich was a great speaker at meetings, never afraid to say what was on his mind.

---

[1] Animal spirits
[2] John Poker
[3] Gilbert Rich, John Poker, Sam Napeo and Philip Rich
[4] Shaman

In April 1997, I was at my desk writing this book when our secretary, Ipun[1] Asta, came into the office. She stayed about ten minutes and left again. All the staff of the Innu Nation were supposed to be at work that day. A few hours later I heard she had committed suicide. I didn't want to believe it. She'd been at the office only that afternoon. We went to her residence but the RCMP wouldn't let us in. The weather was bad the next day so they couldn't take the body out to do an autopsy. They kept the body in a cool place in the RCMP storage house.

I went to see Ipun's parents the next morning. At first I sat with her father Miste-Etuet. Then her mother Manteskueu[2] came in and started to cry. I was crying too. I couldn't help it. I knew how she must have felt losing a second daughter. A few years before another daughter had died from an overdose. Her son-in-law, Ipun's husband, had also committed suicide in this same house.

Only thirty-four years old, Ipun would still be alive if it had not been for alcohol. It was tragic to see these things happening so often. The healing workers were doing their best but they couldn't handle all these problems. Maybe they didn't have enough staff to do all the work. If I'd been a leader I would've advised the workers to make home visits once or twice a week so the people who were suffering would know that others cared about them.

I wondered why so many people were dying before this move took place. Would the deaths continue to happen after the move? No one had the answers. One elder told me the move was not good. He didn't want to leave the place where his parents and other relatives were buried. He believed there was a reason so many people were dying before relocation. I was tempted to believe him. A few elders who were very anxious to move to Natuashish had already died. It was difficult for me to understand this because I didn't have the knowledge of the elders.

---

[1] Yvonne
[2] Mary Georgette

It wasn't long before problems started with our relocation plans. The band council was supposed to be in charge of relocation but the Mushuau Innu Renewal Committee (MIRC) quickly took over the control. I attended MIRC meetings. The consultant tabled a proposal, did all the talking and then asked the committee members for their thoughts. He warned them that if the proposal wasn't approved it would be too late to start the project that summer. Some committee members got scared. They didn't want to be blamed for any delays. One member popped up and said, "It's a good proposal and I give it my approval." The rest of the committee all said yes too. The consultant then wrote down on his paper that the committee had given its approval.

The MIRC members didn't always really know what they were approving. These elders needed good translations and good explanations of what the *Akaneshau* advisors were saying. They needed more time to understand what the *Akaneshau* person wanted, what he could do to help the community.

One day I went to visit an elder who was going to attend an MIRC meeting. I felt sorry for her because I didn't often see her say anything at meetings. I was sure she didn't always agree with everything that was being discussed. I felt the other elders also thought they had to always say yes. One MIRC member told me he was no longer interested in attending meetings because the consultant always wanted his way.

We as Innu didn't know any outside contractors to do the work of the relocation. The consultant was the person who recommended the best contractor. We had no idea how well he knew this contractor. I thought maybe the guy was his friend or someone he knew in the past. I didn't like that the Chief was always taking the consultant's advice. He was invited to our meetings and the Chief always said yes to him. Was his advice better than the councilors'?

People in the community also didn't always know what was happening with relocation. One time I went to see a worker at the relocation office. He wasn't there and another guy was sitting at his desk. He said he was the new project manager. No one knew what was going on behind MIRC doors. No one knew how much money this new person was making. I ran into another new person in the band council office who told me he was working with a consulting business and hired to develop job descriptions for all the employees in Davis Inlet. I thought it was crazy to bring in someone from the outside to do job descriptions for an Innu community. It was a waste of money to pay for his travel expenses. The band council could do its own job descriptions.

Other problems were brewing over the relocation money. Some leaders were doing a good job but others just wanted to be elected to help themselves to more money. At one band council AGM[1] I asked the leaders how much money they made in a year. I wanted to know the salaries of all the *Akaneshau* people who worked in the Band office and with the MIRC. They wouldn't tell me. A friend of mine stood up to point out that one of the band council staff was trying to control everything and giving jobs to most of his children. The Chief responded that he didn't hire his own relatives. His wife was not working and he'd never tried to find her a job.

There were also rumours about joint ventures. I asked a question about this conflict of interest, which was a new thing for the Innu. Some Innu had partnerships with non-Innu companies. How much money would Innu involved in joint ventures get from relocation? Some leaders looked at each other. Finally the Chief said it was true there were a few Innu joint ventures but he never gave us names.

I thought if an elected leader was involved in a private business like a joint venture, he was in a conflict-of-interest position. Leaders were elected to look after the community and the interests of all Mushuau Innu, not to look after themselves. Leaders were the servants of the people. At the same time I didn't think leaders were in a conflict of interest if they hired their own relatives or friends. The community was small so most people were related to each other and many were friends with the Chief and Council. It wasn't really a conflict to hire your friend or relative. But when the Council gave a contract to non-Innu friends – if it was an under-the-table deal and they stood to gain from it – then it really was a conflict of interest.

I told my friend it wasn't worth sitting around at the meeting to listen to all the cover-ups. I left to go do my work at the Health Commission. After I left, the Chief talked about an alcohol ban in the community. I knew the Chief was trying very hard to get this ban but other Councilors didn't support the idea. It was sad to see the Chief not get support from his councilors for such a good idea. No wonder he quit his job. I wish he'd stayed on longer. He would've been re-elected for a second term.

---

[1] Annual General Meeting

Once again it was frustrating to see our leaders always quitting. We'd elect a good Chief with a majority vote but he or she always quit before the term was up. It affected the whole community. People were finding it hard to trust each other. One election was held when six people ran for Chief and twelve people for councilor positions. Most of those who got elected used alcohol to buy their votes. We were still lucky to have elected a sober Chief again but the vote was very split between all six candidates. The winner received only 74 votes, far from a majority. It was a good thing people didn't know much about majority or minority votes.

I kept thinking about how for so many years people from the outside didn't care about Davis Inlet. Why this sudden interest with relocation? They were seeing dollar signs and suddenly very interested in working with the Innu. Some of these non-Innu contractors had complained so long about the Innu but now they were using us to get housing contracts. After relocation we'd never hear from our joint venture friends again. They'd have enough money and they wouldn't care what happened to us. Leaders and outsiders would benefit the most from this relocation agreement. Some leaders went back to school to get a higher education so they could help our community but others went back to school just to make more money. Some leaders now had their own businesses through joint ventures so they had no worries about the future.

In a way I couldn't blame them. There were no Innu contractors for the relocation work, only Innu joint ventures with *Akaneshau* contractors. One joint venture with a Quebec partner had the lowest bid and brought its own men from Quebec. Davis Engineering was the project manager for relocation and subcontracted different parts of the project such as water and sewage, roads, the airstrip, rock crushing, concrete and housing. Emery Construction and Colby's Construction hired a lot of local people but the Innu were not the ones benefiting the most from the relocation agreement.

Yes, most people would get good houses with water and sewage facilities but nothing else. Low-income families would suffer the most. They wouldn't be able to buy the things they needed for their homes such as chairs, a table or beds. Most Innu people would be working during the move but what would happen after? Those who had no education would have to work very hard to feed their families. Many would still be on social assistance. I worried that our real advisors, the elders, would not be with us very long. If young leaders were not careful about what they took and what they gave to the community, they could make huge mistakes that would really hurt our people.

As a band councilor I attended one meeting in St. John's with federal officials, the MIRC and the project manager. Everyone had a chance to speak. I was very happy to be invited and when my time came to speak I had my notes in front of me. I told them that in 1967 when the government built the houses in Sheshatshiu, I remembered the Innu got a free house but it was just an empty house with no furniture. The government may have paid for some second-hand furniture from the military in Goose Bay – beds, mattresses, chairs and tables that I helped move at the time. I didn't think the relocation budget included money for furniture and suggested we could still make a proposal so that every household could be furnished for one time only. Everyone around the table supported this idea.

It was our relocation money. If we were to work together we had to learn to respect and care for each other. I also wanted to see us make the decisions about how to pay labourers for their work on the relocation site. A person who did hard labour was a very hard-working person but he made less money than an office worker. Some people who worked in offices did nothing, just sat around playing computer games, talking and laughing, yet they collected a pay-cheque every week and made more money than people who worked really hard. In *Akaneshau* communities and big cities, office workers made more money than labourers but they were qualified and they worked very hard. In our community some office workers were not fully qualified to do their work.

As well some people were being hired just enough weeks to qualify for their unemployment insurance (U.I.) benefits and then laid off. These people suffered the most. They had to send their application to see if they qualified. A week or so later they'd receive their U.I. cards that they then had to send back to St. John's. Another two weeks later they'd get their first cheque. While they waited for this payment they couldn't receive any social assistance or get any credit from the Innu store. I don't remember whether the concerns I raised at the meeting were addressed.

With all our elections we weren't always able to elect the best Chief. At one point many people were complaining about one chief because shortly after he took office he and one of his councilors set up a business. I wondered where the Chief and his partner had gotten the money to start up that kind of business. I figured it was probably from the relocation funding.

I also wondered how much this Chief supported the healing of our people. Shortly after the election another mobile treatment program was being offered out in *nutshimit*. I was very interested in attending that kind of treatment with my whole family. One of my daughters was confirmed to go so she wrote a letter to the council to apply for a leave from her job. She was told she'd have to go on her holiday time. She wouldn't be allowed to take holidays during the summer. She decided not to go. Other employees were refused leave to attend the program.

I thought this was crazy. The band council should support anyone who wanted to heal him or herself. This was the first time I'd seen this. If a council wouldn't support the healing programs, nothing would change after our move to Natuashish. We'd have to suffer another two years with this Chief before another election was held.

One day a former councilor came to tell me a lot of things about this new council. We'd voted for this Chief so that he'd help his community, not just himself and his friends. We both thought we'd made a mistake. We just laughed. I thought it was too late to do anything, but my friend thought different.

"So many people are complaining about this new council," he said. "Some people are thinking about organizing a protest against the council."

"It's true that the people have all the power in this community, not the band council," I said.

"What will probably happen is that the new Council will give people something to keep them quiet," my friend predicted.

The band council started to purchase ATVs or boats and outboard motors for everyone. People could choose. I asked the financial manager where this money was coming from and he told me the band council had a surplus for the year. The truth was the money had actually been overspent. The council then decided to build 25 houses in Davis Inlet and not at the new site. These houses could easily be assembled in a matter of weeks because the wiring was already installed in the walls. After relocation they could be taken apart and moved to the new site for other uses, such as a church, teachers' residence or a hotel. A councilor told me these houses were not being paid for with relocation money but from a separate fund.

We didn't know what would happen from one day to the next with this council. They made a plan one day and the next day their plan had already changed. People were angry and frustrated. A group of protesters decided to go to the Band Council building to ask the Chief and councilors to step down and resign. Nothing happened.

Two letters addressed to the Chief, deputy Chief and councilors were released to the media. One letter stated that the people wanted the leaders to do the honorable thing and step down from their positions. The second letter stated: "When are you going to open your eyes? Don't you know what is happening in our community? Everyone knows that since you were elected things have gotten worse." The majority of the people had sent a very strong message to the leaders. They had no idea what would happen but they were hoping for the best.

Only one councilor resigned. I couldn't understand why the Chief and other councilors wouldn't listen to the people. Instead they decided to have a leadership retreat at Flowers Bay. I was asked to co-ordinate this workshop but I didn't think it would work. Many people didn't want to attend this retreat so the leaders decided to hold it in the community. I don't know how many people went. A consultant from Halifax was invited to help out. I thought this guy had no business at this retreat and that the Innu could solve their own problems. There was too much anger in the community.

Another protest was organized outside the band council building. I watched the protesters walk back and forth inside the building by the Chief's office. I thought the leaders should resign. They should do what the people wanted before something serious happened.

IN THE MID 1990S MY SON NAPEU started to sniff gas. Ever since he was a young boy I kept telling him he should go into a treatment program. He was only sixteen but he was a good hunter. I thought he should go out to treatment to see if it could help him stop sniffing. When I mentioned it to him he said nothing but a couple of weeks later he made arrangements to go. He was on a waiting list for a treatment centre in Quebec, and his counselor David Nuna would tell him when there was a bed available. He was very anxious to go but had to wait a long time. Finally he got the news he could go. Napeu was very excited although I had mixed feelings. I was very happy but also worried about him. I was really going to miss him.

"My son, I'm very proud of you for going to get some treatment to heal yourself. You've made a very good decision," I said to him. "My hope for your future, for the future of all your brothers and sisters, is that you'll all be well-educated and that you'll keep your culture and way of life. You all know how much I care for you and love you."

I drove him to the airstrip to catch his plane. We waited for about a half an hour but it felt like minutes. When the Twin Otter arrived I hugged him and told him to take care of himself and to do his best. He said he'd try hard to heal himself. I had to wait three weeks before I could talk to him on the phone because of a treatment program rule. When I was finally able to call, he said he was okay and he'd try to stay the whole three months. His counselor told me he was doing great and they weren't having any problems with him.

At the end of July the youth counselor called to say Napeu was ready to come home. They wanted me to come to the centre for four days of family therapy. I asked him why Napeu was coming home two weeks early. I was glad to hear that Napeu had never gotten angry with his counselor and had participated in all the different aspects of the program.

I traveled to meet up with my son, escorting a young fellow from Sheshatshiu headed to the same treatment centre. We arrived in the evening and I didn't expect to see my son that night but the counselor asked me if I wanted to. They took me to the living room where he was waiting. He stood up and walked towards me. I hugged him and kissed him and told him I was very proud of him. We talked for about twenty minutes and a van came to take me to the place where I'd stay for the next four days. The counselor told me to be ready to start by 9:00 the next morning.

During our therapy together I could tell that my son had learned how to show respect to people. His counselor told me that Napeu had always shown his respect for the program. One evening we had a sweat with other clients and an elder. The elder asked the boys, including my son, to sing a traditional song. He sang with the drum. He must've learned this song from the elder. In our culture I'd never seen a young person sing a traditional song. Innu songs come from our dreams. If a person dreams about the same song three times then he or she can sing it. Anyway, I had to show my respect for other people's culture. I was happy that my son had learned new things from another Native culture.

When we got back to Goose Bay my eldest son Gerry told us he was going to Innu Nikamu, the Innu music festival that happens in Sept Isles every summer. Napeu wanted to go along. I told him I was very worried about him but the decision was his. He decided not to go. We stayed the night in Goose Bay and I went to a bar called Maxwell's not to drink but to meet up with a couple of friends. When I got back to the Friendship Centre where we were staying they told me I'd received five calls about an emergency back home. I tried to call but there was no answer. I went straight to our room and found Napeu watching television. I didn't want him to notice that I was upset or to tell him about the calls. I was very worried, wondering why my wife was calling in the middle of the night.

I called first thing in the morning and my wife told me our house had almost caught on fire. My son Pien had been sniffing gas in the basement and left a lit candle unattended. Fortunately the local fire-fighters managed to put out the fire. They'd done a super job with little equipment. I was happy to hear that no one was hurt. I told Napeu about the near mishap.

My daughter was at the airport with her daughter to meet us when we arrived that day. I was surprised that my wife wasn't there to meet our son. When we got home I was even more surprised when Shanut didn't even hug him. I felt frustrated about this welcome but I didn't say anything. I know hugging someone, even our children, is very new to us and not part of our culture. Innu people kiss each other on special occasions like on New Year's or when a person is leaving for a long time or returning after a long absence. The only time I'd seen people hug each other was after a healing meeting. Anyway, we were all very happy to see Napeu back home.

With Napeu home again and the problems with Pien sniffing, we decided to go into *nutshimit* with a couple other families. I thought it would be best for my sons to be in *nutshimit*. I was working with the Innu Nation and had one month's holiday coming to me as well as a month of cultural leave. I thought it would be nice for my sons to be in *nutshimit* in the fall to help with their healing. I wrote in my journal many days that fall.

AUGUST 31, DAVIS INLET

Patnik[1] Rich left on a Twin Otter this morning with his family and father-in-law for nutshimit. The plane returned and we quickly loaded our gear without noticing that the tide was going out so fast. The plane was grounded. We should've pushed the plane out with every load. The pilots said we'd have to wait for high tide. They should've started up the plane and tried to move forward but they were new to the job. I never met them before. I told them it would be at least three hours before the water would begin to rise again. We left around 5:00 in the evening and it took us about forty minutes to reach the camp at Kassitakaikan. As the plane circled to prepare for landing I could see Patnik making a fire. No tent was set up and I wondered why. The pilots beached the plane. One of the pilots grabbed the rope, quickly jumped out of the plane, tied the rope onto the rear of the floats and threw the rope to Patrick's family. They pulled it to turn the plane around. We unloaded our stuff and decided to set up just one tent before dark. This is temporary and we will move somewhere else once we have our canoes. There are seventeen of us in one big tent. Patrick has already killed three caribou. It didn't take long to set up the tent because all our children helped. Napeu and Pien are very happy to be here.

SEPTEMBER 1

Weather: partly sunny, snow and high winds later in the day. Shanut and I went to cut some wood and then I skinned a caribou Patrick killed yesterday. We heard a plane fly over our camp on its way to another one

---

[1] Patrick

nearby where Tatesh[1] Rich has set up his tent. Within an hour the plane landed on our beach and dropped off an outboard motor and a few pieces of plywood. Shina[2] Rich, her three children and Shushep[3] Gregoire were on board. The pilot told us that as soon as the wind died down he'd pick up our canoe in Davis Inlet and drop it off to us. Patrick killed another caribou today.

SEPTEMBER 2

Weather: sunny periods and windy. We were expecting the plane with our canoe but the winds were too high. My son Napeu went fishing and got one lake trout. Our elder Mishta-Penashue[4] and my son Gerry each caught a fish too.

SEPTEMBER 3

Weather: cloudy with light winds from the northeast. We saw seven caribou this morning and killed three. In the afternoon the plane finally arrived with the canoe and gas. At about 4:00 we went looking for a place to camp. We cut a few sticks of dry wood for our tent poles. We'll move tomorrow.

SEPTEMBER 4

The weather was mostly sunny with a light northwesterly wind. We killed a caribou as she swam across the lake. We saw six more at the other end of the lake but we don't want to kill too many at this time of the year. We cut more sticks and around 3:30 we moved to our new campsite, a nice spot. The skies clouded over in the evening, then turned into lightning and thundershowers.

SEPTEMBER 5

Weather: cloudy and a little windy. I'm supposed to go to Davis Inlet to attend a meeting but no news yet about the plane. This morning we cut some sticks for a scaffold to smoke some meat. Napeu and Pien cut sticks so I can build a matutishanitshuap[5] to have sweats and to serve as our

---

[1] Thaddeus
[2] Sheila
[3] Joseph Mark
[4] Francis Benuen
[5] Sweat lodge

storage tent. The plane arrived in the afternoon. Pinip Rich and Sam Mistenapeo were already on board. Sam was sick and needed to see the nurse in Davis Inlet.

SEPTEMBER 6

The Innu Nation board and Band Council arrived for the meeting about noon. We started at 2:30 but the meeting resolved nothing. I had nothing to do in the evening so my daughter Shakanin and I played radio bingo. It was mostly cloudy and windy today.

SEPTEMBER 7

Mainly sunny today with a little bit of wind. The meeting was supposed to start at 9:00 but it was 10:30 before it got underway. The main issue on the table was only resolved late afternoon. Jacqueline and I went to the store to do some shopping. We were told the plane would arrive at noon the next day to bring us back to our camp.

SEPTEMBER 8

Weather: cloudy and windy. The plane arrived around 11:00 and Pinip, Sam and I returned to our camps. I sat in the front with the pilot and as we landed I could see caribou swimming across the lake. We killed three of them.

SEPTEMBER 9

Weather: cloud, but calm winds all day. We made a Makushan today with five caribou. In the afternoon, Gerry, Jonah, Roman and I went fishing. We paddled across the lake. Gerry caught two fish but one got away. While we were fishing a caribou stag suddenly appeared from the woods. My cartridges were in the canoe with my 22 rifle. We saw another caribou up on the hill from our camp. Patrick and I crossed the lake and walked from there. We only had 22s but we killed the caribou. We had lake trout for supper and invited Patrick and his family to eat with us in our tent. This is an Innu tradition. Lake trout is a sacred fish and has to be eaten where it is cooked. It rained in the evening but not much.

September 10

Weather foggy early this morning, but it cleared up in the afternoon and then rained in the evening with winds from the north. This morning we boiled the crushed caribou bones for the Makushan. It took about three hours. Then I went with Napeu, Pien and Patnik to the other end of the lake to cut firewood and haul it back by boat. We cut enough for two loads in a 16-foot freighter canoe. Shanut spent her day drying and smoking caribou meat.

SEPTEMBER 12

I was up at 4:10 this morning. It was so cold I had to make a fire. Shanut and I went to pick boughs. Nishapet and Shanut laid a new floor of boughs in the tent. I went for a walk halfway up the mountain. I looked back to where our tents stood. I could see across the lake over the mountains to a couple of big lakes beyond. It brought back a lot of memories from my childhood. It made me wonder how my parents and grandparents had managed to survive with just wild meat and fish to live on for a whole year in nutshimit. I decided to walk back down the hill, forget about what was on my mind. I walked into our tent and laid myself down on fresh boughs.

SEPTEMBER 13

Weather: mainly sunny and very windy. Pien, Shanut and I cut some wood. Shanut started to scrape the meat off the caribou hide. All the children went berry-picking. In the evening, Patrick and I pumped gas from the oil drum into five and ten-gallon cans. Our elder Mishta-Penashue got sick and we tried to contact Davis Inlet but no one could hear us. Shanut and I spent most of the night in Patnik's tent to keep an eye on Mishta-Penashue. He was very sick all night.

SEPTEMBER 14

Weather: mainly sunny with high winds from the northwest. We continued to try to contact Davis Inlet on the radio but still no one could hear us. Francis was feeling a little better this morning. A plane came to Tatesh's camp around 5:00 so I asked Francis if he would like to go to Davis Inlet to see the nurse. His daughter Shushan[1] was away from the camp so he preferred not to go. When Shushan returned she encouraged him to go so he changed his mind. We called over to Thaddeus's camp to

---

[1] Suzanne

tell the pilot to pick up Francis. He could hardly walk when we took him to the plane.

SEPTEMBER 15

Weather: cloudy this morning but the wind picked up in the afternoon. We went to collect boughs in the morning and then decided to go caribou hunting at the end of the lake. We saw two caribou but when we tried to shoot we missed. Patrick said it was a short portage over to the next lake. We had to haul our freighter canoe over and then return to bring the motor, the gas and the rest of our gear. We went on our way again and soon spotted a caribou, a big stag. Patrick shot him. I cleaned the guts and left him there. We continued to the end of the lake where we spotted a lot of caribou. We killed only two. We would've killed more but it was getting late and we wanted to get home before dark. We picked up the other caribou on our way back.

SEPTEMBER 16

Weather: cloudy with a light drizzle and windy. We went caribou hunting again. Shanut and Shushan will dry the meat. First we had to get some wood. Napeu, Pien, Patnik, and I set off in the boat. We didn't have to go far when we saw five caribou. The boys shot all five. It was too windy to load them all in the canoe so we left them on a small island. We'll return tomorrow to fetch them.

SEPTEMBER 17

Weather: cloudy, cold and windy. While we waited for the wind to calm down we prepared for a Makushan. We had only twenty-four bones so it didn't take us that long to scrape the meat off. Patnik crushed the bones around 7:30 this evening. We were ready to have a feast but I thought we'd wait for Uniam[1] Katshinak and his family who arrive tomorrow.

SEPTEMBER 18

Weather: mainly sunny early on and very windy. Clouds moved in during the afternoon. We finally managed to pick up our five caribou on the island. Patnik, Shushan, Shanut, Napeu and I crossed the lake and walked about a mile. Halfway to another lake, Shinapiu-miskumi, we saw

---

[1] William

172

a small herd of about sixteen caribou, mostly female. We decided not to kill any because there was no stag. Besides that, we didn't want to kill too many caribou and waste any meat. We heard on the radio that Kanikuen Rich was sent to hospital in St. John's.

SEPTEMBER 19

Weather: cloudy with calm winds, a little foggy to the east and a light drizzle in the afternoon. Uniam and his family arrived. The plane barely made it because of the poor weather. We helped unload the stuff. Later I asked Napeu and Pien to help me set up my fishing net. Both were very excited. I asked Patnik if I could use his boat. I needed only my net, an axe and a gun. The spot where I wanted to set the net was about 10 minutes away. We walked up the hill just to look around and saw a caribou about a half a mile away. I wanted to check my net before we headed back to camp. I didn't really expect to find any fish yet but I'd already caught two kukamess[1]. We headed home and helped cut sticks for Uniam's tent. We also set up our sweat lodge but we couldn't sweat because it was raining.

SEPTEMBER 20

Weather: foggy day with drizzle and calm winds. We expected a plane to bring in Uniam's canoe but it never came because of the fog. Napeu, Patnik and I went hunting and killed one caribou. On our way home we checked my net and found eleven lake trout and four speckled trout. Later Napeu, Pien and I canoed across the lake to cut dry wood. We helped Uniam set up his tent and ate trout for supper.

SEPTEMBER 21

Weather: snowing with winds from the north. Patnik, Kevin and I went hunting, hoping to see a black bear that we'd spotted last night. On our way back I checked my net and pulled out five speckled trout and ten lake trout. The boys went partridge hunting. They saw a lot but said the birds were very wild.

SEPTEMBER 25

Weather: partly sunny and cold with high winds. The first thing we did was pick up the caribou we killed yesterday. In the afternoon we had a

---

[1] Lake trout

sweat. Pien heated up the rocks and we helped him bring in some dry wood. Nine of us sat around inside the lodge. I was in charge. All our kids were there. At first there seemed to be no heat. We'd built it using boughs on the ceiling and walls to make it dark. Every time I poured water on the rocks the hot steam would go up and not come down again. I told Patnik it must be the boughs on the ceiling that were causing our troubles. We removed them and continued to sweat. This time the lodge got very hot. None of us could stay very long inside. We heard by radio tonight that the plane was coming to all the camps tomorrow.

SEPTEMBER 26

Weather: mainly sunny with light winds from the northwest. Shanut pounded the dry meat to make niuiniken[1] this morning while Pien played his guitar – a very quiet morning. We were expecting the plane around 2:00. Nishapet, Kevin, Anishen, Roman and Lisa went back to Davis Inlet. Later we saw three caribou headed to our camp and we killed all three. They were nearby so it was easy to haul them back right away.

SEPTEMBER 27

Weather: nice day, but cloudy and windy. Shanut made pancakes for breakfast, which we ate with molasses. We were tired of eating deer meat. A plane brought some of Uniam's stuff but he said he wanted to go back to his camp at Kaishtatutet. The pilot had to pick up families in other camps. He said he'd return in the afternoon if he had time to help Uniam move. Pien was sick so he had to go back to Davis Inlet. The pilot also wanted to drop off stuff for Tatesh at our camp because he didn't have time to get to the other camp. He was in a hurry to get back to Goose Bay. We quickly unloaded the four boxes of junk food and Patnik, Jonah, Gerry and I hauled them to the other end of the lake. Ankiss[2] Penashue had called us earlier from the other camp to say he'd come and pick them up. While we waited we walked up the hill and saw a lot of caribou on both sides of the lake. About an hour later, Ankiss, his wife Kanani and two kids came to pick up the boxes. We headed back to our camp. Shanut and Shushan were working on the deerskins and drying meat on the open fire. Napeu, Patnik and I went to get wood before sundown.

---

[1] Pemmican
[2] Hank

SEPTEMBER 28

Weather: cloudy with light winds. A Twin Otter came to pick up Uniam's belongings. The pilot had two drums of aviation fuel so he would make another trip here and to the camps at Kakutukutapitak and Ushpuakaniss. My three sons went back to Davis Inlet. Patnik and I went to pick up a couple of caribou we'd shot two days ago. Patrick forgot his rope and I lost my knife. He found his rope but I never found my knife. The plane came back around 3:30. Tatesh and his two kids were aboard. The women boarded the plane to go back to Davis Inlet. Only Patnik and I stayed. It didn't take us too long to set up the small tent left behind.

SEPTEMBER 29

Weather: cloudy with light rain and winds from the southwest. After breakfast we packed our gear and piled it on the beach to wait for the plane. It was still raining a little. We cleaned up the campsite. It took us about five-and-a-half hours. My tent was still standing. We hoped the rain would stop so that the tent would dry. It didn't stop until later in the evening so we took the tent down after supper. We burned the dried boughs from the floor. We saw a caribou swimming across the lake as we were working on the tent and decided to get this one last stag. We shot it in the water and shared the meat between the two of us.

SEPTEMBER 30

Weather: partly sunny with light winds. The plane landed around 10:00 with two drums of aviation fuel so he couldn't take us with all our gear. I told the pilot we were prepared to stay but we'd send the gear on this flight. He got most of our stuff on board, including the meat. I didn't think a single Otter could carry so much stuff. As we were loading up, the rear floats touched ground and as the plane moved into deeper water it sank. I thought the plane was overloaded. Patnik figured it wasn't our fault. The pilot should know what he was doing. We both laughed. We weren't going to worry about the plane. The wind had started to pick up by the time the pilot headed towards the end of the lake and turned around to take off. It went a long way before it was finally airborne. All we had left was a bit of grub, blankets, one-and-a-half drums of gas, the canoe and the outboard motor. On his second trip the pilot went to the camp at Ushpuakaniss before coming to our camp. He couldn't open the fuel drum so he broke it with an axe. I asked him if he could make another trip but he said he didn't have enough fuel and would return tomorrow to pick us up, weather permitting. He was headed to Tatesh's camp to pick up Ankiss Penashue and his family. We had nothing to do, just hope for the plane to come tomorrow. We walked up the hill but there was no sign of caribou. We saw geese but we never had our shotguns with us.

OCTOBER 1

Weather: clear and windy in the morning, but the wind picked up and the sky clouded over. We heard on the radio that Tatesh's father Nian[1] was sick last night but he appears to be better this morning. About 9:30 Patnik's wife Shushan called to say she was drinking. Patrick was very upset and frustrated. I felt sorry for him. I knew how he felt when he heard his wife drunk on the radio. I would have felt the same way. The wind was blowing stronger but we heard the plane was on its way. The pilot headed to Pinip's camp first. I spent the day thinking back over the thirty-two days we'd just spent in nutshimit. We'd killed forty-two caribou. Nothing from these caribou had been wasted. We could've killed more but we didn't want to waste any meat. We wanted to respect our way of life. I walked around the campsite to take a final look. It brought back many memories of my father's time. The frame of our sweat lodge was still standing. We wanted to leave it as is with the frame, the boughs on the floor and the rocks. When people came back to this site in years to come they'd see the frame and know we'd come before.

I had many things on my mind as I looked at the skeleton of the lodge. I wondered if my children would continue to come back to this place. What about the things I'd taught them? Would they continue to pass on these teachings to their children? Or would their children live more like Akaneshau people? It really hurt inside of me to think about these things. I looked down at the rocks we had used to generate the heat in the sweat lodge. I whispered to the rocks, "Make us come back here with our children." I knew the plane would be here soon. I could've stayed longer and hoped that I'd come back to this very same place next fall.

About 2:00 in the afternoon the plane arrived. The pilot told me about how the plane had been overloaded yesterday. I told him we'd noticed and

---

[1] Leon

he laughed. He said he couldn't take the canoe because it was too windy. I asked him if he'd pick it up next time he was up this way. I sat up front with the pilot and as the plane began to move I looked down to where our tents had been. I can't describe how I felt when the plane took off. My only wish was that I'd be able to come back with my family and friends. We arrived around 3:15 and I walked home to my family. This evening I am finishing up this writing in my diary.

IN JULY OF 1998, two local Innu researchers and a co-ordinator from outside were hired to do a survey of how the Davis Inlet Innu felt about an alcohol ban and the use of intoxicants such as gas and glue. They had nineteen questions and interviewed eighty-eight people. People who could write English also submitted completed questionnaires. A referendum on the ban was held in August. Sixty-two percent of voters said they wanted a ban but voter turnout was low. The Band Council should've had a public meeting before the referendum to explain the situation to people.

I was in favour of the ban but I had many unanswered questions. A ban was not going to be easy to enforce. The community was too divided and people were not working together. I read a newspaper quoting a Chief from Manitoba who said a ban would do more harm than good. As a recovering alcoholic I knew what it was like when someone needed alcohol. Businesses in both Nain and Hopedale now had licences to sell beer. They were only two hours away on a fast boat. In the winter people could travel there by skidoo. Would people continue to go there to buy their booze? Would they have to drink it outside the community? Something might happen to them in the winter if an unexpected storm turned up. In the fall the water could get very rough to travel by boat. I was worried about boating and skidoo accidents.

At the same time I thought with no alcohol in the community there would be no more fighting or arguments. The Innu would work together and the government would hear only one voice. If we could get rid of gas sniffing there'd be no more vandalism, no more break-and- enters. We'd no longer need so many police officers. Children would go to school. They'd be well-educated and prepared to become future leaders. Our culture, values, traditions and Innu way of life would be very important to this generation.

I thought this was one time the band council was doing what they could to make our community a better place to live. Something good was bound to come out of this first-time effort to ban alcohol. I hoped we'd eventually figure out how to make the ban work. Everyone had to work together and never abandon our goal.

The idea for an alcohol ban had been first discussed in 1992 when the People's Inquiry report came out. It was an idea from the community, not the Chief. Before a referendum ever took place all the issues should've been on the table for us to discuss as a community. Everyone needed to be involved in the decision, not just the band council. Who would take the blame if something bad happened? The researchers should've talked to more people. We didn't know what everyone thought about this issue. The research team was also supposed to visit other Native communities that had gone dry to gather information about enforcing a ban. The research was never finished and the referendum just went ahead. Afterwards nothing happened.

As I sat in my office one day, I wondered what our new community would look like and if it would be a dry one. The Chief came in with a letter in hand. I knew he'd resigned even before I looked at the letter. I wasn't surprised. He was getting too much pressure from the community. I personally had no concerns whatsoever about his work as Chief. Only he knew his reasons for resigning. To me a Chief was not a special person but just like any other employee. The only difference was that he was elected and had to take direction from the community. He couldn't steer the course alone.

For years I continued to worry about my sons sniffing gas. It wasn't only my son Napeu who sniffed. At night especially in the winter I'd never get a good sleep because I worried about whether my son Pien might fall asleep outside and freeze to death. I also worried about suicide. If he was too high on gas he might walk out into open water or he might jump off a cliff. Every time someone knocked on the door in the early morning I just couldn't get up to answer it. I would wake my wife up to go. I always thought there'd be bad news about my son.

I wouldn't go hunting on the weekend if Pien didn't come along. I didn't want to leave him in the house alone or lock the doors because he needed a place to eat and sleep. I didn't want to shout at him or hurt him. I always loved him as much as I loved my other kids. I worried about him day and night. When I was at work and the receptionist paged my name for a phone-call my first thought was that there'd be bad news about my son.

I was happy when I saw Pien working and keeping busy. It reminded me of all the times we went camping. He was a good kid. He could do a man's work and was very interested in hunting. He was also a singer and played the guitar and keyboard. One time he and his group were invited to play at the Innu Nikamu festival in Sept Isles. Now it seemed like he'd lost interest in these things.

As a parent, what I felt when I saw my children sniff gas is something between love and anger. I'd see my children sniff gas and sometimes I'd feel very angry inside. I never wanted to say a word to them because I worried that if I said anything I'd be reminded about the kind of person I was like when I was still drinking. I thought I was the bad person, not my children. I knew they remembered my history of alcohol problems. My wife and I were paying the price. If I hadn't drank when my children were young they wouldn't have these problems. I felt very sorry for them and I hoped one day they would heal themselves. The only thing I could do was try to talk to them. I knew they weren't listening to me but I wanted to show them that I cared about them and loved them.

One time one of my sons was high on gas and very angry with me. He grabbed the axe. This is the child I really loved most, more than the other ones.

"Son, you want to be safe," I said to him. "I want to help you in any way I can." I was only about three feet away from him. He still had the axe in hand as I continued to talk to him. He slowly put the axe down and walked out. He said something but I didn't hear him. I had no angry feelings against him. My love for this son was stronger than ever. I felt very sorry for him because he was such a nice boy and a good hunter. He'd always learned so quickly what I taught him about hunting. He'd also been doing really well in school but had started to miss a lot of school-days.

I was hoping someday he'd quit sniffing like his sister. My daughter had sniffed but quit. I loved my children just about all the same, but there were times when I loved this son more than the others. He respected the elders, attended school and helped us in many ways both outside and inside the house or tent. I always thought he'd finish his education and work for his people but I knew that the only way he and my other sons would quit sniffing was if they decided for themselves.

Over the years I saw many kids sniff gas anywhere, like on the road. I'd ask them to throw away their bags of gas. Sometimes they did and other times they refused. I wondered why there were so many kids sniffing gas. My son

Napeu had gone to a solvent abuse program in another province. While he was in Goose Bay with his brother he went to school and never sniffed but when he came back to Davis Inlet he started to sniff again within days.

I wasn't only concerned for my own children. I thought kids were sniffing gas because we were in an isolated community. There was no place for them to go to have fun like playing hockey, swimming, playing pool or going out to restaurants. I thought the kids themselves needed to talk to the leaders to tell them what they wanted to see in our new community. If we didn't pay attention to the kids no expert in the world would ever solve the problem.

One day I found a typed note on my desk with fourteen statements from concerned people in the community. The first statement was that the council had failed to deal with the gas sniffing crisis. This was exactly what I thought. Many times at council meetings I'd said the biggest problem in our community was gas and glue sniffing but the Chiefs never seemed to hear my concerns. I felt like we were standing by, watching our very own children suffer. The alcohol and solvent abuse problem was in our hands to solve. We couldn't depend too much on *Akaneshau* people or other Native people from the West. We had to try to heal our community in our own way.

I thought many young people must feel left out and that no one cared for them. Many told me about their feelings. We needed strong leaders who seriously wanted to find ways to heal our community. The most important thing was to find staff to work with the young gas sniffers, people who were serious about helping troubled youth and who wouldn't get tired of them. The best people to do this work were former gas sniffers who'd quit. Their own experiences with solvent abuse might be able to help other kids. Every effort was worth a try to help our young people.

The year before we moved to Natuashish both my sons Pien and Napeu quit sniffing but now they had a different problem. These two sons and so many other young people in Natuashish started having problems with drugs. There were also still gas sniffers in the community. Not much had changed.

IN SEPTEMBER OF 1998, plans were underway for a third leadership retreat in Border Beacon. The retreat was going ahead even with the resignation of the Chief. Two other retreats had already been held in the previous year, one in Flowers Bay and the other one in the community. The Chief had invited me to attend these retreats but I never stayed long at either one. I wasn't interested because it seemed to me like we were just playing a game.

I decided to give this retreat another try although I didn't really expect anything good to come out of it. I didn't expect it to work but as I participated in meetings every day I began to think this retreat was very important to every one of us. I started to think the retreat could be very worthwhile. We tried to address all the problems we were having with our leadership. I could see people were very excited about this retreat. Part of me still had concerns. I didn't know why this retreat had to be held in Border Beacon. It was very expensive to move all the people there. I knew if we could only work together we could improve relationships in the community. Would we be able to do that after the retreat? I took the minutes on what was being and wrote a short report when it was all over.

When the facilitator of the retreat, Jerry Kerr, introduced himself and his partners he said they all had experiences as Chief and Vice-Chief in their communities. He told us that the four of them did not have any answers to our problems. He talked about how many people had come in the past to tell us what to do but he believed that we needed to run our own affairs. Outsiders had thought they could do a good job but they didn't know our culture and way of life. When people from outside gave us advice, it couldn't work because everything had to come from our people to help our community heal. He gave the example of children being sent out to treatment programs. Some came back in good spirits but others hadn't changed at all. Jerry said he and his partners were invited guests. The community had decided to hold the retreat and they were there to help us plan for our future. Everyone there understood that we had serious problems. Jerry told us we'd have the opportunity to all hear from each other about how we saw these problems. We'd talk about how we could work together and how we could make things work. It was up to us to make this retreat work. If we didn't, our problems would only get worse. Jerry and his team couldn't make the retreat succeed. It would have to come from the people. He told us that he had twenty years of experience doing this kind of work and this was the first time he felt a retreat like this might not succeed. How long the retreat would last was up to the people.

At first the retreat was more like a teaching session than training, not what I had expected. One facilitator talked about how man and woman came to live on earth, about the Creator, the Spirits and the seven laws of creation: love, kindness, sharing, respect, truth, humility and courage. He used many examples of other Native peoples' cultures. I thought he was trying to tell us how to run our own affairs. As he talked I began to understand why he was using all these examples, but I wasn't very comfortable with what was happening. Our elders were there and they were our advisors. I just listened and wondered whether this person had any respect as he tried to teach us these things. I wouldn't have felt this if the elders hadn't been there. Sometimes it sounded funny and weird when he used too many examples and stories of other cultures.

Then this guy started talking about the three groups in the community: the Band Council, the staff and the public. Each had their own opinion and didn't want to talk about them. Young adults especially could understand what he was saying. The band council was not in the habit of providing information to the community and many people didn't know what was really happening. We were divided and not working together. Too many people were complaining too much. The band council was misspending funds and the people felt frustrated and mistreated.

The facilitator talked about how expectations, values and pressures created communication problems. He talked about clans within the community. He told us this workshop would be tough, that the problems that led to the need for this retreat were serious. He advised people not to attack each other over personal issues. We had to deal with our communication problems. Some people wondered whether we would make decisions at this retreat and we were told we would at least make a plan to deal with the problems.

A former Chief got up to say she'd written a letter on behalf of the community to this last Chief not because she was angry at anyone but because she felt she had a right to know how the council was spending money. She said when people stood up at a meeting to express their concerns it didn't mean they were angry or their comment was a personal attack. She said for the community to be healed we had to speak up.

We split up into four groups. My group talked about the position of a band bouncilor, what authority a councilor had and what his duties were for his people and community. The other three groups talked about the roles of the Chief, the staff and the public. We all came together to share our separate discussions. We didn't agree about everything but it was very helpful and easy to understand what other people thought. Everyone had a chance to say something.

The facilitator also talked about how the band council should hire people, how positions had to be advertised in public places. The person who applied for that job had to be a good person. Some of us wondered what was meant by the word "good." We were told it meant a person with qualifications. I asked what happened if the brother or the sister of the Chief applied for the job. If that person was qualified, should they be hired? It was suggested the Chief should not be present during that hiring process. The hiring committee would make that decision.

The role and responsibilities of the Chief were discussed. When a big issue arose in the community, whether good or bad, it was not just the Chief's responsibility. For example, if a protest took place in the community and someone was hurt, who would take the responsibility? We couldn't blame the Chief. We had to blame ourselves. When something serious happened in the community, like an accident or gas sniffing, it didn't only affect only one person or family. It affected the whole community.

We talked about how politics were very new to us. They weren't part of our way of life in the past. We talked about life in *nutshimit* and life in the community and who our leaders were in the old days. Akat Piwas said that when they were in *nutshimit* they felt comfortable and happy because the land was so beautiful. There was clean water to drink. They felt healthy. There was no alcohol. People got along well with each other. We ate fresh meat and life was very quiet. In the community, people didn't often visit each other. There was drinking, children sniffing gas and many different bad things were happening to people. In the old days, people looked after the elders and had respect for each other. Did people share as much when they were in the community? People did share a lot of food but not things like televisions.

In the past an experienced hunter would be the leader or *utshimau*. A person who killed the most animals would automatically become an *utshimau* and the person who decided when people should move from one place to another. The retreat facilitator said that the federal government didn't want to negotiate or make a deal with an expert hunter – with someone who had killed a lot of caribou. They had to deal with people who had more control, like a band council.

I thought about how politics had created a lot of problems in our community, how some leaders felt they knew better than anyone else how to do things in the community but that wasn't so. We all knew what we wanted for the future of our children but we were keeping everything inside. We weren't talking to each other and that was really hurting us. Some people were afraid to talk; others felt shame. They felt useless. All Innu were equal. We were all very strong but we just didn't see that. If all Innu worked together we would have one strong voice.

We talked about whether we should have an elder for Chief. We could have a new policy that only an elder over sixty years old could run for Chief. One elder, Uniam Katshinak, said he thought it would be good because it wasn't easy for young people to negotiate with governments. An elder would have more experience and know how to answer all the questions about the Innu in the past, the present and the future. Some people thought that a person with a criminal record should not be allowed to run for Chief. By criminal we didn't mean someone who'd killed a caribou when hunting season was closed but a person with a serious criminal record.

The facilitator told us that in his community a person running for Chief had to be thirty-five years old (or older) and had to speak both his language and English. This person had to have a lot of experience or already have been elected councilor. When the Chief was elected they held a peace pipe ceremony. The Chief would hold a sacred thing in his hand, something like a *teueikan*[1], and say: "I commit myself to listen, hear and work with the people and to follow the truth of my people. The Creator is watching. As Chief I am here to do what my people want me to do. I am your servant."

Uniam thought the facilitator was giving us too much advice and trying to tell us what to do. His words weren't translated so the facilitator never knew what was said. Uniam wondered about decisions being made during the retreat. What about all the people in Davis Inlet who didn't know what was going on here? We would have to let them know what had happened.

Kiti Rich thought it was a good idea to have a ceremony for the new Chief and suggested holding a community feast to recognize the new Chief. Akat Piwas also thought we should have a feast when the Chief resigned so that

[1] Innu drum

he'd feel respected and leave his position in peace. It would be a ceremony of special thanks to show our appreciation for what the Chief had done. This would help people work together more closely.

We also talked about the roles and responsibilities of the councilors. They were there to share the leadership with the Chief. They could be given specific responsibilities such as health or education.

The following day the deputy Chief resigned. When I arrived for the session his letter of resignation was posted on the wall. The Innu decided to meet without the facilitators that morning. Only one person did the talking. I thought it was a waste of time. He talked about his personal problems and how past leaders had spent the money. He said that as a leader he had tried to help the elders one time but when people had started to complain he hadn't bothered to help them anymore. He never said what he'd done to help them. He accused some people of saying bad things about others in small groups at this retreat. He said he'd run for councilor in this next election. He thought whoever was elected Chief would never be able to make a difference. Things would only get worse. People would fight each other and the council building would get beat up. He thought nothing would change. He left and no one knew why he'd said these things. Maybe he didn't quite understand what the leadership retreat was all about.

The facilitators joined our meeting again and we went on to talk about conflict of interest. This was starting to be a big issue in our community with all the joint ventures and relocation. People were having a hard time understanding what was meant by a conflict-of-interest. It wasn't easy to translate because we didn't have any Innu words for it. The facilitator told us that everything could be a conflict-of-interest for leaders with the size of our community. I disagreed with him. Past and present leaders knew about conflict-of-interest and people had a right to complain about this issue.

We were told that an elected Chief or councilor was not allowed to get involved in any businesses or joint venture to avoid any conflict-of-interest. A councilor couldn't have a job with the Band Council but he or she could work anywhere else. Another policy was that only Councilors who didn't have a job would get an honorarium for attending a council meeting.

We also talked about how decisions should be made at a full council meeting, not just between the Chief and a couple of councilors. If a decision was required about a really big issue, a public meeting should be called to get the community's input. The Chief and councilors should not do favours for their friends or relatives, nor should they provide alcohol to the community. They should stay sober and free of drugs, not only from Monday through Friday but right to the end of their term.

The voting age was another topic of discussion. In Sheshatshiu the age was sixteen. We decided to keep it at eighteen. We also agreed that a person should be thirty-five to run for Chief and twenty-one to run for councilor. We decided there should be six councilors and one should be appointed Acting Chief for when the Chief was out of town.

We talked about budgets and the problem of spending money on things that weren't in the budget. Another problem was the requirement to send back leftover money at the end of the fiscal year. One elder asked why the money had to be sent back when we had so many financial difficulties in the community. The last time he'd gone out to hospital he had to pay his own way home when he was finished with the doctor. Non-insured benefits from the federal government used to cover almost any health-related issues but now there were limits. Health Canada would only pay so much for prescriptions, for glasses, transportation, drugs, treatments and escorts for children to go to hospitals.

With education funding the more students attended school, the more funding we got. Adult education was very important for our community. Many drop-outs were coming back to upgrade themselves. This was a good sign for life at the new site.

One elder asked about band council purchases of ATVs. We were told that the band council would pay a subsidy and each person would pay the rest of the cost. Where was that money going – to the dealer or the band council? We were told the money from the community member and the band council went directly to the dealer.

Jerry Kerr talked about the present council's budget deficit and how we were only halfway through the fiscal year. He warned us if the council kept spending at this rate the Federal Government might decide to appoint someone from Indian Affairs to control our spending the following year. The government could also decide to take over relocation funding.

The good news was that the council had negotiated additional funding with Indian Affairs. Our leaders would have to be very careful about how they spent the money. They might have to lay off some employees and cut expenditures. Some of us wondered where funding for healing would come from and we hoped council would still have funding for treatment programs.

Everyone seemed to understand what was going on at the retreat. The only minor problem was that not many people spoke up. Most of the people who spoke were former leaders or elders. This was okay because they spoke on behalf of the community. This was the first time I'd seen a meeting go so well. Only one person had tried to interrupt, but without success. No one was disturbed by his action. Those attending understood the importance of the meeting for all the people of Davis Inlet including those not present. We knew about our past mistake of not working together.

One comment made by a woman really touched me. I could feel every word she said. "When we are in *nutshimit* we are very close together. We respect and support each other. In the community we're divided. We hear many different stories which turn us against each other."

People who had been upset and angry were able to talk about the lack of communication from the leaders. We knew money wouldn't solve our problems. Words and actions were much stronger. People had to start talking to each other more. News traveled fast when the leaders were against each other. It hit the media and everyone heard about it, including our *Akaneshau* supporters and the governments. When the leaders and the public were against each other the governments just relaxed. This was good news for them because they knew we were going nowhere while we fought with each other. We needed to understand how the governments were playing these kinds of games with us. The new council had to understand that it couldn't do whatever it wanted. It needed to take issues to the public for their approval. Leaders needed a lot of feedback from the community to do good work.

Although not all the leaders were present at this retreat, I thought it was well organized and the facilitators did a good job. I was especially thankful to the elders attending the retreat. It was very important to hear their stories of the past. I thought it was about time that we gave them something in return. We often said that we respected our elders but we didn't show it. What could we do to make them feel respected? It had to be something from our culture. Maybe we could fly them out in *nutshimit* for a week or two, or a month. The council could hire sober people to work for them while they were out there if they couldn't do things for themselves.

On the last day of the retreat the Chief or band councilors were not present. Two more councilors had resigned and the remaining councilor had no power at all. Band council elections were called for October, 1998. Nine people ran as councilors and two people ran for Chief. I was elected councilor.

In January 1999, our council submitted an eight-point plan for healing to the governments. The Mushuau Innu Healing Strategy outlined six issues we wanted to address: 1) Mushuau Innu governance, 2) policing, 3) justice, 4) youth forum, 5) recreation and 6) family treatment. We hoped our plan would work out okay before relocation.

In March we had another community gathering about forty kilometres from Davis Inlet in a beautiful place called Miste-shuapi. After the leadership retreat in Border Beacon, Jerry Kerr and his team had prepared a report and recommendations. They were invited to the gathering. Most people were hoping the recommendations would pass but only a few people showed up at the meeting. One leader suggested we hold a public meeting in the community in June when all the people were back from *nutshimit*.

We continued to have problems with the way our bandcouncil was run. I figured these kinds of problems would continue to happen until Mushuau Innu governance was in place.

W HILE WE CONTINUED to have problems with our council, the Innu
Nation had developed into a strong organization. It was a good thing the
Innu Nation was working with both band councils of Sheshatshiu and Davis
Inlet. Innu Nation leaders were meeting with governments on the very big
issues of land rights, the hydro development of the Lower Churchill, the Trans-
Labrador Highway, the Voisey's Bay mine project, forest developments and
others. I didn't want to see the Innu Nation collapse. Without it the band
councils had no power against governments. I hoped the Innu Nation would
always be front and centre in our struggles, with the two band councils at its
side to back it up and show all their support. If the people supported the Innu
Nation, the band councils had no choice but to also stand behind it.

Some of us understood that developments might not happen for a number
of years but we had to be prepared. Our leaders couldn't just wait for these
things to happen to react. The Innu Nation and the band councils needed to
have a long-term plan. If a company decided to start a development, what
action would the Innu take? Would they sit down with the company to
negotiate an Impact Benefit Agreement?

We had so many issues to deal with. In 1996 a land rights framework
agreement was signed in St. John's after the Innu Nation held a referendum in
both communities. The board of directors along with Innu Nation staff and some
elders attended the signing ceremony. We knew there was nothing to get excited
about and we still had a long way to go. The agreement was only the list of
things we all agreed could be talked about at the negotiation table. We figured it
would take at least another five years before a final agreement was reached.

According to our lawyers, the government's land claims policy stated that
if we got more land through a final agreement we'd get less money for
compensation. If we went for less land we'd get more money. I thought it was
better for us to get more land for the future. It would be nice to have a piece
of land for our grandchildren and their children. I worried that money would
only create more social problems in our communities.

In the spring of 1998, a big land rights meeting was being held in
Sheshatshiu to discuss land selection – what land the Innu would legally own if

they signed a land rights agreement. The meeting was part of a community consultation the Innu Nation was holding to let the people in both communities know the details of what would be included in a land rights agreement and what self-government would look like. Two Twin Otters were chartered to bring people from Davis Inlet to Sheshatshiu for the meeting. I didn't attend, although I was invited. I thought thirty people from here were enough.

Both federal and provincial negotiators were there to listen to the people's concerns. Or so they said. What the Newfoundland government was proposing for Innu lands meant nothing to us. The government was prepared to give only forty-five square miles. Any person could walk that distance in one day. This offer was totally unacceptable. How could they offer us this size of land when they knew the land belonged to the Innu? No Innu had ever signed any papers to give away any of our vast territory. There was no way we could accept this measly offer. We needed a much bigger piece of land to survive with our culture of hunting, fishing and trapping.

For co-management lands – lands to be managed by both Innu and government – we were told two Innu would sit on the management board along with two representatives from the province and two from the federal government. The chairperson would always have the final say, whoever that person was. We could see this was the governments' proposal and they had the most members on that board.

It was always very hard for the Innu and governments to talk about the land. I thought governments and companies should've been proud that there were so many different kinds of animals in Labrador. Governments especially should've been trying to protect them like the Innu had done for thousands of years. We'd always survived from the wild animals. The foods we ate come mostly from these animals. Berries and medicines come from the many different kinds of plants and trees. We believed the land, the trees, berries, the animals, the water were sacred for everyone on earth. Many Innu had landed in jail trying to protect our land and animals.

Governments were trying to tell us they could rebuild the land after they damaged it but the land and the animals aren't like machines. Once the land was destroyed or polluted it became a dead land. Once the environment was poisoned, the habitats of the animals were no longer safe. The food they ate was no longer safe.

We knew, for example, if mining went ahead at Voisey's Bay that the lakes in the area would become dead lakes. The government never understood what our respect for the land means. In our language, the word for respect of the *Aueshish-utshimaut*[1] and of the land, wild plants, rivers and lakes – this kind of respect – is a very big word *Ishpitenitamun*. This word means respect for the elders, respect for Mother Nature and all its animals. My late father used to say to me, "Respect the snow, water, any kind of weather. Don't ever fool around with it. If the Spirit is angry it could take your life. Most importantly you must always respect the animals you kill. The meat must always be shared with others. It must never be wasted." This is the kind of respect we meant with this word.

Every time we told the government we wanted to protect the animals and the land for the future of our children they talked about cows, sheep and chickens – how these animals lived near big cities and there was nothing wrong with them. I thought governments should've known better than to tell us these lies. We knew farmers had to inject their animals with antibiotics to protect them from disease. When animals ate plants from polluted areas, diseases could spread quickly from one animal to another and then possibly to humans who ate the meat.

For thousands of years before any *Akaneshau* man set foot on our Native Land, which they now called Canada, Aboriginal peoples survived from wild animals and fish. There was no such thing as flour, tea, sugar and butter on this land. Now the government was trying to control everything in Canada. Over the centuries Aboriginal people were forced to negotiate with governments for their land rights. I thought this was not right. Governments were the ones who should be coming to us to negotiate and prove their claim to our land. All of Canada was Aboriginal peoples' land. In order for us to keep our culture and to survive as Innu I thought we should we never extinguish our rights. This is what the government was asking us to do if we signed a land rights agreement.

An elder appointed to represent us at the land rights negotiation table told me once he thought the Innu would be the ones to make the decision about how much land we wanted and how much we would offer to the governments. After attending a few meetings he realized that we were negotiating with the governments for our very own land.

"It's very strange to me," he said. "I've never seen this kind of negotiation in my life. To make our children hunters and trappers and to keep our culture

---

[1] Animal Spirits or Masters

alive, we'll need a large piece of land for the future generations. What are the government people thinking?"

I felt the same way. For over twenty years we'd been sitting at this land rights negotiations table. I don't know how many different Innu negotiators we'd had over the years but we always had the same lawyer at the table. When I worked with the Innu Nation I attended most land rights meetings in Ottawa, St. John's, Sheshatshiu or Davis Inlet. Always there were arguments between the three parties. Sometimes it was about how the wording needed to be changed, sometimes about when the next meeting would be held. It was looking like the talks would never resolve anything. Would it take twenty-five years or more? This was a long, long time to have to negotiate something that really belonged to us already. Many elders and young people passed away during that time, never to see the final settlement. The province and federal government didn't really care how long it took because they just let big developments like mining, the Trans-Labrador Highway, the Lower Churchill hydro project keep right on rolling. The land rights negotiations still had a long way to go. No one knew when a settlement would be reached. We just waited, hoping there would be Innu lands left to negotiate for the future of our children and their children. I wondered what would become of our young people when our elders were gone. Who would take the lead? I hoped our culture wouldn't get lost between this and the next generation.

I worried that money was becoming ever more powerful in our community. Our leaders seemed to be more and more interested in forming partnerships with big companies to make money for themselves. Money was a good thing. We all needed money to buy necessities for ourselves and our communities but money could also create a lot of problems. It made people go against each other and divided communities. It created inequalities and jealousies. It was used to buy alcohol and drugs. People who could buy these substances could also buy boats, trucks or skidoos and accidents could happen. With more drugs and alcohol we'd see more suicides. I worried that only a few of us thought like this and we'd be unable to stop our leaders from signing away our land because partnerships and money were leading our leaders astray.

Our problems with the provincial and federal governments continued. They were always trying to get their own way and making all kinds of decisions on behalf of the Innu people. We knew what was best for us. They had no right to make decisions for us. Sometimes they had us cornered. In the late 1990s, the Innu began negotiating with Canada about getting registered as Status Indians. This was after we received a letter from Indian Affairs in 1996. The letter stated we had to be registered as status Indians under the Indian Act in order for Canada to recognize us as Innu. The letter also talked about setting up reserves for our communities. The letter meant nothing to me. I didn't know if our leaders would accept this proposal. I was hoping they wouldn't. I was sure the Innu Nation would never accept it but I didn't know where the two band councils stood on this issue.

I'd met many Native people from across Canada. Most were registered and lived on reserves. I asked them about their life on reserves and how they managed as their population grew. What happened when there was no more space to build any more houses on their reserves? They had to build houses on Crown land and then their people had to pay taxes like everyone else who lived off-reserve. One good thing about reserve status is that people didn't have to pay income tax or sales tax. There were many stores off reserve that didn't accept their status cards and they had to pay taxes when they bought things from those stores. I told them how useless my status card was in Labrador. I had this card because my late father was registered in Quebec. When the Quebec Innu were registered, some Sheshatshiu Innu families – the Andrews, Gregoires and Ashinis – were also registered because we must have been baptized in Sept Isles.

For a number of years none of us ever thought about our status cards. It was nothing to get it since it was only a short distance to walk to the band council office when we were in Sept Isles. One day I decided to go to the band office – *Innu-mashinaikanitshuap*.

"Where can I get my status card?" I asked one of the girls.

"Right here," she said.

She never asked me that many questions, just my name, my father's and mother's names and my date of birth. She looked at the files.

"You were born on September 15, 1946," she told me.

"In Labrador my date of birth is registered as September 6, 1946," I said to her. "But since I was baptized in Sept Isles you must have the right birth date. There's no other George Gregoire in Labrador."

"Do you have a picture of yourself?" she asked.

I had to go and get my picture taken. Once I had the picture it didn't take long to issue my card. It was only good in Quebec and useless in Labrador. I was certainly not more Innu now that I had a card.

Governments had no right to tell us we weren't Innu because we weren't registered under the Indian Act. They should've known better. They knew our people never came from Europe or any other foreign land. We'd always been here on this land called Nitassinan. We had our own culture, values, language and way of life. Aboriginal people in Canada weren't Indians. *Akaneshau* people might have called us Indians like we were from India or tribal names such as Mohawk, Naskapi, Montagnais or Mi'kmaq, but we had our own names for our peoples in our own languages. If we spoke to the government people in our own language, they wouldn't understand a word we said. What kind of proof or evidence did they need before they recognized us as Innu?

I thought if the Innu were forced to live on reserves it would be like being put in jail. Our culture and Innu way of life would disappear more rapidly. This was why Canada was offering us registration and reserves. They might recognize us as Aboriginal people but they wanted us to live like *Akaneshau* people. Reserves would be the end of the road for us. But while I didn't think we should have to be registered for governments to recognize us as the Innu of Labrador, I also didn't think we should have to pay taxes. Anything purchased by the Innu outside the community but delivered to an Innu community should also be exempted. Innu people who worked in the community shouldn't pay income taxes but an Innu person working outside the community should pay. I knew that in one year in Davis Inlet we received about $3.6 million from the government but over half a million went back in taxes.

When Minister Tom Irwin, Premier Brian Tobin and our leaders Kiti Rich and Peter Penashue met to discuss the issue of tax exemption, the Minister said that taxation should be discussed at the self-government table in our land claims negotiations. Sheshatshiu Chief Pun[1] Rich thought the issue should be discussed before self-government was ever resolved. We didn't know how long

---

[1] Paul

land claims negotiations would take. With self-government we'd have to pay taxes in order to run our own government.

Our lawyer told us that our land rights negotiations wouldn't be affected if we accepted registration and reserves. Reserve status would be eliminated once a final agreement was reached. If we were status Indians we'd also qualify for different program funding from Indian Affairs that we couldn't access now.

We did decide to get registration when we moved to Natuashish, which was made a reserve. In the end it never made much difference. Status meant that we didn't pay taxes but only inside the community. Our deductions on our pay-cheques were not as high as they used to be. I still thought that living on a reserve was a type of slavery. Registration was nothing to be proud of. Innu on social assistance still got the same amount of money. Sometimes people got purchase orders from the band council but only for food. The province still ran the school and social services. It's not like the dollars started rolling in as a result of registration.

One morning I went to visit our land rights negotiator, Penute Michel, who was from Sheshatshiu. I asked him when our land rights settlement would happen. He said the target date for an agreement in principal to be signed was December 2000.

"What about the people here?" I asked him. "Do they know what is going on at these land rights meetings?"

"No," he said. "But once the agreement in principle is signed there'll be a community referendum in Sheshatshiu and Davis Inlet and people will have to vote yes or no."

"Why not explain to the people first what you think is going to happen if they vote yes or no?" I asked. "If the yes vote wins you'll have no worries but if the no vote wins what will the leaders do?"

"That's going to be a real problem because there are other Aboriginal people on the waiting list ready to negotiate land claims. Maybe the government will just suspend our talks."

"This is the reason the Innu Nation should hold a big meeting with the two communities and explain to the people where the Innu Nation stands. It's only three months away before you sign the agreement in principle. You need to talk to the people now, not later."

Penute had been working with the Innu Nation for years. I told him he should finish with that work. He said he was interested in working with a private business. But if he quit who would take his place? The money and business could wait. I told him it was way more important to see our land rights settled for the future of our children and the next generation.

IN OCTOBER 1998, I went to James Bay with an Innu delegation to visit a Cree community and hear their side of the story about Hydro-Québec. First we went to the hydro town of Radisson, about an hour's drive from the Cree community of Chissassibi to look at the hydro dam. A van was waiting for us to tour both inside and outside the hydro plant. A young gentleman from Hydro-Québec showed us around. It was sad to see how much land had been flooded by Hydro-Québec. I asked him if he had any information about the 10,000 caribou that drowned in the Caniapiscau River in 1984. He said that no water was released from the dam when those caribou drowned. They'd drowned because of heavy rains that lasted for many days. I didn't believe him. I knew that nature's heavy rains wouldn't drown that many caribou.

"Were there any gravesites in the area before it was flooded?" I asked. Before answering my question our guide walked us over to a monument.

"What's this for?" I asked.

"Yes, there were gravesites on the land that was flooded," our guide told us. "Hydro- Québec asked the Cree people if they wanted to move any graves before the land was flooded. The Cree people told Hydro-Québec they didn't want to disturb the graves." The guide went on to tell us Hydro-Québec had put up this monument in memory of the people who were buried in the flood area. The gravesites were all underwater now. I didn't ask another question.

The next day, Hydro people showed us around inside the Control Centre. I wasn't very interested to see everything on computer. They explained how their machines worked, things we knew nothing about. This wasn't what I expected to see or hear. I was hoping to hear about the impacts and benefits for the Cree people in James Bay, who I knew were the owners of the land.

We had lunch at the community centre in Chissassibi, where a Cree elder came up to ask us what we were up to.

"We're here to get all the information we can about Hydro-Québec and the flooding of your land," I told him.

"I'm sure no one around here feels good about it," he said.

I told him what our guide said about the caribou drowning.

"That's another crooked story from Hydro-Québec," he said. "As far as I know the dam at Caniapiscau was opened and the water released drowned the caribou. Not only 10,000. There were 23,000 that actually drowned. Inuit and Cree people were there after it happened."

"This morning when I was talking to the Hydro guy I had a feeling he didn't tell me the whole story," I said to the elder. "This is the information we really need. Thanks for sharing it."

"Do you guys need a ride to the airport?" he asked us. I was with George Nuna. On the way to the airport I asked him his name.

"George Rabbitskin," he said.

"My name is George and my friend here is also George," I told him.

"We three Georges on the way to the airport," he said, joking.

At the Montreal airport I met a friend, a French guy I hadn't seen for twenty years or more. He'd stayed at my house in Davis Inlet. Now he worked for Hydro-Québec.

"You look like a king now, the way you dress," I told him. "Is that because you're working with Hydro-Québec?" He laughed and didn't say a word.

Our trip to Chissassibi gave us information we could use in negotiations between the Innu Nation, Newfoundland Hydro and Hydro-Québec about developing hydro projects at Gull Island and Muskrat Falls on the Churchill River. The two companies were planning a partnership. They knew the Innu would give them grief if they didn't try to negotiate with us. Not long into these negotiations the Innu Nation election rolled around and the new president, David Nuke, pulled out of the negotiating table. He also wasn't interested in talks about an Impact Benefit Agreement with the Voisey's Bay Mining Company. He said he didn't want to take his people into dark places. He thought land rights and Innu self-government should be settled first before any big project went ahead. He said his people elected him knowing where he stood on these issues.

The Innu had never received any compensation or received any share at all of the profits from the massive Churchill Falls hydro project. Hydro-Québec received most of the profit, selling the electricity to Americans for hundreds of millions of dollars every year. It reaped almost all the profits and Newfoundland got a little. Innu land was damaged a lot while Americans were happy with their light bills.

We knew we'd made a lot of mistakes in the past, that we had to learn from them. I remembered the work I'd done in the Meshikamau area during the 1960s and '70s, paddling from the overflow Piastepeu, to Lobstick, Sangirt, Flour Lake and eventually Churchill Falls, where the town is now. We'd portaged from Flour Lake to many different ponds and the last pond where we camped was where the dykes were built near Churchill Falls. After the flooding the area was totally unrecognizable. The beauty of the land and ponds was no longer. The flooded area was now like a dead lake to us.

If the Lower Churchill development went ahead, I knew that Winikapau Lake would now be a second dead lake. It would be wider and longer but useless for hunting and trapping. The beautiful forest on each side of the lake would become a wasteland. Over half a million cords of wood would be wasted. Small animals would move to higher grounds. Many would die of drowning. The waterway would now be a reservoir and not a river, changing the habitat of the fish and the animals. Lower water levels down river would mean that rapids would no longer be safe for canoeing. Unseen rocks would make it too dangerous for canoes. New roads would bring more outsiders and locals who'd build new cabins for hunting and fishing. There'd be less fish in the rivers and the surviving fish wouldn't be safe to eat anyway because of the methylmercury. There'd be a lot of clear-cutting for transmission lines. Forestry companies would use the roads to clear-cut more trees. Nothing good would happen to the environment. I thought maybe there'd be some good things for outsiders but not for the Innu.

We'd already taken a stand with the hydro company. In 1993 the Sheshatshiu Innu ripped out their hydro meters to protest against Newfoundland Hydro and the Churchill Falls hydro development. They wanted to make a statement about how they got nothing, no compensation at all for the land they lost with the Churchill Falls hydro development. Provincial Justice Minister Ed Roberts suspended land claims talks when he heard about this action. I agreed with the Sheshatshiu Innu. They could keep begging for compensation at the negotiation table but they'd never get anything. Only the courts could decide who was right and who was wrong in this situation.

In 1999 we were invited to a meeting with Hydro-Québec in Sept Isle. Hydro-Québec never showed up. The company thought they were meeting with the Innu from the North Shore and Schefferville. When they found out the Labrador Innu would be there they decided not to come. Our meeting went ahead without Hydro-Québec.

That same year the Innu Nation decided to hold a community consultation to let the communities know what the Lower Churchill development would look like and what some of the impacts would be. They received money from Hydro-Québec and Newfoundland Hydro to do this. The problem was that the Innu Nation was already negotiating with the hydro companies. I thought the community consultation was supposed to come first, before any negotiations. Did the people have enough information to make a decision about this development?

What was going to happen when the community consultation report was finished? Would Innu negotiators listen to the people. Would they try to negotiate for the benefits people wanted or would they just look after themselves? The Innu had always tried to protect their land. I couldn't understand how we could become partners with the hydro companies. It would be like helping them destroy our land. I had many different thoughts about this. If compensation funding went to the Innu Nation or the band council no one would know where all that money would be spent. They might try to use that money for their own private businesses. I felt very sorry for my people, who didn't know what was going on inside the Innu Nation.

I worried the Innu Nation would give away too much and kill our culture. The leaders probably believed their culture was no longer useful. We could never go back to our way of life fifty years ago but we needed to continue to practise our culture and teach our children about our traditions. If there were too many developments on our land, where would we practise our culture? There was the threat of the Lower Churchill hydro project for the people of Sheshatshiu and Voisey's Bay on our side in Davis Inlet, and in the west we already had the Churchill Falls hydro project and the Wabush mine. In every direction there were developments: the Trans- Labrador Highway, the South Labrador Highway, forestry developments, low-level flying, national parks. The only way out was to the open sea but we couldn't practise our culture out on the open sea.

Maybe a few Innu would get short-term jobs on a hydro project but most jobs would be too technical. We heard the word "training" many times. Every time the government came to the a negotiating table with the Innu the first word we always heard was "training." They used that word just to make us say "yes" to any development. I agreed that training was important but would Innu get jobs once the training was completed? Some might but outsiders would always be number one on the list to get jobs. The Innu would always come second.

If we decided we should try to get something rather than just stand on the sidelines, I wanted the Innu Nation to make sure all Innu got benefits. The most important thing was for funding to go directly to individuals. At least people would feel respected and be able to buy things they needed like trucks, skidoos and boats. They'd feel free to go to *nutshimit* to practise their culture. The bad things from this kind of compensation would be dangerous drugs, alcohol, suicides and family problems. We could solve these if we hired professional people who could educate our people. I also wanted to see some compensation go to the band councils for cultural as well as education and training programs.

During the consultation I warned leaders to be careful. "Don't make too many trips down the slippery road of compensation just to give away what we depend on – the land that belongs to every one of us," I wrote in the questionnaire passed around the communities to find out people's opinions about the development and what the Innu Nation should do about it. I thought if the Innu didn't get what we wanted we should protest again against the hydro project or go to court.

During the consultation a group of Innu went to Churchill Falls for a tour of the project. We drove to the dykes on the top of the hill. From where we stood on the dyke I could see all the different lakes – Lobstick Lake, Sangirt Lake, Flour Lake – were now all flooded into one huge lake. For a thousand years, Innu from Quebec and Labrador had used this land for hunting and trapping and now it was a wasteland. I thought governments should be ashamed of themselves. How much profit had they made over those thirty years while the Innu just waited and suffered hoping that one day they'd receive compensation? Before another dam was built on the Churchill River the Innu had to get compensation for the Churchill Falls hydro project.

As we were leaving the building after the tour one of the Hydro ladies said to me, "Many visitors from other countries come in the summer. They really like Labrador. Most of them say the land is very beautiful around Churchill Falls."

"Why don't you tell them it was even more beautiful before Hydro flooded the land? That is what I'd tell them," I said to her. She nodded in agreement but she didn't seem so sure about my suggestion.

During the summer of 2000, my sister Tshaukuesh invited me to canoe with her from Churchill Falls to Gull Island to protest against the Lower Churchill hydro development. The trip was very interesting although we didn't portage at all. It brought back many memories. We took over a week stopping often and setting up our camps early in the day. Sometimes it was too windy to paddle especially around Winikapau Lake. We hunted a little. Everywhere we camped we had to find a small brook for drinking water because we knew the river was now contaminated with methylmercury because of the hydro dams.

On both sides of the river the trees, mostly black spruce, were so tall. Although I'd seen many trees in Labrador, this was the first time I saw this kind of tree, almost the same size in diameter from top to bottom. I thought those kind of trees only grew near rivers but I climbed a very steep hill and I was amazed to see all the trees up top just like the ones near the river. I found a nice spot to sit and looked down at the river. The first thing that came to my mind was my friend saying how all the trees would be cut down for use at the sawmill. It seemed impossible to me to cut all the trees that would end up underwater after the dam was built. It would take many years to do that work. Cutting the trees down didn't mean the forest would be saved, only more damage. With a 300-foot dam, a lot of trees would drown on both sides of the river.

For many years, my sister had been trying to save the land, rivers and its animals. At first the leaders were much more involved. Now they didn't seem to care. I didn't know why. Maybe they were seeing too many dollar signs at the end of the road they'd now decided to take.

Once when I was headed to Labrador City with my sister Nush[1] I noticed a road being built down to the river just a few kilometres away from Goose Bay.

---

[1] Rose Gregoire

"Do you know anything about this bridge?" I asked Nush.

"I'm not sure," she said. "It's probably for another forestry development on the other side of the river now that they're no longer cutting off the Grand Lake Road."

"This is just like the road from Goose Bay to Cartwright. It was never really discussed, not with the communities anyway," I said. "And do the elders sitting at the land rights negotiations table know anything about this road? Does the Innu Nation have any say about it?"

My sister never responded. I asked her another question.

"What do you think about national parks?"

"As long as the Innu can use that area I don't have a problem with them," she said.

"We know national parks are protected areas but you can't do any hunting in a park. I hope the Innu will be allowed to hunt for small game or probably we'll be allowed to fish in the lakes. Anyway, we don't know what will be in the agreement."

I was not against having an agreement as long as the Innu Nation and the governments could settle on one that wouldn't be a problem for us.

THE YEAR 2000 BROUGHT MORE TRAGEDY to our community. The first was when one of our elders passed away – my wife's mother Meneshkuesh. I was at meetings in St. John's when I heard she was very sick. The Chief and his two brothers had to go back to see their grandmother. I stayed behind with another councilor to finish the meeting. On Friday I took an early flight to Goose Bay and went straight to the hospital to see my mother-in-law. She was on oxygen and had an IV in her arm but she still recognized me. My wife and her sister were sitting beside her.

My wife told me her mother had asked to see all her grandchildren and great-grandchildren before she died. The next day they all arrived from Davis Inlet and came to the hospital. Every one of them gave their grandmother a kiss.

On that day, the 7th of January, my son Gerry and his girlfriend Shirley had a baby girl. The priest came to baptize the baby and my mother-in-law agreed to be her godmother. I watched her look at the baby, moving her hand and arms as she tried to hold her. With a smile on her face she looked happy to receive this special gift of being the godmother of my son's baby girl. The baby was also named Meneshkuesh, meaning "Pretty Girl." I looked at my wife and saw tears in her eyes. She must have thought many things in her mind about how her mother had taught her so many traditional things in her life.

On Saturday my wife was very tired so I told her she should rest and spend the night at the hotel. The next morning we were just about to go for breakfast when the phone rang. Shanut had to hurry to the hospital because her mother was now spitting blood. I'd already ordered breakfast with our children so I cancelled Shanut's order. I told her I'd be there as soon as I could. My mother-in-law was already unconscious and breathing with an oxygen mask when I got there. I knew how my wife and her two sisters felt as I stood in the hallway.

"Please try not to cry," I said to my wife. "Your mother has suffered enough. Don't expect her to live many more days."

On January 30th I stood by the doorway and watched my wife hold her mother's hand. Moments later I heard people crying inside the room. I recognized my wife's voice. I squeezed into the room. My father-in-law,

Tshenish, was still holding his wife's hand as Shanut and her sister Akat cried.

That evening, Shanut told me about the deep pain she'd felt watching her mother suffer. Although she missed her she was relieved that her mother's suffering was over. The body was flown to Davis Inlet on Sunday afternoon. On Monday we all returned home and the funeral took place on Wednesday.

In 1994 my mother-in-law had been very much involved in a protest in Ottawa. She wanted to show our young Innu leaders there was nothing to fear when there were land and animals to be protected.

"I'm here today because of everything that grows on earth," she told them. "I'm here because of everything the animals eat that is part of our own food too because we eat every kind of animal. That is why I'm here to protect the land."

In June another very sad day fell on our community. Shanut called out to me that she saw black smoke coming from somewhere in the middle of the community. I looked through the window and saw the smoke but I wasn't worried. I thought someone was just burning garbage. I gave my daughter the keys to my ATV to go see what was happening. Within minutes she came back to say Eric Mistenapeo's house was on fire and Eric was in the house. When he came out he was badly burned and taken to the clinic. He never made it.

The next morning I went to see Eric's mother and father. How many times had I gone to visit them in the past? I was hurting deeply when I saw them sitting in their bedroom. Edward was looking out of the window toward the spot where his late son's house had been. Manteskueu was crying. I sat between the two. Manteskueu started talking. She told me she'd been at the relocation camp at Natuashish when the chopper came to pick her up. I asked her if her son was conscious when she saw him at the clinic.

"Nikaui, I recognize you," her son said to his mother. "From now on I don't care what happens to me. It doesn't matter if I die because I have too many problems with my woman."

Those were the last words he said to his mother. She said her son had been very angry when he returned from the mobile treatment program. She didn't say why. Her son had poured diesel on the floor and tried to light it. Two people had witnessed him do this but had left him alone in the house.

Manteskueu said they should have stayed with him or invited him for a walk. I held her hand and told her I knew how she felt.

"Your son was such a nice young man," I told her. "I always respected him because he always showed respect to everyone in the community."

Given the size of our community everyone is deeply wounded when one person dies. I felt very sorry for the Mistenapeo family because their two daughters and son-in-law had already committed suicide. I wasn't sure whether this fire was an accident or a suicide. I kept wondering when these tragedies would stop. There'd already been too many suicides in the community. The message we were getting from our young people was unknown but I think they just wanted to be respected and loved. Kids were sniffing and no one seemed to care about them. When tragedies happened, people seemed to wake up but only for a short period of time. Sometimes it looked like leaders were trying to use the victims to get more money from the governments. This didn't solve our problems. The money was not going to bring the victims back to life.

One day after my mother-in-law passed away I told my wife that we should go to our camp the next day to check my fish net. I thought she'd be really excited about this trip.

"I planned to wash clothes tomorrow but I'll come anyway," she said.

We left early and crossed the neck north of Davis Inlet about five kilometres away. Shanut was driving my other skidoo so I waited for her. I asked if she remembered to bring cigarettes and matches. She checked the bags – no cigarettes and no matches.

"You keep going," I told her. "I'll go back to pick up cigarettes and matches. Wait for me at Daniel's Rattle."

I unhitched my komatik and went back to Davis Inlet. About an hour later I caught up with her. We arrived at our camp and after we had something to eat I told her we still had three hours of daylight, time enough to check one of my nets. We could check the other one the next day.

As I pulled out my net she never said a word, although I had twelve big chars.

"I'll leave the net for another week," I said to her. "Next time I'll pull it out for good."

Afterward I decided to go and cut some dry wood for the night. We ate fish for supper. Just before we went to bed I had to say something to Shanut.

"There's something strange going on with you," I said to her. "It's not about our relationship as man and wife. What's the problem?"

"I love to be out camping," she replied. "But every time I see the places where my late mother was before, I feel very lonely."

"Well, no matter where we go we won't ever find a place where your late mother has never been," I said to her. "We both know she's been everywhere in this part of Labrador."

"What if we moved back to Sheshatshiu?" she asked.

"That's going to be a very difficult decision for us to make," I replied. "But maybe you're right. We should move. It's been thirty years since I first came to Davis Inlet."

She wanted to continue talking about it.

"It's too early to talk about moving to Sheshatshiu," I said.

"Why?" she asked.

"Because in Sheshatshiu I'll need to find a job and we'll need a house."

The next morning we were up early. As I made the fire I looked outside to a beautiful day. Not so cold. At 9:00 I told Shanut I was going to chop a hole in the ice to check my other net while she finished washing the dishes. I'd wait for her there.

When I got to the ice I realized I'd forgot my ice chisel. I didn't bother to go back to get it because I knew Shanut would bring it when she came. I started to chop the hole with my axe. About a half hour later Shanut had still not shown up. I wondered what was holding her up since she'd almost finished the dishes when I left. The ice was too thick to chop with an axe so I decided to go get the ice chisel since I was only about a half mile from the tent. About halfway there I saw her coming. She'd brought the chisel and it didn't take long to dig the holes. I had 26 chars in my net. We put the net back in the water and drove back to our tent.

As we arrived at the camp I noticed one of the komatiks had been pulled away from the skidoo. I didn't see what was in the box. The tent was still warm but the only thing left was a kettle with tea on the stove, some bread, butter, sugar, a knife and spoon and a little leftover fish.

"Is the tea still warm?" Shanut called from outside the tent. "Should we eat before we go?"

"Leave for where?" I asked.

"For Davis. The stuff is all packed in the komatik and ready to go."

"Why are you doing this?"

"I thought you said we were going back today."

"Yes, but not this early," I said.

Shanut had always liked being in *nutshimit*. She never liked having to return to the community. She was always prepared to stay another night. Now she seemed too anxious to get back to Davis Inlet. I understood what she was feeling. There were many special reasons why she missed her mother so much. Most of the time she'd looked after her mother very well.

Both my wife and children continued to pressure me a lot to move to Sheshatshiu. I had two choices: to move to the new community of Natuashish or to relocate to Sheshatshiu. When I came to Davis Inlet in 1969 it was a nice quiet community but things had changed a lot in 30 years. The culture was still the same but the old ways were partly gone. Sheshatshiu also had many social problems. I didn't want to move because of the culture or social problems. I just thought thirty years was long enough. It was time to move back to the place where I really came from and where my late father and mother were buried. I would move to show my respect for the many things they'd taught me in my life – the best gift I could ever receive.

At the same time I really wanted to see what the new community would be like. I knew living conditions would be much better than in Davis Inlet. I wondered if we'd be able to afford the monthly rent. I thought alcohol and solvent abuse would be the biggest problems if they weren't solved before the move. A new treatment centre in Sheshatshiu had opened its doors to serve young people, not only Innu from our two communities but also Aboriginal youth from all Atlantic provinces. I hoped the Innu counselors would do a good job. I also hoped that things would change after the move.

CONSTRUCTION OF A WHOLE NEW community at Natuashish went on for many years as costs rose steadily. In the spring of 1999, I attended a meeting in Ottawa with the federal government's Treasury Board about relocation funding. We were told we had to cut $13 million from our proposal. We had to give up our plans to build an indoor rink that would've cost $4 million. We still wanted to do our best to build the arena no matter what it would cost because our children needed a facility for recreation in winter and summer.

Both the CIBC and the Bank of Montreal offered to help us raise money for things that weren't in the agreement. We also knew that an Impact Benefit Agreement for the Voisey's Bay mine was on the table and negotiations were starting about the Lower Churchill hydro development. Money would come from IBA and we'd be able to pay back a loan.

As we saw the houses going up, people in the community began to get excited about the move. This would be the first time that Mushuau Innu lived in houses with running water, a shower, and enough room for all our own children. We still hoped this wouldn't change the Innu way of life for a number of years yet. I hoped we wouldn't forget our culture, and people would still want to live in tents in the summer and winter, including young people.

At the same time I had growing concerns about what would happen after the move. There was the big problem of people having to make monthly payments. For how long? I didn't know. I had no idea what would happen if people couldn't afford to make their payments.

In July 1999, our healing co-ordinator arranged for a number of us to meet in Goose Bay with the RCMP and Social Services to look at gas sniffing, alcohol and the children. We also wanted to discuss a proposed by-law to ban alcohol in our community. The meeting didn't go anywhere because too many different issues were on the table at the same time.

The next day we had another meeting with the consultant, Jerry Kerr, and the Sheshatshiu band anager, Marcel Ashini, to discuss housing policy. Marcel explained that our housing policy would be the same as the one for Torngat Housing, Melville Native Housing and Newfoundland and Labrador Housing.

The meeting continued all morning with Jerry Kerr's consulting group. I thought we should be meeting other Native people who'd experienced relocation. We could ask them about their housing policies. We wouldn't have to use their policies but we could get an idea of how their policies worked. I couldn't understand why our housing co-ordinator hadn't even been invited to the meeting. He worked for the Housing Authority whose mandate was to look after housing policies. The Housing Authority was a new department appointed by the band council to be responsible for all issues related to housing. The band council had also decided that one councilor would oversee the Housing Authority.

The federal government told us at this meeting that they would only cover half the cost of each new house. Where would the rest of the money come from? It wouldn't be hard to get additional funding but how would we pay it back? We'd never had this kind of policy before. It would be very difficult to enforce because we now had free housing. I thought people shouldn't be surprised to have to pay rent but surely the people couldn't afford to pay $700 or $800 a month. There were two ways to do this. One option was for the Band Council to own the houses, rent them out and take responsibility for maintenance. The second option was for people to pay a monthly amount to eventually own their home after a number of years – like a mortgage. In that case maintenance would be the homeowner's responsibility. The Housing Authority would have to decide what they thought was best for the community. No decision was made at the meeting.

After the move no one was asked to pay the rent. Instead people over 60 years of age received free fuel for heating. I thought the new Housing Authority was doing a good job. Did they come up with money to cover the rent? I didn't know but I thought whatever they were doing was good for our new community.

In the meantime, we were still struggling to make our community stay healthy. Part of the problem was that we could no longer control our children. In the past, parents could control their own kids. Now the young people were controlling their parents. We weren't afraid of our children but we just couldn't punish them anymore because if we did we'd end up in jail. Now no matter how old the child was he or she would report their mother or father to the police. We couldn't touch our children because of government laws. Part of our problems, such as solvent abuse, could be blamed on these government laws.

In Davis Inlet alone a lot of money was being spent on mobile treatment programs, on Nechi training for counselors and to send people to outside treatment centres. Some people completed the programs and managed to stay sober for long periods of time but then slipped again. Gas sniffing seemed to be getting worse. If we hadn't depended on outside treatment programs, Nechi training and outside elders, the money could've been better spent in our community or in *nutshimit*. Our elders would've had a better idea of how to heal our community if they'd been consulted but our Nechi trainees thought outside counselors and elders were better qualified to help our people.

Governments also didn't recognize our elders as healers. I didn't think governments would ever approve funding to pay for the involvement of our elders in our healing programs. Governments believed experienced counselors and outside elders would solve our alcohol and solvent abuse problems but these people didn't understand that their culture was different. During our many meetings, government officials continued to tell us what we should do for our communities. They claimed to know our way of life so well but I thought that when an *Akaneshau* person gave us advice, in his mind he was thinking about the *Akaneshau* culture and his own ways.

"Okay, here is the money," the government might say. "Join the Voisey's Bay Mining Company and you'll make a lot of money for your communities. Your troubles will be over."

That advice wouldn't work because money was not the answer to our problems. Maybe if we knew how to spend money properly it might help us with our healing. We had to learn how to work together to remove the block that kept us from coming together – alcohol. I thought if we were to heal ourselves we had to use our own culture. We needed to consult our elders to find our healing through our way of life. In counseling we had to use many different aspects of Innu culture.

How many people stopped drinking or sniffing gas? No more than ten people who'd been to the Poundmakers Lodge were still sober today. Had any kids stopped sniffing gas? Millions of dollars were spent on healing. I looked at the money spent on mobile treatment programs – on charters, plywood and lumber, skidoos and private radio phones. We couldn't continue to spend the money on programs that weren't working.

To me the truth seemed to be that there were more people who'd stopped drinking on their own than those who attended treatment programs. Those who'd stopped on their own must've felt proud of themselves because they did it for their children. The Health Commission decided to honour these people. Each of them got a certificate from the Alcohol Program for the number of years they'd stayed sober. I was very proud of the Health Commission for recognizing the people who had stopped drinking on their own. The Health Director, Katnen[1], was doing her best to make this community come together to solve our community problems. I knew it must be a frustrating job but she was doing her best. I thought we needed to do more for our young people or we could expect more suicides. The recreation directors were doing what they could to help young people.

I worried that we'd be taking our social problems with us when we moved. The new community was not going to be so healthy because only the business people, their relatives and friends would be working. The majority of people would be left out, with no jobs and no income. If most people were unemployed and living on social assistance it would be very hard to solve the gas sniffing and alcohol problems. People wouldn't want to accept short-term jobs and lay-offs. Children would suffer the most and feel angry and very frustrated. Only God knew what would happen to our young people.

In the meantime, I decided to move back to Sheshatshiu in 2000 after having spent thirty-one years in Davis Inlet with my family. The reason I moved was very simple. I again slipped back into drinking after being sober for three years. I drank for about three months and quit again. My wife was also drinking. Our marriage almost fell apart. It was all my fault because I had an affair with another woman. Eventually my wife and I managed to patch everything up before it was too late. I can't say why and how it happened. My life was miserable during those three months. I had to go to court for assault. My wife laid the charges.

In spite of what I thought about treatment programs, I had to ask for help. During the month of April I decided along with my family to participate in a

---

[1] Kathleen Benuen

family treatment program in Sheshatshiu. The program really did something for us but six weeks was too short. I really found out for myself about the waste of money to bring people from the outside to solve our problems with all the travel costs, accommodation and their expensive fees. The program I attended with my family was an Innu program. Only *Innu-aimun* was spoken for six weeks. All the clients and counselors knew each other. If I'd gone to a B.C. or Ontario Aboriginal treatment centre I would've spoken only English. I wouldn't have been afraid to speak about myself because no one from the program would know the kind of person I was.

When I was in the family treatment program I spoke about myself. I wanted my family to hear my story about my past, the pain I kept inside for so many years. This was very hard to do. At the same time Shanut heard things she never knew before. She was also very open and told her story about the pain she'd covered up for so many years. I was deeply hurt when I heard her story. I guess she felt the same way. It took courage to talk and listen to each other but sharing our stories and our hurts was very helpful. We forgave each other. If I'd gone to treatment outside the community without my wife I could've talked and talked without worrying about my wife hearing the details of my past.

It was very important that we could do our healing work in *Innu-aimun*. We could be comfortable speaking our own language and not having to use translators to communicate with the counselors or others in the group. My wife, for example, would not be accepted to go to a treatment program outside because she doesn't speak English. Even if she was, she wouldn't understand a word of what other people were saying. Some government people think all Aboriginal people have the same culture and language.

The family treatment program really gave me a lot of strength to stay sober for many years to follow. All the counselors in that program were Innu and they were all qualified. I was so thankful to my wife for all her support during that program. It wasn't easy but we did it because we supported each other.

Later that summer the federal government made a commitment to the Sheshatshiu Band Council to purchase the Lobstick Lodge located west of Churchill Falls and to fund the family treatment program for the next five years. I applied for a job with the family treatment program and I was hired as a support worker and counselor. I don't know how many of us were hired, maybe twelve, with a mix of both men and women. Although I was never trained to do this kind of work, I had a lot of personal experience with alcohol and family problems and I felt very confident that I could do the job. Most people hired were young. One older woman was a little over sixty years old and I was fofty-five. I was very interested in my new job because the treatment program would be held in *nutshimit* and I always loved to be in *nutshimit*.

In the meantime, whenever I ran into people from Davis Inlet they always asked me the same question.

"When will you be coming back to Davis Inlet?"

"Maybe when the new community is built," I told them.

"If you move back to Davis Inlet we can renovate your house and there's always a job waiting for you," the Chief from Davis Inlet told me.

My position as counselor was very important. I was also working with the Innu Nation to help do land selection for Davis Inlet in the land claims negotiations – also very important work. It involved research with the elders about how the Innu used the land in the past and present. We'd look at maps to point out travel routes, camping areas, meeting places, ceremonial sites, hunting and trapping grounds and burial sites. I liked working closely with the elders and I had no problems talking with them. I respected them just as much as I respected myself. I told the Chief in Davis Inlet that it was very important to do this land selection with the elders because they knew the land better than we did.

In late November 2002, we heard that an order was signed by the federal government opening the way for Sheshatshiu and Natuashish to become reserves under the Indian Act. I'd moved back to Davis Inlet by then. People had mixed feelings. Some were excited but others were not very happy because they didn't know how the Indian Act would affect their children and grandchildren. I saw no reason to get excited because I didn't really know anything about the Indian Act. Maybe only the leaders knew what was good or bad about this new status. All I knew was that for many years the Newfoundland government had controlled the Innu and now control would be moved over to the federal government.

I figured it would probably be good for private businesses on the reserve. In the meantime, Innu people working at Natuashish wouldn't have to pay taxes starting that week but those of us still working in Davis Inlet had to pay taxes until we moved to the new community. In August the engineering company had told us 100 houses would be completed by the end of October and the target date for the move was December 14, 2002. By the end of November only 58 houses had been built. It looked like we'd be living in two communities for awhile yet. Indian Affairs suggested we move before Christmas and double up families in each house until all homes were completed. Two weeks before Christmas seemed a bad time to me to be moving. My house wouldn't be finished until late February or March. But I was happy the elders would be able to move and live in comfortable homes during the Christmas holiday. If I had to move I decided I'd just set up my tent in the new community. I'd been born in a tent and lived in one until I was twenty years old and I could still live in a tent whenever I felt like it.

As planned, people began to move from Davis Inlet to our new community of Natuashish. My children were happy and excited because their living conditions would improve. The new house had hot and cold water, a shower with a bathtub, and an oil and wood furnace in the basement. I decided to move my whole family from Sheshatshiu although my children liked Sheshatshiu better than Davis Inlet. My wife loved Sheshatshiu too but I didn't like it that much. I always wanted to go back to Davis Inlet, so after two years we moved back just before the move to Natuashish. After we moved to Natuashish I soon began to miss Davis Inlet. I'd first come to Sheshatshiu with my family around 1951 but after I married Shanut in 1969 I moved to Davis Inlet. It became my real home. It was hard to describe how much I missed Davis Inlet. I had so many friends who'd passed away there. It was a beautiful place to live, and the elders I spoke to felt the same way. Young people were the ones anxious to move to the new community.

THE NEW MILLENNIUM BROUGHT more and more worries about the kind of job the Innu Nation was doing. Our strong leaders were beginning to change. The president had fought for relocation and he'd been really outspoken during the protest against mining at Voisey's Bay. Although the company said it was only doing exploration work, it was still the beginning of a mine to us. This president was well respected in both communities but he began to lose support and eventually he stepped down from the position. He went on to work with the Sheshatshiu band council and moved to St. John's. He was now in charge of negotiating the devolution of services, part of a federal government plan to hand over the control and operation of education, health and social services to the Innu. Later he became involved with the Voisey's Bay Nickel Company.

In June of 2002, a referendum was held for a yes or no vote regarding the Impact Benefit Agreement for the Voisey's Bay mining project. I was working with the family treatment program in Sheshatshiu and I attended a public meeting at the band council building. Not many people got a chance to talk. The meeting was the just-sit-and-listen kind. I tried to bring up my concerns but I was told to let the lawyer and then an advisor finish. I knew I'd never get a chance to speak so I left before the meeting was over. I was deeply hurt and very frustrated. Most of us believed young people needed jobs but most Innu were not educated and had no skills to get well-paid jobs. Innu hired at the mine would only get labour jobs.

I later attended an elders' meeting at the Innu Nation office. I asked the Innu Nation consultant whether there'd be any training dollars for the Innu. He said there was $1.4 million set aside for training Innu people. I asked if this would be for every year over the next thirty years. He said this was one-time only funding. This seemed like a very small amount of money to me. What about the kids who didn't know what was going on today and the kids yet to be born? Would there be anything for them when they grew up? I thought the leaders only cared about the money, about their private businesses and things they could benefit from themselves.

In August that year I was back in Davis Inlet and out at a Daniel's Rattle relocation campsite. A friend of mine showed me a cheque worth $600 made out to his aunt.

"Do you know what this cheque is for?" he asked.

"I have no idea," I told him. "Maybe it's from the Voisey's Bay company." All Innu over sixty got $600 from the Innu Nation or wherever the money was coming from. I didn't know. Was this for every month for the next thirty years? It was probably a gift to the elders for having voted yes to let the Voisey's Bay project go ahead.

News soon started floating around the community that we'd received $1 million from the Voisey's Bay Nickel Company. The money went to the Innu Nation and no one really knew what was going on. Some people said skidoos would be purchased for every couple in the community, including common-law couples. Each couple received a request form to complete to get $6400. The form couldn't be processed until it was signed. Once the form was submitted we then received some kind of a voucher, not cash. We could choose from three items: a skidoo, an ATV or furniture. I signed the form along with my wife's name and chose to buy a skidoo. My daughter Jacqueline faxed it to the vice-president of the Innu Nation, Jimmy Nui. The balance owing on the purchases had to come from our own pockets.

After fifty or so people had signed the form, an Innu Nation employee came to my office with some documents in hand. He showed me a summary release form that each of us had to sign before anyone received the item of choice. Our lawyers had prepared this form that was part of the compensation deal in the Impact Benefit Agreement. I read all the pages and I was in total disagreement. I couldn't sign that form on behalf of my children or grandchildren. If I signed, I was agreeing never to sue the Innu Nation, the Voisey's Bay Nickel Company or Inco, or any of the people who worked for them. Even if the project turned out to have a lot of negative impacts on Innu harvesting in the future, the company or the Innu Nation would be able to tell the courts that any claim against them was not valid because we'd accepted this small compensation and signed their release form.

I told the Innu Nation employee that my signature would remain on that document for the next thirty years but my skidoo would only last two years or less. This compensation agreement really confused me. Why did I have to sign something now that could affect my children and grandchildren for decades?

A friend in the office told the guy from the Innu Nation not to get involved in this issue.

"Let the vice-president handle these forms himself," my friend advised him. "People in the community don't really know what they are signing. When they find out, the Innu Nation will be in trouble and they'll blame you."

That was the end of their conversation. I wrote a letter to the vice-president to explain how confused I was about the agreement. That very same day I received a response from both the vice-president and the lawyer but neither of them answered my questions. I wrote a second letter to the vice-president and this time I got no response at all. Later I heard they got rid of the release forms. We only had to sign a form confirming we'd received the items. I thought this compensation agreement would continue to be a big issue if people didn't know how the rest of the money was being spent. But for now most people had a skidoo that would help them make the move to our new community of Natuashish.

The Lower Churchill hydro project continued to loom just around the corner and the Innu Nation continued its negotiations with the hydro companies and the Government of Newfoundland. I happened to run into one of the Innu chief negotiators at the land rights table. He said he'd quit his job as negotiator because he didn't want to be in a conflict-of-interest position. I asked him what he meant.

"I'm involved in a private business with a company from Labrador City," he said.

"Most leaders are involved in businesses, too," I pointed out to him.

"I don't want people to complain," he told me. "My son is also working with the company, but it's not working out very well."

I asked him who his partner was and he told me it was another leader who'd also quit his job with the Innu Nation.

"We want to set up a private consultants' business," he replied.

"Do you think you'll succeed with this?"

"I'm not sure but now that I quit I never have any money. I think I might have to apply for that job again."

"Some people might already have applied for it."

A few days later I heard these two leaders had been rehired to work with the Innu Nation. People in Sheshatshiu couldn't believe their ears. I felt sorry for the other people who had applied for the two positions.

A few months later the Innu Nation disappointed me once again and I had to send a letter to its board of directors. I'd been a long-time employee of the Innu Nation. I felt I had a right to speak up. I was really upset about a decision they'd made to lay off a number of employees. I had no idea of the reasons for the lay-offs. Maybe the Innu Nation was short of funding or the money was being spent on something else. The decision was made during a teleconference meeting of the board with only one person from Davis Inlet present. The other Davis Inlet board members were all in *nutshimit*. I was in the office alone when the minutes from the meeting were faxed to our office the next morning. I was shocked to see the fat raises the leaders had given themselves. The negotiators also got a raise, and board members were to get back-pay from January for their attendance at meetings. Other Innu employees got nothing. There was no discussion about these employees or raises for them in the minutes. I would never have known this if I hadn't been standing by that machine.

Shortly after this meeting the Innu Nation implemented its decision to lay off some of its Innu employees. Some Innu employees were well-educated in the *Akaneshau* way. Others were not but they still had their own education in their way of life. Innu education could be far better than *Akaneshau* education in some situations. The president was well educated in the *Akaneshau* education and should therefore have known better about the conflict-of-interest of some leaders involved in business who also got fat raises. Employees who complained about the Innu Nation were recognized as bad people. Soon business people would be running our organization. Were these leaders just using the Innu Nation to be successful in their own business? They had nothing to lose. If they failed they'd still have their jobs. If they succeeded they'd quit and forget about us all.

A lot of money was also being spent on outside consultants. I often wondered if they really wanted to help or were they just playing a game with us. Maybe they were only interested in the money. I worried about the Innu people being laid off. How were they going to pay their loans at the bank? Our leaders were betraying their own people.

I never got a response to my letter to the board. If I had been an *Akaneshau* I would have got a response right away. There was nothing I could do. The way the leaders were running the organization didn't look good. Some leaders who'd been fighting hard for our people for years were now brainwashed by private business and government money. They'd get their way. We needed to order t-shirts with a picture of a dollar sign on them. That might be the only way to make the leaders listen to us. Money now had the power over the Innu Nation.

My thinking was that any Innu person could decide to either work for their people or work for a company. That was the choice but they should make up their mind. Joint ventures were not necessarily good or bad. Innu had to find a partner to start up a business because we didn't have the start-up money or know-how. Outside businesses were interested because they knew a partnership with Innu people would mean contracts with the band council or Innu Nation.

I could see a lot of problems with joint ventures. We saw it happen with the relocation contracts. *Akaneshau* business people were buying Innu people and using them to get these contracts and benefit from our communities. Some money went into the pockets of some Innu. Businesses hired a few local people. But I agreed with one friend who said that the rich were getting richer and the poor were getting poorer. In the 1970s, very few dollars were available in our communities. Now, in the 2002 relocation, the mine at Voisey's Bay and the Lower Churchill hydro development, *Akaneshau* business people all wanted a piece of the action and the only way to get it was to use Innu people.

People just didn't know what was going on. Joint ventures were creating a lot of divisions in both communities. Our people were against each other. Money was a power dividing the community and sending different groups in many separate directions. It made me sad to see this happening. My only hope was that we'd work together to heal our communities. I supported Innu companies 100 percent but I wanted Innu companies to do work on their own, not with outside interests. If the company succeeded, Innu people would own the business 100 percent, not 49.

At the same time, our elders were beginning to lose their voice. When I worked for the Innu Nation we always brought along an elder to every land rights negotiation meetings. Leaders were not inviting elders to those meetings anymore. Did they actually think they could negotiate better without an elder? Or were they too tired to look after the elder? Maybe they just didn't care what happened. In the old days our elders had used the land in many different ways to survive. Before any *Akaneshau* had set foot on our land all our foods and medicines had come from Nitassinan. For thousands of years our culture, our values and our way of life had been passed down from one generation to another. Our young leaders had to recognize that the elders were our special advisors. Without elders we'd get nowhere with these land rights negotiations. In meetings I attended, when we had difficulty answering a question from the governments we just gave our elders a chance to speak. They spoke from their hearts as experts about the land and wildlife. They spoke of things the government didn't like to hear but had to listen.

During one such meeting in Ottawa, a Sheshatshiu elder and I shared a hotel room. Early one morning we were sipping our coffee as he sat on the bed and I sat in a chair. I told him I had one important question to ask him. I knew he could easily answer a question about the land but I wasn't sure he could help me if my question was about anything else.

"I want to know about earthquakes, volcanoes, floods, tornadoes and landslides. Why are these natural disasters happening so much in Canada and elsewhere in the world?" I asked.

"Those things are happening and will continue to happen because Mother Nature can no longer watch the land and the animals being destroyed by big developments." he said to me. "Mother Nature has to fight back. The worst is yet to come. The ocean is not angry yet but when the ocean becomes angry many big cities will be flooded. The government will no longer have any protection from these angry Spirits."

His words amazed me. I didn't ask any other questions. I just told him we should go for breakfast. This answer from the elder stayed in my mind as I sat through the land rights negotiations.

IN 2006, THE LABRADOR INNU experienced the first of a series of losses, which left families and our communities reeling. It would take us a long time to recover. The first bad news came in July. At the time, Shanut was in Ste Anne de Beaupre in Quebec with a group from Natuashish. I told her to go on with our son Gerry to Sept Isles and wait for me there. I left for Sept Isles with my daughter Nishapet and her two kids, Mario and Rocco. We left Labrador City early in the afternoon and I noticed the transmission oil was leaking. We barely made it to Gabriel, the next community with a gas station and hotel. By then it was 1:00 in the morning.

"There's nothing we can do," I said to Nishapet. "We have to spend the night and try to contact Gerry in the morning." The lady looking after the gas station was very nice to us. She gave us all the sleeping bags we needed and the keys to a house for us to stay. I asked her if I could make a call and she gave me her phone to use. I called Gerry and he said he would leave early in the morning to pick us up. We ate our breakfast in the hotel restaurant and waited for Gerry. We expected him around 10:00, but he never showed up until 1:00 in the afternoon.

While we loaded the truck I went inside to thank the lady who gave us a place to sleep. I told her we'd leave the truck and asked if she would keep an eye on it until the tow-truck got here.

"Don't worry. I'll look after that," she said. I thanked her again for her kindness.

We were almost in Sept Isles when Gerry's cellphone rang. When I answered it I recognized Tapit Nuke's voice.

"Penute Michel has left us for good," he said. I knew what he meant. Penute had died. I told Gerry we had to go to the hospital. When we arrived, Tapit, Penute's wife Tshanet[1] and his two daughters were waiting for us outside the hospital. I felt hurt deep inside when I saw Tshanet. I walked straight over to her. She stood up and I have her a hug. She was crying and I couldn't help crying too.

---

[1] Janet

"We must try to accept God's way although we know it is a great loss to the Innu Nation," I said to her. All the way from Gabriel I thought about Penute Michel and where I might find him – in Sept Isles or Maliotenam. I wanted to ask him if the Innu Nation could pay for half the cost of the tow truck. Those thoughts were gone now.

Penute's body was shipped back to Sheshatshiu for the funeral. The Innu Nation chartered an aircraft for us to go to the funeral. A group of Quebec Innu had their own charter. The funeral held in the school gym lasted from 3:00 in the afternoon to 8:00 in the evening – the the longest service I ever attended. There were so many people who spoke and so many letters to read out from others who couldn't come but wanted to pay their final respects.

I thought about how Penute would be remembered. He'd been President of the Naskapi Montagnais Association before it became the Innu Nation. In those early days he'd done his best to work with Innu from the Quebec North Shore on land issues but he never got anywhere because some of their leaders wanted their own land claims. Other leaders believed that the Supreme Court was the best place to settle land issues but there was no guarantee the Innu could win in court. Negotiations on land rights went on for years and Penute served as chief land rights negotiator until he was elected president of the Innu Nation in 2004. After a year-and-a-half of his term he left us forever but I knew his vision, direction and goals would live on.

Penute was well-known amongst many non-Innu people across Canada. He always had time to talk to people. No matter where – in the office or at home – Penute always made a point of answering anyone's questions in a very honest way. He and I didn't always agree on some issues. We argued but in the end we always remained friends.

I remember very clearly when Penute was just a young child. He was always dressed funny. As teenagers we called him Kauitentakust and then everyone in Sheshatshiu began to call him that name, which in English means Funny Man. I never thought at the time that Penute would become one of our great leaders. He never dressed like an *Akaneshau* person, not with a suit or tie, even when he was in the office. He usually wore jeans or jogging pants, a t-shirt and running shoes. He dressed the same way as when he was in *nutshimit*.

But when Penute met with government officials he was a different person, not in the way he dressed but in the way he spoke. He would speak in a very low voice and take a few seconds before speaking the next word. I guess he wanted to be careful about what he said. He did a lot of speaking. Maybe he was our best spokesperson. He was our voice at meetings with governments, with support groups, churches and media all over Canada and more than once in Europe. He was not a shy man. He was always telling our story, talking about Innu history, about colonization, Innu Nationhood and our rights, how we never signed any treaty. His words helped us to stand up as Innu people and fight for our rights. He talked about Gandhi and his peaceful protests and Nelson Mandela and how they fought for the rights of their people; how the Innu had the same struggle. In meetings with the Innu, when someone asked him a question Penute would wait until the person was finished and then he would stand to give his answer. Since we don't have words in *Innu-aimun* for a lot of political talk, Penute had to do a lot of explaining. Sometimes he used parables to make the person understand. I never heard him shout at anyone when he spoke at a meeting. Penute will be remembered well in many years to come by both Innu and *Akaneshau*.

Penute was not only interested in politics. He was a hunter too and loved to be in *nutshimit* with his family. I know the place where he usually went in the springtime to hunt geese and ducks, somewhere between Churchill Falls and Wabush on a river called Ussukumenuan. That was Penute's hunting grounds. He never thought to build a cabin there because he loved to live in the tent with his family. At Ussukumenuan there's a small island where Penute would usually wait for geese to land. He had so many friends, Innu and *Akaneshau* who now call that island Penute's Island.

One time when I went to visit Penute at home I told him I had to get something to eat.

"Can you wait?" he asked me. "Tshanet is cooking and we want you to have dinner with us." I accepted his invitation. While we waited for dinner we continued our conversation.

"Shuash[1], what do you think about some of our former leaders always talking about me behind my back?" he asked.

"Yes, I've heard about it but that doesn't interest me," I told him. "We're the voters. We voted for you to be our leader. That's what counts. We know bad news travels fast but most people know better than to pay much attention to gossip." I told him that people would see he was going in the right direction.

"One day the people who talk about you will come to you for your help," I said to him. "Don't let the gossip bother you."

---

[1] George

"I understand that," Penute said. "I'm trying to be fair to anyone and I'll continue to do so until the end of my term."

I told Penute I had to go visit inmates at the Correctional Centre. He asked me if I was going to Innu Nikamu, the music festival in Sept Isles held in August.

"I'm thinking about it," I said.

"I'll see you there. Keep in touch."

I nodded without saying a word. That was the last time I talked to Penute in person. A month and a half later he died in Sept Isles. It just happened so fast. He'd be sadly missed by many Innu in Labrador and Quebec and by Settlers, Metis and people far away. My late sister Nush had often said that Penute was overworked, that he was too nice to his people. He never liked to use the word "no." He wanted to help people in any way he could. Nush said she felt very sorry for his father and mother. I told my sister that unexpected things were bound to happen. There was nothing we could do.

I never expected to hear very bad news about my sister Nush only months after Penute died. It was January 2007, and after having been sober for nearly seven years I fell off the wagon again. For a little over a month I was back on the bottle. This was when my sister got sick. She had never really complained about her illness. She only told me once that her doctor said she had gallstones. Sometimes she had pain in her joints, like in her arm, and she thought it was arthritis. She never seemed worried. She always wanted to be happy when she talked with anyone.

Nush was a very kind person and always helped any person in need. One summer I was staying at her house when the phone rang around 1:00 in the morning. I got up to answer. A woman asked to talk to Nush and I told her my sister was asleep. The woman said it was important she talk to Nush. I knocked on Nush's door to give her the message and headed back to bed. I never heard the conversation, only just before she hung up I heard her say, "We'll be there." She came to my room and said we had to go see this couple. As a former addictions counselor I had to support my sister's work.

It was a cold winter night and I had to warm up my truck before we could be on our way. I knew the couple very well. The man seemed more upset than his wife as he paced back and forth in the living room. Nush talked to the woman and I talked to the man. After a while they were able to talk to each other. We told them we'd be back in the morning. When we returned the two of them were happy and joking with each other.

I usually stayed with Nush when I was in Sheshatshiu, so I knew she got many calls at night. Sometimes I'd just drop her off to see a client. She didn't always invite me to come along because she was dealing with a confidential matter. Sometimes she'd spend the night with her client at the women's shelter. She did this work for many years, helping people in Sheshatshiu, not only the women but also inmates at the Correctional Centre. She helped many people to start talking about sexual abuse. She was an Innu healer. I knew Nush was overworked and very tired and that she needed to take a few weeks' break. I asked her once if she had enough overtime hours to take some time off. She did but she said she couldn't because it would be like leaving people with no one to care for them. Some Innu leaders didn't like the work she was doing to help women but that didn't bother her at all.

Nush was also very involved in the protests against low-level flying. She was one of the women who spent time in jail. One time a bunch of women were arrested and convicted. All of them were sent to the women's correctional centre in Stephenville. They were sent home after a couple of weeks but Manimat Hurley had to stay longer because she was arrested more than once and she'd signed an undertaking that she wouldn't protest on the runway again. A month or more passed and Manimat sent a message to the leaders in Sheshatshiu saying more women should protest at Goose Bay. If they were arrested they'd be able to join her in Stephenville. I was in Davis Inlet at the time when my sister Nush phoned me. She told me about the message from Manimat.

"Tomorrow us women will protest and see what happens. See how many of us will be arrested," Nush said on the phone.

"You yourself will be arrested," I said. "This is your second time to be arrested so this time they won't release you now until your court date. Whatever action you take it's in your hands. I'm not going to try to stop you because I know Manimat will be happy to see other women from Sheshatshiu."

"I feel very sorry for Manimat and the women talked about it," Nush said. "We want to be in jail too so the Government of Canada can see we are arrested because we are trying to protect the land and the wild animals. The saddest part is to see Manimat still in jail and her children she had to leave behind."

Nush was also involved in the occupation of the bombing range at Minipi Lake. My sister was never really involved in politics, not like a politician, but she had a very strong voice. She wasn't afraid to speak out on behalf of her community. She spoke at many events and during speaking tours across Canada. Many people outside Nitassinan learned about the suffering and struggles of the Innu because of Nush's voice. She was fighting NATO, the biggest military organization in the world, with her words. She wasn't afraid to stand up and tell the judge exactly what she thought of his court, his government, its laws and the war games being practised on Innu land.

Nush was the person who gave other Innu people a lot of courage.

In February 2007, a few days after I'd stopped drinking again, it was my turn to ask my sister Nush for help. I was still sick and shaking. No one answered when I phoned her. I tried many times to call and finally I phoned my other sister Tshaukuesh who told me Nush was staying with her son Chris in Goose Bay. She didn't know why. I was kind of worried.

A couple of days later, Nush was admitted to the hospital in Happy Valley. The very next day she was taken by medevac to the Health Sciences Centre in St. John's. I didn't want my wife and children to see how worried I was. A couple of days later Nush's daughter Shanet[1] called to tell me the sad news. She wanted to know if there was any way I could go to St. John's because her mother had a very serious health problem. I was not expecting to hear this news.

"It's not good news," I told Shanut. "Nush has liver cancer and she might not live long. Janet is trying to make arrangements with the Chief for us to go to St. John's as soon as possible." In the meantime I went to the Innu Nation to see if they could help with airfares. That very same day they made arrangements for us to travel. We caught the afternoon flight to Goose Bay and went on to St. John's on an evening flight.

We spent the night at the Holiday Inn and got up early the next morning. By the time we ate our breakfast and reached the hospital the receptionist told us Nush had been moved to intensive care. I was even more worried now, wondering if I'd be able to see her without crying. We met my other sisters and my two nieces and nephew on the third floor. Only two people were allowed to see Nush for each visit.

I walked into her room and saw her all hooked up to different machines. I went straight to her bed. She smiled when she saw me and waved her hand

---

[1] Janet

for me to come closer. I gave her a hug and kissed her on both cheeks. I told her I loved her. I couldn't help it. I started to cry. I looked over at Shanut and she was crying too. Nush asked us about our trip and who was looking after the kids. She asked about other people, wanting to know that someone was taking care of them.

We left to join the rest of the family in the waiting room. My oldest sister suggested we pray together. Shanet wanted us to ask the doctor if Nush could be sent back to the Goose Bay Hospital so her family and friends back home could see her. I had mixed feelings about this request. I wanted to ask the doctor directly to find out what he thought about the idea. The next day I happened to be alone with Nush when the doctor was doing his rounds.

"You must be George Gregoire," he said to me.

"Yes, I'm Nush's brother." I replied. The two of us walked away from the bed so she couldn't hear us. I asked him what would happen if we took Nush home to Goose Bay. He said we could but she had very little time left. I wondered if she was well enough to travel. She might die before she got to Goose Bay. I explained to the family in the waiting room what the doctor had just said. I couldn't tell Shanet because she believed her mother was going to live long enough to see her brother Chris and his girlfriend's baby due only a few short months away.

The next morning I got up and had my breakfast with Shanut before heading back to visit Nush.

"I'm very tired," I told Shanut. "I just don't have the energy to watch my sister fight for her life. Maybe we should go back to Natuashish in the morning, but I want to go talk to Nush first." Shanut said she'd support whatever decision I made.

Nush was happy to see me. She managed to eat some breakfast that morning, the first time since she entered the hospital. I didn't tell her about my plan to leave. Later I sat with my sisters in the waiting room and told them I was leaving the next day and my reasons why. Everyone was very accepting. I had so many things on my mind but there was one more thing they had to know.

"I had a strange dream last night," I told them. "I went for a walk with Shanut and Nush down along the docks here in St. John's. There were so many different ships. One wooden ship had no motor, like a schooner or maybe like the ship John Cabot used when he first discovered Newfoundland. I asked Nush and Shanut what the ship looked like on the inside. We got on board to have a look. I thought that surely the ship would have no motor but it had everything. The cabins were like a hotel suite, with a bathroom, shower and mirror. Each cabin had its own computer and TV. I told Nush I thought it was strange that the boat would have all these things but no engine. When we stepped outside we noticed one of the masts was broken. I told the women I couldn't see how they could replace a pole that size and weight. Nush said they'd find a way. We continued to walk and look at other ships. When we reached the end of the harbour I stopped to talk to Nush, but when I turned around Shanut was all by herself. 'What happened to Nush?' I asked. 'Maybe she went back to the old ship?' Shanut said. We returned to the ship but it was gone. We looked everywhere but there was no sign of Nush. The old ship had headed through the narrows and directly out to the open sea. We could barely spot it on the horizon. I told Shanut that Nush must have sailed away on that old ship. At this point I woke from my dream and quietly got up to go the bathroom, trying to not wake Shanut. I was crying. I knew the dream had a message for me."

No one in the room said anything for a moment. Finally my sister said, "Your dream is telling us something, but is it bad or good?" I tried to give them strength by telling them not to worry but I knew the dream was telling me that Nush would not be with us much longer. I left to call and change our reservations.

That afternoon they moved Nush to the fourth floor. I was worried. Why were they taking her out of intensive care? Was it because there was nothing more they could do for her? I went to see her that evening for the last time. Back at the hotel I asked the front desk for a wake-up call the next morning.

A little after midnight I woke up to the phone ringing. I quickly answered and it was Shanet asking us to come to the hospital right away. I told her to wait for us in the lobby. "Get dressed," I said to Shanut. The cab was waiting for us and minutes later we were at the hospital. I gave the driver twenty dollars and told him to keep the change. When we arrived on the fourth floor my nephew Peter Penashue was in the hallway. He came up and put his arms around me. "It's bad news," he said. "It's all over." I couldn't believe it. I thought I'd get the chance to say goodbye to Nush. I walked into her room and she still looked so much alive. I took her hand and kissed both her cheeks. "I love you Little Sister," I whispered. I knew she couldn't hear me but in my culture I believed her spirit could.

In this moment I remembered my dream. I wasn't the only one in the family who was so deeply hurt after Nush passed away, but since we were the youngest I was the one who was always so close to her. Whenever I had a problem she was always there. When she needed help I was available by phone or in person.

As we left the room I saw a doctor standing by the nurse's station. I thanked him for doing his best to save my sister's life. He thanked me too. The whole family gathered in the waiting room and I told my sisters, nieces and nephews that we should thank God for taking Nush so peacefully before she'd suffered too long. He'd done this because He loved us. We should accept God's way. My eldest sister echoed my words.

I never slept again that night. The next morning Shanut and I caught a plane to Goose Bay. I phoned my nephew Tanien Ashini and he agreed the Innu Nation would charter a Dash 8 to bring the body and the family back to Labrador. The following day her body was prepared for burial at the funeral home and brought to the church in Sheshatshiu in the evening. The funeral was planned for the following afternoon. In our culture we had to watch over the body for one night before the funeral.

We expected a big crowd for the funeral so the leaders arranged for the funeral to be held in the arena. My family ate breakfast at my sister's and headed out to the arena for two o'clock. A woman from Natuashish came over to ask if she could say a few words for my late sister. I told her I would announce when she could speak. We were sitting in the front. I was crying when Father Chris spoke about Nush. An elder came up to me. "Don't feel too sad. God takes care of everything," he said to me. "We're born to live in the world only temporarily. Not forever. When our time comes, we're all going to die." I thanked Father Chris after the service.

When I returned to Natuashish after Nush's funeral I felt so empty with nothing to discuss, no one to talk to, no place to go. Before she died, Nush called me almost every morning so every time the phone rang I thought it must be her. I pictured her sitting at her table with the phone in her hand talking and laughing as she did whenever I visited her. I've only been inside her house once since she passed away.

In June 2007, the Innu of Labrador suffered another great loss. I was in Goose Bay to visit inmates in the Correctional Centre. I visited my friend

Apenam[1] to ask him if he was holding a sweat that afternoon. I told him I'd be there. Around noon I was passing by the hospital and noticed there were many people from Sheshatshiu standing outside Emergency. I decided to go find out what was happening. An ambulance had just arrived with Apenam, who'd suffered a stroke. I couldn't believe what I was hearing. I'd only just been talking to him.

Later that day when I returned to the hospital, Apenam was all hooked up with an oxygen tube going into his nose. I couldn't tell whether he was sleeping or unconscious. A young fellow who'd been helping out with the sweat told me Apenam was just sitting on a log when he arrived to unload some wood. He said Apenam was talking to his wife but she wasn't there. The ambulance was called to take Apenam to the hospital in Goose Bay. Later he was transferred to St. John's and put on life support. I was very upset to get the news from his nephew by phone that Apenam had passed away. I made my own arrangements to attend the funeral of this good friend of mine, a drinking buddy at one time and later a friend who helped me and many others stay sober.

"Why are these things happening?" I asked my wife Shanut after the funeral. "In less than a year we've lost all these people from Sheshatshiu." Penute, Nush and Apenam were very qualified leaders. A Sheshatshiu elder later told me the passing of three great leaders was a warning to us because we were not working together. We were always against each other, not like the old days when the Innu always helped each other out.

Apenam was well-known in both communities. He'd traveled to many different communities across Canada, including the North. He'd been sober for over twenty years. Apenam was always available when someone needed help. He held a regular *matutishanitshuap*[2] as a healing ritual. We used to sweat together often. Apenam was a healer, not like a shaman or medicine man, but his words were very strong. I remember one time when we had a sweat at Lobstick Lodge. It was pitch black in the *matutishanitshuap* and we couldn't see each other. I was sitting next to Apenam and I was the first person to do the sharing. I didn't realize what I was saying. Apenam interrupted me.

"Shuash," he said. "You are here to deal with you and your problems, not someone else's problems. Talk about yourself and no blaming."

There were other clients inside the lodge and I felt ashamed when he said that because everyone knew he was my good friend. As I continued to share I

[1] Abraham Pone
[2] Sweat lodge

had to be very careful about what I said. I could only talk about myself. More than once I heard him shout these words out to anyone in the sweat, not just me. He made us work hard to heal ourselves. I learned a lot from him. I managed to stay sober for up to seven years at a time and then I'd slipped only once during that time before I was sober for many years again.

During that treatment program in Lobstick Lodge an elder would open the circle every morning with a prayer. Then Apenam would stand and say, "Remember what you see and hear here, stays here. And no politics." He gave us a hard time during the day but in the evening he was a different man. He joked and said things that made the clients laugh. Sometimes he'd ask clients to play games just for fun to make us laugh. "Laughing is part of healing," he said.

One very interesting thing he did was to ask us to do role-plays. For example, I'd play the drunken father, a woman would be my wife and younger clients would play my children. The role-play would help us to understand what it was like to have alcohol in the family, to show what I was like when I was drunk. Others did their own role-play too. We were told not to laugh although some people couldn't help themselves. After the role-play we discussed what it was like when the person was drunk and how the woman and children were scared. It opened us to see what it was like to be an alcoholic and how it affected other people close to us. Sometimes the women cried when they saw the role-play. This is the kind of work that Apenam did and why I say Apenam was a healer. He was a mentor to many Innu and helped many of us change our lives, especially the men. He wouldn't listen to any crap from us and we respected him for that.

Apenam also worked on justice issues, trying to support Innu people who were having problems with the law. He managed to get the okay from the provincial minister of justice to hold a *matutishanitshuap* at the Correctional Centre. Both the minister and the Chief Justice thought this was a good idea. Apenam told them anyone would be welcome into the *matutishanitshuap* – Innu, Inuit, Settler or Metis. Apenam and I held a sweat twice at the Correctional Centre before he passed away. Apenam was my boss when I lived in Sheshatshiu and worked as a counselor. After I returned to Davis Inlet and then Natuashish, we continued to work together on justice issues and visit inmates in the Correctional Centre. We were the first ones to bring the Supreme Court to Natuashish to hold a sentencing circle.

In a sentencing circle the community has a say in what happens to the offender. The circle is made up of the accused, the victim, the family of the accused and the family of the victim, elders and other interested community members. Everyone sits around in a circle – the judge, defense lawyer, prosecutor and policemen also sit in the circle. The judge asks an elder to say a prayer. Everyone has a chance to talk. The circle discusses the offender, the crime and various sentences that might be suitable. The judge makes the final decision. This was a new way of doing justice. We thought it could help both the victims and the offenders and their families heal.

Apenam was very well-respected by people outside Sheshatshiu too. In 2001 he received an award from the Newfoundland Law Society for his work with the justice system. Apenam always said that what we needed was our own Innu justice system with an Innu judge and Innu lawyers, a system based on our own Innu values and traditions.

Apenam was always on the move looking for ways to heal not – only his community and the Innu but anyone who had problems with alcohol, drugs or the law. He was often invited to share his experience in Quebec North Shore communities.

"I heard you took a course to be a welder years ago in Ontario," I said to him one day when the two of us were traveling together to Esker. "Did you ever finish that course?"

"I did," Apenam replied. "I got my certificate."

"Why didn't you ever work as a welder? You could've made a lot of money. In Voisey's Bay a welder gets paid a lot."

Apenam didn't respond right away. Then he laughed. "Money doesn't solve problems, Shuash," he said. "I could've made a lot of money and watched my people suffer with the law, alcohol and drugs. I've been down a very rough road. I killed my aunt by accident because of the alcohol. Now I'm sober. I want to do something to make it up to my people. I want people to see and hear about my experience. I've been able to help many young people with their problems, including you. That's why I do this work."

"Whatever direction you take, I'm with you," I said to him.

Together Apenam and I also made a proposal to provide counseling services at Voisey's Bay to help anyone who had an alcohol or drug problem. Apenam also recommended to the company that it hire the services of financial experts to help people learn about money management. In our proposal we clearly stated that the counseling service was not just for the Innu but for everyone. Our proposal was rejected. The general manager told us the company planned to bring in their own counseling services. A couple of years later when I was in Voisey's Bay I asked the manager about their counseling services and he told me they had none. I didn't bother to bring up our proposal again even although I knew Apenam's dream for counseling services at the Voisey's Bay camp was still a very good idea.

Apenam's main goal was to help heal his community but he was also very interested in hunting and sharing wild foods with the elders. I continued to help out with sweats in Sheshatshiu after Apenam passed away. Some of his former clients would call on his spirit for help during sweats. In our culture we believed a person's soul could contact his or her friend or relative through dreams. We also believed we could contact a dead person's spirit.

After Apenam passed away, clients and co-workers continued to do the work Apenam began and to continue in the direction in which he led us. Apenam's name would not be forgotten. I would always be thankful to my late friend. Without his help I wouldn't be sober today.

Sadly, on October 13, 2009, we lost another great leader. Tanien Ashini was my nephew and also my godson. Tanien was well-educated in the *Akaneshau* ways and also very well educated in Innu culture, or I would rather say the Innu way of life. This made him a very good leader. He served as Chief of Sheshatshiu, president of the Innu Nation and he was the chief land rights negotiator for a number of years. But what he really liked to do was hunt in the fall and spring. He was a great hunter just like his late father Penute. And whenever Tanien returned to the community he would share his kill with the elders just as the Innu always did in the old days.

In meetings with governments you never saw Tanien dressed in a suit and tie, but when he spoke he was a person to respect. He never had a long speech but he spoke from his heart. He was doing his best to protect the land for the future generations. I attended many land rights meetings with him. As chief negotiator sometimes he'd ask for a caucus meeting with us. Many times I heard him say to our lawyer, John Olthuis, "Okay me son, what do you think?" During Innu meetings, he took notes on what people said. When his time came to speak, he would go back to his notes and try to answer all the questions if he could. If he couldn't answer a question he would ask another leader to respond. He could read any book or file and debate any *Akaneshau*. He knew his stuff and he made people sit up and listen. People did not interrupt him when he spoke. They just listened.

The day Tanien passed away, I was in Natuashish. I had just arrived at my friend's house when the phone rang. It was Tanien's brother Shuash. I couldn't understand what he was saying because he was crying.

"Is Tanien okay?" I asked him.

"No, he just passed away about ten minutes ago," Shuash said. When I hung up the phone I wondered if I should call Shanut right away. She was working and it took me a while to make my decision whether to wait until she got home. Finally I thought it best to call her and she started to cry when I told her.

I was feeling very sad about Tanien. Although he was a heavy drinker at times, he always showed his respect to anyone who talked with him. He was very much involved in fighting for Innu land rights, in the protests against low-level flying, in the fight for compensation for the Lower Churchill hydro development, in the fight against clearcutting and the mine at Voisey's Bay. He spent time in jail for the protests. He showed his people how much he cared for them. He was at the table fighting for the Tshash Petapen agreement. He never lived to see the agreement come to pass. Tanien was a great leader, a father and a hunter. Many of us would remember him as an honest leader and a person who loved to spend time in *nutshimit*.

"That's the sixth leader we lost in just three years," I said to Shanut on the phone. I was thinking about Penute, Nush, Apenam, Tanien, and Kanikuen Penashue, another great leader who I wrote about earlier in this book. There was also Manimei[1] Osmond, who worked a lot with Nush and Apenam to help the people heal from their addictions and other social problems. These six great leaders were not old. They were in their forties or fifties. They all came from Sheshatshiu. I cannot describe how the Innu felt when their leaders passed on to the other world. They could never be replaced. They were fighters for their people. There would never be other leaders like them. I thought we Innu should pick a day to remember them. We didn't have to wait for the government to recognize that day. We could do it on our own to show how much we respect these leaders. Their relatives would be happy.

---

[1] Mary May

I N 2007, CHIEF PROTE POKER was elected and he appointed a new band manager, Phil Jeddore, a Mi'kmaq from Conne River, Newfoundland, who couldn't speak *Innu-aimun* but could understand a bit. I soon received a letter from him saying the Chief and council would no longer fund my position. That was it. I was no longer an employee of the Band. I accepted this but when my employment insurance ran out I went to see the Chief about work.

When I sat down to talk to him he wanted to know what I thought about banning alcohol in the community. I told him I didn't drink and I was not opposed to by-laws in the community but I was not in favour of a ban. I told him I was worried a ban would drive people outside the community to drink in the winter. Or they might drive to other coastal communities to get alcohol. This could get dangerous in the spring and fall during break-up and freeze-up. I also pointed out that it was not safe for people to drink when they were in a boat during the summer. In the winter, people could have accidents on their snowmobiles. They could get lost or go through the ice. When I finished, the Chief told me why he'd let me go.

"You were bootlegging. That's the problem I have with you."

"I'm no longer doing that," I said. "Some people say I'm still bootlegging but it's not true. Bootlegging is not the biggest problem anymore anyway. Not so many people drink like they used to now. The real problem is drugs, especially for the young people with jobs and money." I told him I knew who the drug dealers were. We all did. I had no plans to report them to the police because they were my people. It was the police's job to find out who they were. I didn't mind reporting my own children sometimes, but not other people. I never laid charges against my children, but sometimes they needed to be locked up for the night.

Before our meeting ended, the Chief suggested I work for the Healing Lodge. They needed someone to look after the *matutishanitshuap*[1]. He said he'd talk to the Healing Lodge director and get back to me. I was happy to do this work to help my people talk about their problems and heal. I'd worked so

---

[1] Sweat lodge

many years as an alcohol counselor in both Davis Inlet and later in Sheshatshiu. There was a lot of help available for people here in Natuashish now. A number of qualified counselors worked at the Healing Lodge. I would help out and look after the *matutishanitshuap*.

The first part of my job was to build the *matutishanitshuap* and it was not was that easy. It was hard to find the sticks to get started. I had to find the right kind of small green tree that easily bent without breaking. I looked for trees that were about two-and-a-half inches in diameter from the bottom and half-an-inch on top. I could use any tree: spruce, juniper, willow or birch. The best sticks to use were small birch, but they were hard to find. I needed about 17 or 18 sticks to build the lodge. It's hard for one person to build a lodge. I had to find a helper to hold the sticks in place while I bent them and tied them together to form a dome – a round shape like an igloo. The sticks were tied with cotton line, not with rope which wouldn't last long in the heat. The entrance had to face the spot where I'd make a fire to heat the rocks. I covered the frame with three layers of black canvas. Plastic tarps could never be used. Once built, the sweat lodge was about 12 by 12 feet and inside about four or five feet high. It couldn't be too high or it would be hard to hold enough heat. The last thing to do was to spread a cushion of spruce boughs to make a floor.

I started to hold sweats and invited people to join me. The only problem was the location of the lodge a few kilometers away from the community. Sometimes I'd get so many calls. People wanted to know when I'd be doing my next sweat. My boss wanted me to keep a list of people who came to the sweats, not their names, just the number of people who participated. The lodge could hold as many as sixteen of us doing the sweat together.

In the summer of 2009 we decided to build a house near the healing lodge that we could use for sweats. I built a second *matutishanitshuap* inside that house so it would be easier to hold sweats in the winter. I also wanted to have a *matutishanitshuap* in *nutshimit,* so I built one that was a little smaller at Daniel's Rattle. The two *matutishanitshuap* were for the whole community. Anyone was free to use them.

Today there is a new Chief, Simeon Tshakapesh, and I'm still organizing these sweats although most of the other people working at the Healing Lodge were let go by this Chief. Sweats can last as much as three or four hours. It's dark inside the *matutishanitshuap*; the only things you see are the red-hot rocks. I use about thirty rocks the size of a soccer ball. Small rocks cool off more quickly. When water is poured on the hot rocks, the steam goes up and comes right back down. People in the *matutishanitshuap* might find the steam intense and like it's burning them but it's just hot steam. The person leading the sweat often calls the rocks "grandfathers" and welcomes all those who are joining him. He pours water bit by bit and lets the hot steam go out. The person watching the fire must wait outside. Then the one running the sweat asks the person outside to close the flap. The ceremony starts with a prayer. When water is poured on the hot rocks, people must sit still and not move around. If you move you will feel burning, which is just the hot steam. The intense heat lasts only a few minutes but it's still very hot inside. The leader then explains to the participants that what is heard within the *matutishanitshuap* must stay there. What people say is never to be discussed outside the *matutishanitshuap*. When a person's turn comes up to speak, he or she is asked to say their name to begin.

Some women don't like to sweat with a man. I don't know why. When I sweat I welcome everyone: man, woman, police, judge, priest, lawyer, politicians, doctor, nurse or anyone from another country. Anyone can do a sweat. If the premier of Newfoundland felt like having a sweat with the Innu, I would welcome her too.

I also hold a sweat when I visit inmates at the Correctional Centre in Goose Bay. I still do this work even when I have to pay my own airfare to get there from Natuashish. The band council never has any money in the budget to pay for this travel. My old boss at the Healing Lodge said he'd ask Health Canada if they could provide funding for me to travel to Goose Bay every two weeks or at least once a month to visit the inmates. Health Canada agreed to pay for the airfare but they wouldn't pay for any expenses. I can find a place to stay but a per diem would be good. The really good thing is that they set up a tent and built a *matutishanitshuap* outside the Correctional Centre. The inmates do good work inside that *matutishanitshuap*.

A land rights agreement called the *Tshash Petapen* or New Dawn Agreement was signed by leaders of the Innu Nation, the two band councils and the province at the end of 2008. It would take another three years to work out the fine print and for the federal government to finally sign on. No one in the two communities really knew what was in the agreement. All we knew was that the piece of land that would now belong to the Innu was a very small area. The leaders said there would be a referendum in the two communities to ratify the agreement. People would get to say yes or no to this deal. We started to hear about the details of the agreement, including a deal over the Lower Churchill hydro project. If we voted in favour of the agreement we'd be giving our go-ahead for another development.

I thought the government was brainwashing our leaders, and our leaders wanted to do the same thing to our people. I attended an Innu Nation meeting where they presented a map showing where the dams would be built and outlining the land that would be designated Innu. They talked a lot about money but they didn't talk at all about the wild animals and all the land used by the Innu for thousands of years.

The people of Sheshatshiu and Natuashish didn't really understand this Tshash Petapen Agreement. What benefits would we really get? If we looked at the Voisey's Bay mining development, how many Innu were working there? Very few, and none from Natuashish. One time I visited my friend Shimuniss[1] Andrew in Sheshatshiu when the Grand Chief of the Innu Nation was speaking on the community radio. He said there were still three issues that needed to be resolved before the agreement could be settled. He spoke of the Lower Churchill hydro development, a mining development near Bloom Lake in Quebec and a new mine not far from Schefferville on the Labrador side of the border. The government was insisting the Innu would get rich. My friend laughed when he heard that.

"Do you see what I'm cooking, Shuash?" he asked me. "These are my last three potatoes. You think this agreement will make me richer?" We laughed.

"It's probably true our leaders will become rich but the people are the ones who'll suffer," I said. "One day there'll be no place for the Innu to hunt or fish. Who knows how many more hydro or mining projects will happen in the future?"

I didn't think the Lower Churchill hydro development should be part of this agreement. I saw it as a separate issue. I was concerned that the piece of Innu land was way too small with our population growing so quickly. I thought we needed strong leaders to speak on behalf of their people, not leaders who'd make sure they got richer while the people got poorer. I didn't think leaders

---

[1] Simon

should be signing anything without first consulting their own people. The leaders were supposed to be our servants working for us. The communities were the leaders. I also thought about how this agreement was dividing us. The leaders should've known that things would never get better unless we worked together. They needed to figure out how we could come together and stop the fighting.

On June 30, 2011, a referendum was finally held in the two communities to ratify the Tshash Petapen Agreement. I wondered if people supported the agreement. Would the Innu agree to the $6.2 billion Lower Churchill project with dams at Gull Island and Muskrat Falls and so much flooding of our lands just because we'd get 5 percent royalties? The agreement said we'd get $5 million every year before and during construction and up to $400 million in construction contracts. How many jobs would we really get? In terms of Innu control over traditional lands, the agreement said we'd have hunting rights in 34,000 square kilometres. In the end, the Innu cast their vote in the referendum, and support for the Tshash Petapen Agreement reached 96 percent in Natuashish and 84 percent in Sheshatshiu. This was more support than anyone imagined. I thought it must be the high numbers of young people in our community who voted this way.

I have no idea now what will happen with our Tshash Petapen agreement. I know other First Nations people who signed a land claims agreement have problems enforcing it. They are always in court with the governments. I know some Innu will benefit from the agreement but others will get nothing. Maybe our children and their children will try to protect the environment and animals. Others will probably go after the money. As for myself and my family, I hope my children and grandchildren will benefit from this agreement. At the same time I would like to see the land stay clear for hunting and as feeding grounds for the animals. I also worry about the Innu in Quebec who still use their land in Labrador. What are they thinking? Some of them want to protest our agreement. What will happen with that? I will wait and see if this agreement is a step forward for the Innu.

I continue to struggle with my addiction, although I have been doing pretty good for more than 12 years. Sometimes I slip but not for long and I quit again. I still worry a lot about my children, and now my grandchildren and other small children in our community. For years it seemed like most children had stopped sniffing gas although more young people were doing drugs and hard drugs too. Since the fall of 2010, children started sniffing in large numbers again. For so many years the number of kids sniffing was very small. Now some of the sniffers are only six years old. What happened to make so many people turn to doing such a dangerous thing again? Maybe it was because of so much fighting in the community.

I keep thinking the problem is that our children don't know enough about being Innu. There aren't enough education or cultural programs. This must be part of the reason they're turning to gas sniffing and drugs. It seemed for years parents were starting to take more responsibility for their own children, really doing a good job of looking after them, making sure they went to school every day. Where are those parents now? Children seem to be controlling their parents. They tell their parents they'll go to Social Services or they'll commit suicide if they don't get what they want. These children know they are protected by Social Services. They know their parents cannot punish them, so they are always doing things like stealing, breaking and entering, gas sniffing. The one good thing is that there is no more homebrew in Natuashish. We also have times when the community is very quiet and peaceful and there is no drinking at all. We have to work together for the community to be like this more often.

We need to find every way we can to protect our culture, to make sure our children learn about who they are. Many times Shanut and I talk about life in the country. She tells me stories about her family when they were in the country. So I share mine too. As we get old we both know we'll never be able to go back to the old ways again. This is a very sad situation for the elders in Natuashish and Sheshatshiu but the younger people are finding new ways to keep our culture alive.

In 2009, I heard Kestiniss[1] had decided to make a film about Tshiushuas, an Innu legend. I found out when I drove my truck to Mistinatuashu, a spot at the end of the Access Road outside Natuashish. I parked the truck and as I walked along the beach I noticed two tents had been set up – a regular tent and a teepee in a wooded area. Nobody was around. I wondered what was happening and then it came to my mind what I'd heard. Was Kestiniss really

---

[1] Christine Poker

going to make a film about an Innu legend? As I thought about this film my excitement grew. The next morning I ran into Shinipest[1] and told him about the teepees at Mistinatuashu. Shinipest is Kestiniss's first cousin. We drove down the Access Road all the way to the site. This time there was a big crowd on the beach: elder women, boys and children.

"This is going to be interesting to watch how movies get made," I said to Shinipest. "This isn't Hollywood where they make cowboy and Indian movies. This is an Innu film about an Innu legend."

Kestiniss welcomed us into the tent. She told her sister to give us something to eat. Later she asked me if I could join them. She wanted me to play the father in the film. Shutit[2] would play the mother. At first I thought she was joking.

"I could play Meminteu," I said to her. I was laughing, thinking about this very bad character in one of our Innu legends.

"No this is the Innu legend of Tshiushuas," Kestiniss said. In Davis Inlet, when Kestiniss was young she'd stayed with my family one time when her late father Tumi[3] was still alive. She was like a daughter to me.

"Okay, everyone get dressed. We're going to start shooting soon," Kestiness called out later that day. Everyone dressed up in their costume: kids, boys and elder women. At the end of the day we went back to the community. The next morning before we left for the film site I went to my boss, Reuben Pillay, and explained to him what I'd be doing that day and why it was important for me to help Kestiniss with her film.

The film tells the story of Tshiushuas, an orphan boy with no father or mother. He falls in love with a girl. I played her father in the film. The girl soon becomes pregnant and a baby boy is born. No one knows who the father is and this upsets the girls' parents. The people decide to send the couple away, believing they won't survive but they do because Tshiushuas has spiritual power given to him by *Missinak*, the Spirit of all the water animals and fish. When the couple returns, the baby grows up to love his grandparents and the grandparents love him too. All is forgiven. Tshiushuas has the power to help his people learn to respect and help each other.

It took about a week to shoot this film. Sometimes the weather was bad and we had to wait for a good day. The place where they chose to shoot the

---

[1] Sylvester Rich
[2] Judith Rich
[3] Tommy Rich

film is a very beautiful spot – a long sandy beach where a small brook runs. You can see the mountains beyond the big lake. There were about 25 people, including elders, involved in making the film. We were all dressed in Innu costumes, made to look like traditional Innu clothing. Some people were dressed in caribou hides and held a bow and arrow in their hands. It was interesting to watch how they shot the scene with Tshiushuas and his wife and baby on the wooden raft. One cameramen had to canoe out to the end of the pond with his camera rolling, while the other cameraman hid behind the bush to stay out of the picture. Kestiniss, as the director, worked very hard directing the film crew. Sometimes we were told to do the same scene over and over again until she thought it was just right. I didn't mind that because I knew we were making this film for our children.

In the past, elders always told this story to their children to make them understand how Innu lived in earlier times. Innu always respected and helped each other, like sharing the food they killed. The reason the film was made is to show the importance of sharing and helping to our children, grandchildren and their children not yet born. The film is teaching our children a better way to heal the community.

As an elder I think this kind of film can help our young people understand where we really come from and who we really are. I'm happy to see the National Film Board of Canada support this kind of film and to see Innu people making our own films. These films are going to be around for good and can be used by future Innu generations.

In 2012, Kestiniss made another film, also about an Innu legend, called *Kaianuet Kills Meminteu*. This time I actually do play Meminteu. Ben Rich plays Kaianuet. Maminteu was an *atshen*, who was like a human being – bigger and very bad, who killed people and ate them. Kaianuet was an Innu man who killed Meminteu, someone who was able to do what no one else could. He saved the people.

It is very interesting for the young people, and especially the elders, to see these films. I can safely say that if our community can work together, like we did on these films, we can find a way to revive our culture before it is totally lost.

Now as I finish this last chapter I think about the years I worked writing my story and why it was so important for me to publish this book. I want people to read my book, both Innu and non-Innu, to know about my way of life. I want people to know about my life when I was younger and what I learned about trapping and hunting from my late father. I want them to know about our land rights, our protests against low-level flying and other developments on our land such as mining and hydro projects. I shared stories about Innu leadership, both the good and the bad. Some former leaders might be uncomfortable to read my book but the things I've written are a true story. In some places I didn't use people's names, so I could protect their privacy.

I've also shared stories about how I became an alcoholic. Maybe in the future many Innu children will grow up and read my book. They will learn how alcohol affected my life, my community and my children. They'll also learn about how strong the Innu could be without alcohol when they were living in the *nutshimit*. They'll know how strong the Innu were in their fight with the governments over their rights. Now money has replaced the power of the Innu. The children need to know about their history. We know *Akaneshau* education is important for the Innu nowadays but our language and culture are also very important. If future leaders could continue to learn both the Innu way of life and the *Akaneshau* education, they will have the power to be better negotiators for their people. If our culture and language are lost, governments will say there are Innu people but they don't have any culture and no language. That is one thing I hope never happens.

INNU GLOSSARY

Akaneshau:	English-speaking white person
Atshen:	Similar to a human being, only bigger and very bad, who killed people and ate them
Aueshish-utshimauat:	Animal Masters or Spirits
Innu-aimun:	Innu language
Ishpitenitamun:	Respect shown by the Innu for the Animal Spirits/Masters and the natural world
Kakushapatak:	Shaman, person with spiritual powers (one who does the shaking tent)
Kamiteut:	Spiritual powers, and the gift of supernatural powers
Kukamess:	Lake trout
Miteu:	Spiritual powers (not in lexicon, see above)
Mishtapeu:	Spirit Master
Missinak:	Master or Spirit of the Water Dwellers
Matutishanitshuap:	Sweat lodge
Makushan:	Feast of the Caribou
Mushuau Innu:	People of the Barrens
Nikatipenimush:	Caribou Master or Spirit
Nikaui:	Mother

Innu-Nikamu:	Innu festival or Innu singing
Innu teueikan:	Innu drum if spelled innu-teueikan
Innu-mashinaikanitshuap:	Innu office or band council office
nipinamushiu:	Summer water or water that never freezes along the lake or river shore
Nitassinan.	Our homeland or Innu homeland
Nutaui:	Father
Nutshimit:	The bush or the country
Pimin:	Bone marrow, obtained from boiling the crushed bones
Tshash Petapen:	New Dawn, as in the New Dawn Agreement, the Labrador Innu Land Rights Settlement agreement with Canada and the province of Newfoundland and Labrador
Tshishiku-napeu:	Sky Spirit
Uhuapeu:	Porcupine Master or Spirit
Utshimau:	Leader or boss
Utshimassiu:	From Utshimassits, the Innu name for Davis Inlet

ACKNOWLEDGEMENTS

Deep in my heart I want to thank Camille Fouillard, who in her spare time did a lot of work typing and editing my writing. She is well-known in both Natuashish and Sheshatshiu. I met her in the 1980s during the protests against the NATO base and military low-level flying in Labrador. We became good friends. Many times she came to Davis Inlet, Natuashish and Sheshatshiu to work with the Innu. We worked together on the People's Inquiry and the *Gathering Voices* book that came out of that. I also would like to thank my friend's husband, Bruce, who also always welcomed me in his home and allowed me to use his fax machine when I had papers to send my editor (Camille). Bruce and Camille have two children, Esmée and Léo, who one day I hope will read my book and know a little bit about the Innu.

Tshinashkumitin also to Peter Armitage for producing maps with Innu names of all the places I write about in my book. The spellings of Innu toponyms in this book are consistent with those in the *Pepamuteiati nitassinat* (www.innuplaces.ca) database. Thanks also to Marguerite MacKenzie for standardizing Innu spellings.

Thanks to the people who gave me photos to use in this book: Virginia Collins, Prote Poker, Marie Wadden, Camille Fouillard, Pat Kelsall, Annette Lutterman and Bob Bartel.

Finally, I am thankful to the Canada Council for the Arts for its financial support through its Explorations Program.

ABOUT THE AUTHOR

George Gregoire (Shuash Kanikuen) was born in 1946 in the Meshikamau area of Nitassinan, the Innu homeland that covers much of the Quebec/Labrador peninsula. He was raised mostly in the country with occasional stints to Sheshatshiu where he attended school a few months every year until his final year in grade 10. He has always been very interested in reading any kind of book or magazine. In the meantime he was well educated in the knowledge and the ways of the Innu and became a hunter. He has served as addictions program director, Band Manager, Band Councilor, land rights negotiator, interpreter, actor and now works for the Healing lodge in Natuashish, organizing sweats and providing support for inmates at the Correctional Centre in Happy Valley, Labrador. He is married to Charlotte (Shanut) Gregoire and has 7 children and 17 grandchildren.